The Rhetorical Presidency, Propaganda, and the Cold War, 1945–1955

Recent Titles in the Praeger Series in Presidential Studies
Robert E. Denton, Jr., General Editor

Leadership and the Bush Presidency: Prudence or Drift in an Era of Change?
Edited by Ryan J. Barilleaux

The Presidency and the Persian Gulf War
Edited by Marcia Lynn Whicker, James P. Pfiffner, and Raymond A. Moore

The Press and the Bush Presidency
Mark J. Rozell

Jimmy Carter as Peacemaker: A Post-Presidential Biography
Rod Troester

Presidential Frontiers: Underexplored Issues in White House Politics
Edited by Ryan J. Barilleaux

Heirs Apparent: Solving the Vice Presidential Dilemma
Vance R. Kincade, Jr.

Covering Clinton: The President and the Press in the 1990s
Joseph Hayden

The Rhetorical Presidency, Propaganda, and the Cold War, 1945–1955

Shawn J. Parry-Giles

Praeger Series in Presidential Studies

PRAEGER

Westport, Connecticut
London

Library of Congress Cataloging-in-Publication Data

Parry-Giles, Shawn J., 1960–

    The rhetorical presidency, propaganda, and the Cold War, 1945–1955 / Shawn J. Parry-Giles.

        p.   cm.—(Praeger series in presidential studies, ISSN 1062–0931)
    Includes bibliographical references and index.
    ISBN 0–275–97463–4 (alk. paper)
      1. Truman, Harry S., 1884–1972. 2. Eisenhower, Dwight D. (Dwight David), 1890–1969. 3. United States—Politics and government—1945–1989. 4. Presidents —United States—Language—History—20th century. 5. Rhetoric—Political aspects —United States—History—20th century. 6. Propaganda, American—History— 20th century. 7. Cold War. 8. United States—Foreign relations—1945–1953. 9. United States—Foreign relations—1953–1961. I. Title. II. Series.
E813.P34   2002
327.1′4′097309045—dc21   2001036319

British Library Cataloguing in Publication Data is available.

Library of Congress Catalog Card Number: 2001036319
ISBN: 0–275–97463–4
ISSN: 1062–0931

First published in 2002

Praeger Publishers, 88 Post Road West, Westport, CT 06881
An imprint of Greenwood Publishing Group, Inc.
www.praeger.com

Printed in the United States of America

∞™

The paper used in this book complies with the
Permanent Paper Standard issued by the National
Information Standards Organization (Z39.48–1984).

10 9 8 7 6 5 4 3 2 1

To Trevor

Contents

Acknowledgments

This project is indebted to the tireless work of David Haight, archivist at the Dwight D. Eisenhower Presidential Library. Over the span of this decade-long project, he continually offered notable support, directing me to newly declassified material that he helped prepare for scholarly examination. Moreover, his knowledge of the Eisenhower administration's propaganda activities is unmatched, making him an invaluable resource of the time period and the subject matter. Without Mr. Haight's visible commitment to his work, the insights of this project would be significantly minimized; I want to express particular gratitude to him. I also thank Herb Pancratz of the Dwight D. Eisenhower Presidential Library in Abilene, Kansas, Dennis Bilger of the Harry S. Truman Presidential Library in Independence, Missouri, and Martin Manning of the United States Information Agency Historical Collection in Washington, D.C., for their assistance in the work of this project.

In addition, I wish to express appreciation to other archivists and staff members of the Dwight D. Eisenhower Presidential Library, the Harry S. Truman Presidential Library, the National Archives in Washington, D.C., the United States Information Agency Historical Collection, the Department of Special Collections at the University of Chicago Library, Chicago, Illinois, and the American Society of Newspaper Editors' archives in Reston, Virginia. In addition, I thank Indiana University's Graduate School's Grant-in-Aid program, the administration and faculty of Monmouth College, Monmouth, Illinois, and the Department of Communication (particularly Edward L. Fink) at the University of Maryland, College Park, for partial funding of this project through research and travel grants.

I am also very appreciative of Hans Tuch's willingness to answer my many detailed questions about the activities of the United States Information Agency and to introduce me to the U.S. Information Agency Alumni Association and their various publications. Similarly, I am grateful to Abbott Washburn for offering me further insight into his work with the Eisenhower administration. Gaining the perspective of early Cold War practitioners was invaluable to my comprehension of this historical case study.

I am also most appreciative for the aid of those at Greenwood Publishing Group who guided me through the publication of this book. In particular, I would like to offer my thanks to James Sabin, Betty Pessagno, and especially to Robert E. Denton, Jr., for their notable support.

There are many scholars who offered feedback to chapters, journal articles, or convention papers related to this book project. I am grateful to Thomas Benson, Ira Chernus, Doris A. Graber, Fred Greenstein, David Henry, Randy Y. Hirokawa, R. Gordon Hoxie, Robert L. Ivie, John Louis Lucaites, Elizabeth Walker Mechling, Jay Mechling, Sandra Petronio, Malcolm O. Sillars, William E. Wiethoff, and the late John Wilz. I am particularly indebted to Stacy A. Cordery for her careful reading of an earlier version of this manuscript and to Jan Briggs for her invaluable research support. Martin J. Medhurst warrants particular mention because of his pioneering work on the early rhetoric of the Cold War years. I am most appreciative of his feedback to this manuscript over the past several years.

Others have been unconditionally instrumental to my scholarly development, and I am particularly grateful for their years of support. Richard J. Jensen and James R. Andrews inspirited for me an appreciation of history and public discourse. J. Michel Hogan served as my mentor and friend and taught me like no other how to think and write like a critic. Hogan's unorthodox wit, sarcasm, and humor continue to inspire; I am most thankful for his lasting and loyal friendship. Without reservation, I appreciate these scholars' commitment to teaching as well as their ability to offer a sensible perspective by which to live their lives as academics.

Finally, I wish to thank my family for their continual support. My parents, Phil and Myrna Parry, taught me the value of work and dedication, which made this project possible. My children, Sam and Eli, offer meaning to my work in a way that no others can. And, most significantly, Trevor Parry-Giles showed unwavering endurance through the progression of this project, as he supported my efforts from start to finish. His advice, support, patience, and love made the completion of this project possible and bearable; this book is dedicated to him.

Abbreviations

AEC	Atomic Energy Commission
AP	Associated Press
ASNE	American Society of Newspaper Editors
BBG	Broadcasting Board of Governors
CCF	Congress for Cultural Freedom
CIA	Central Intelligence Agency
CPI	Committee on Public Information
DDEPL	Dwight D. Eisenhower Presidential Library
FBI	Federal Bureau of Investigation
FCC	Federal Communications Commission
HSTPL	Harry S. Truman Presidential Library
IBB	International Broadcasting Bureau
IIA	International Information Administration
IMG	Information Media Guarantee
INS	International News Service
JCS	Joint Chiefs of Staff
KNA	*Know North America*
NBC	National Broadcasting Company
NSC	National Security Council

OCB	Operations Coordinating Board
OSS	Office of Strategic Services
OWI	Office of War Information
POC	*Problems of Communism*
PSB	Psychological Strategy Board
RFA	Radio Free Europe
RL	Radio Liberty
TPIB	Technical Panel on International Broadcasting
UNGA	United Nations General Assembly
UP	United Press
USIA	United States Information Agency
USICA	United States International Communication Agency
USIS	United States Information Service
VOA	Voice of America

Introduction: The Rhetorical Presidency and U.S. Propaganda in the Twentieth Century

In 1982, Fred I. Greenstein altered scholarly and historical perceptions of Dwight D. Eisenhower's presidency through his articulation of the hidden-hand thesis. "Although Eisenhower cultivated the reputation of being above political machination, . . . he was an activist," Greenstein argued, who exhibited "hidden-hand strateg[ies] to conceal his activities from all nonassociates."[1] Eisenhower's successful hidden-hand leadership, though, was aided greatly by the covert apparatus that his predecessor, Harry S. Truman, implemented as part of his Cold War strategy. Truman's creation of the Central Intelligence Agency (CIA) in 1947 and the Psychological Strategy Board (PSB) in 1951, provided the structure in which America's first two Cold War presidents would combat the war against communism with reduced congressional oversight.[2]

Propaganda production and psychological strategy represented key instruments for both the Truman and Eisenhower administrations' Cold War operations. Although Presidents Woodrow Wilson and Franklin D. Roosevelt relied on government propaganda during wartime,[3] Truman and Eisenhower were the first two presidents to introduce and mobilize propaganda as an official *peacetime* institution.[4] In a "war of words," propaganda acted as an integral component of the government's foreign policy operation. To understand propaganda's influence is to grasp the means by which America's Cold War messages were produced and the overall impact that such strategizing had on the ideological constructions of the Cold War. Christopher Simpson reveals the pervasiveness of Cold War planning during the Truman and Eisenhower presidencies, arguing that "the U.S. government's psychological warfare . . . played either direct or indirect roles in several of the most important initiatives in mass communication research of the period."[5] Beyond influencing mass communication research, the institutionalization of propaganda as a primary Cold War device also influenced the practice of the rhetorical presidency, whereby presidential administrations increasingly relied on the public platform (e.g., bully pulpit) for political gain.

The development of America's commitment to a government-sponsored propaganda program not surprisingly parallels the rise of the rhetorical presidency, a twentieth-century phenomenon where U.S. presidents went over the heads of Congress and spoke directly to the people in order to achieve administrative ends. Both the propaganda program and the rhetorical presidency are traceable to the Wilson presidency,[6] and both were altered by the Cold War actions of Truman and Eisenhower. While much has been written about the rhetorical presidency[7] as well as the country's propaganda programs,[8] minimal attention is devoted to the relationship between the rise of the rhetorical presidency and the initiation of government propaganda as a tool of presidential leadership. Similarly, few scholars attend to the contributions that Truman and Eisenhower brought to the practice of the rhetorical presidency.[9] This study intends to fill such voids, centering on how the Truman and Eisenhower administrations strengthened the power of the rhetorical presidency through their institutionalization of a governmental peacetime propaganda program.

Like Wilson, both Truman and Eisenhower increased and restructured presidential power in relation to the bully pulpit. Both succeeded in not only strengthening the practice of governmental propaganda, but in taking such communication activities to new levels.[10] Both administrations likewise used the bully pulpit to circumvent congressional control. Most significantly, both administrations increased the clandestine means by which to thwart such congressional supervision over their administration's Cold War policies, relying on multiple media channels to achieve such ends.[11]

This inculcation of a more covert means of communication represents an important contribution that the Truman and Eisenhower administrations made to the practice of the rhetorical presidency. For many scholars, the rhetorical presidency is limited to activities involving the bully pulpit only.[12] As David Zarefsky argues, presidents have increasingly served "as the chief inventor and broker of the symbols of American politics."[13] Such symbolic power derives, James W. Ceaser et al. contend, from "the visible performance" rather than the "tangible text."[14] Reflecting very explicitly the importance of the bully pulpit to presidential-rhetorical power, Barbara Hinckley argues that the "public record becomes a . . . beginning point for the study of the office" because presidents present "themselves and the office in speeches to the nation."[15] Reducing the rhetorical presidency to the bully pulpit, though, offers a restricted understanding of rhetorical influence, especially in the age of technological sophistication and the increased secretization of presidential actions. To ignore the contributions of the Truman and Eisenhower administrations to the rhetorical presidency is to undervalue their impact on the foreign policy actions of their successors, especially in relation to propaganda, Cold War politics, and covert activities elevated in an era of nuclear proliferation.[16]

In the aftermath of World War II and the publicity of Hitler's well-known "Big Lie" theory, Americans grew more suspicious of government propaganda associated with "half-truths."[17] The negative legacy surrounding the role of propaganda in public politics combined with unique exigencies posed by the Cold War to inspire both the Truman and Eisenhower administrations to lessen public pronouncements connected to their presidencies and to the U. S. government. Instead, the Truman and Eisenhower administrations combined bully pulpit activity with presidentially directed messages voiced by surrogates whose words were as orchestrated by the administration as those delivered by the presidents.

This move toward more covert strategies represented an expansion rather than a reduction in the proliferation of presidentially orchestrated pronouncements, transforming and enhancing presidential-rhetorical discourse. To evidence such a conclusion, I examine the public discourse (e.g., speeches, congressional hearings and debates, propaganda texts, and newspaper articles) along with the private documents (e.g., archival sources: internal memos and directives, reports, minutes) of these two administrations in order to understand how such messages were strategized and ultimately promulgated. Such a holistic analysis reveals the relationship between the rhetorical presidency and propaganda production during the country's "war of words" against communism.[18]

Within this study, I employ a rhetorical perspective in the reading of such public and private discourse. Similar to Francis A. Beer and Robert Hariman's work, this study "acknowledge[s] the factors of 'power politics' while also accounting for discursive power." A rhetorical stance also involves an "appreciation of the dynamics of power" that is evidenced by the private strategizing sessions of the Truman and Eisenhower administrations; it likewise valorizes "both argument and style," which are grounded in the private and public texts disseminated by the propaganda programs. Such a rhetorical perspective emphasizes the ideological as well as the "strategic,"[19] culminating in an analysis that examines the tactical means by which the Cold War ideology of the United States was produced and naturalized through presidential–rhetorical leadership reliant on a prolific propaganda program.

This study ultimately offers four conclusions. First, I call for the expansion of traditional notions of the rhetorical presidency to include covert means of communication. As the Truman and Eisenhower administrations lessened congressional supervision over Cold War planning and propaganda operations, they simultaneously increased presidential command over both. In the process, the two administrations combined public messages emanating from the bully pulpit with discourse controlled by the executive branch but not voiced by the president. The presidential administrations increased control, for example, over such radio mediums as the Voice of America (VOA), Radio Free Europe (RFE), and Radio Liberty (RL); RFE and RL were not even connected to the U.S. government, let alone to the presidents of the United States.[20] The proliferation of presidential policies so vital to the rhetorical effectiveness of a presidential administration could now be conducted by multiple individuals and institutions that allowed for more narrative reiteration and the mirage of popular unanimity regarding the nation's Cold War message.

Second, this study reveals the important contributions that both the Truman and the Eisenhower administrations brought to the practice of the rhetorical presidency, revealing how both presidents integrated the role of public persuasion with institutional imperatives that expanded the power of presidential leadership.[21] Not only did such rhetorical and institutional strictures alter the manner in which Truman and Eisenhower performed the rhetorical presidency, they likewise changed the way in which future presidents combined covert (i.e., secret, behind the scenes) and overt (i.e., public) means of communication to fight the Cold War.[22] Both Truman's and Eisenhower's rhetorical and structural legacies are still evident in the institutional, strategic, and symbolic actions of their successors. An examination of presidential propaganda strategies serves not only as a metonymy of presidential communication patterns, but of presidential governance philosophies as well.[23] Because of the Truman and Eisenhower administrations' work with propaganda, future presidents could mold the propaganda program to fit their individualized foreign policy aims, making propaganda a means by which to expand and alter the rhetorical presidency.

Third, Truman and Eisenhower were able to turn propaganda into a presidential tool because of the move to define it in militaristic rather than journalistic terms. The use of a journalistic paradigm (i.e., where propaganda is equated with news) during the debates over the formation of a peacetime propaganda program helped assuage congressional leaders of the dangers of such a governmental program from 1945 to 1948. The eventual militarization of propaganda from 1950 to 1955, however, aided the presidential administrations in minimizing congressional control and expanding presidential oversight. Just as the president served as the commander-in-chief of the military, so too did he come to serve as the commander-in-chief over a militaristically defined and structured propaganda program. Such a militarized propaganda led to the development of a camouflaged and a defector propaganda, both dependent on a covert means of presidential influence. The military structure consciously and unconsciously changed the tenor of America's international messages, resulting in an Eisenhower administration that privately entertained the replacement of Truman's policy of communist containment with a policy of communist extinction.

Fourth, the Truman and Eisenhower administrations, with the aid of their expanded propaganda operations, helped create a more monolithic Cold War ideology by the time of John F. Kennedy's presidency. Both presidents' mobilization of communication media internationally and their influence over news coverage domestically aided in naturalizing a U.S. anticommunist ideology and a democratic response. Obviously, the communist ideology predated the Cold War, and other political actors were influential in the perpetuation and maintenance of the Cold War ideology. Given the growing power of the rhetorical presidency by the mid-twentieth century, however, the Cold War message of the Truman and Eisenhower administrations helped reify this pervasive and powerful ideological construction, which continues on even in the aftermath of the "war of words."[24]

To fully understand the rhetorical influence of these two Cold War presidencies is to examine their publicly voiced and their privately directed messages. To examine bully pulpit activities only in relation to the rhetorical presidency is limited and misleading in the context of the Cold War. For both administrations, a public discourse of truth and peace camouflaged strident anticommunist rhetoric that was planned and executed by the presidential administrations to support their foreign policy agendas. Presidential surrogates were as influential in inculcating such a pervasive ideology as the presidents themselves. The earliest Cold War presidents thus altered the means by which the rhetorical presidency was practiced from their administrations forward in relation to foreign policy matters and in particular to propaganda production.

PROPAGANDA STRATEGIES, DEBATES, AND TEXTS

In the first part of this study, the Truman administration's use of a journalistic paradigm is examined in chapter 1 as it sought to legalize peacetime propaganda in Congress from 1945 through 1948. The actual propaganda disseminated by the U.S. government during this period is likewise reviewed in chapter 2. Such an examination shows how the journalistic paradigm lessened congressional concerns over a government propaganda program; the analysis likewise demonstrates how the *New York Times* engaged in a public relations campaign of support for the passage of the program. While the domestic campaign was successful in legitimizing a government-sponsored propaganda program, the international messages were less effective due to the diffuse nature of propaganda operations in the intensifying Cold War; propaganda decentralized in the hands of multiple media outlets with too much congressional influence seemingly lacked proper coordination.

By the end of 1948, President Truman sought to lessen congressional control over Cold War operations by institutionalizing a secret CIA-sponsored propaganda structure. Truman's practice of propaganda by 1950 integrated congressionally supervised propaganda activities with his own presidentially directed psychological warfare actions. Part II thus examines Truman's attempt to expand the propaganda operations through legislative channels while developing covert propaganda actions that functioned apart from congressional decision making. The early rhetorical miscalculations of the Truman administration's 1947–1949 propaganda efforts and the intensification of the Cold War led Truman to take to the bully pulpit in support of an expanded propaganda effort. Chapter 3 centers, in part, on the debate over Truman's Campaign of Truth, which sought to expand congressional propaganda expenditures and to intensify the attack against the communist Hate America campaign. During this stage of the propaganda program's evolution, the Truman administration relied on a militaristic paradigm, where the language and the organizational structure of propaganda evidenced a military model. This new Cold War attack was aided not only by the Truman administration's overt propaganda activities funded by Congress, but also by his secretly implemented covert and psychological warfare operations. Chapter 4 assesses the international propaganda disseminated during Truman's Campaign of Truth. Specifically, the chapter examines the VOA broadcasts that exhibited the heightened anticommunist tone and the development of defector propaganda that functioned as Truman's move toward doctrinal warfare. With the latter, the autobiographies of communist refugees or reformed communists were used by the U.S. government as a means of psychological warfare. The Truman administration co-opted these dissident voices through the advancement of an escapee program; presumably, defector narratives assumed higher levels of credibility for people entrapped by communism.

The final part centers on the Eisenhower administration's propaganda activities. It addresses four investigations of the propaganda program in late 1952 and early 1953 and the Eisenhower administration's response to the committees' conclusions. Because Joseph McCarthy's anticommunist inquisitions helped transform the content of the U.S. propaganda program and inspired a reduction of congressional control over its operations, chapter 5 examines the McCarthy committee hearings over the VOA and the State Department's overseas information centers. McCarthy's attacks and increased congressional interference encouraged Eisenhower to reduce and virtually eliminate congressional involvement in propaganda activities, eventually molding propaganda into a presidential operation by 1953.

Chapter 6 focuses on the activities of the Senate Foreign Relations Committee as well as the two presidentially appointed committees (the Rockefeller and the Jackson committees) to assess their involvement in Eisenhower's reorganizational efforts. Eisenhower's inauguration and the work of these four committees helped standardize and militarize a propaganda structure complete with overt and covert strategies. In the end, such a militarized structure encouraged the removal of the program from the Department of State, virtually eliminated congressional oversight of the United States Information Agency (USIA), and secured for Eisenhower and his successors the role of commander-in-chief of propaganda and psychological warfare planning.

Chapter 7 illustrates the longitudinal and massive scope of the Eisenhower administration's coordinated propaganda campaigns by examining the secret strategies and the propaganda texts surrounding Eisenhower's Chance for Peace and Atoms for Peace campaigns. Such expansive initiatives showcase the increased sophistication and secrecy of propaganda under the Eisenhower administration and the need to expand conceptions of the rhetorical presidency. Even though Eisenhower continued to use the bully pulpit to champion his foreign and domestic policies, he simultaneously called on rhetorical surrogates to promulgate his message, often in a covert manner. The militarized vision and structure of the U.S. propaganda program had become so engrained by 1953 that presidential operatives seriously considered the need to extinguish communism. Toward that end, the Eisenhower administration's use of psychological warfare as a means by which to promote a public message of U.S. peace masked the build-up and testing of nuclear weaponry.[25]

This study examines the Truman and Eisenhower administrations' propaganda efforts and their Cold War legacies. These two presidents created and sanctioned a Cold War communications apparatus that remains in place today. Greenstein argues that Truman "was unable to transform" his major addresses "into effective public discourse," yet he made "enduring contributions to the institutional presidency." Similarly, Greenstein asserts that no other president "put comparable effort into structuring his presidency" than Eisenhower, yet he showed less "interest in public persuasion."[26] This study reveals how Truman and Eisenhower integrated public persuasion *and* institutional imperatives with differing degrees of effectiveness, ultimately revising the means by which the rhetorical presidency was practiced from the time of their presidencies forward. To fully grasp the reasons why future presidents articulated messages at odds with their secret activities (e.g., Kennedy and the Cuban Missile Crisis, Nixon and Vietnam, Reagan and the Contras) is to fully appreciate the structure established by Truman and Eisenhower. The conclusion assesses the rhetorical legacies of these two presidents by reviewing the ways in which future presidents structured their propaganda programs according to their own philosophical and rhetorical visions.

The period between 1945 and 1955 represented a tumultuous time in American history. This study demonstrates such tumult as the Truman and Eisenhower administrations sought to locate the proper message and the appropriate propaganda apparatus needed in this new "war of words." By the time that Kennedy assumed the presidency, the Cold War ideology espoused by both the Truman and Eisenhower administrations pervaded U.S. culture. The increased control of the first two Cold War presidents over multiple communication channels secured a unified message about communism, routinized covert operations as a presidential prerogative, and naturalized a propaganda apparatus as an integral part of the government's Cold War operations. In a report that reviewed the performance of the USIA during Eisenhower's administration, the USIA boasted that "never before in history have the words of the President of the United States been so widely disseminated to all peoples of the earth."[27] Because this early Cold War debate institutionalized peacetime propaganda as a presidential tool and expanded the activity of the rhetorical presidency, it becomes necessary to understand the evolution of the debate, the strategies used to achieve the nation's Cold War mission, the means by which congressional oversight decreased, and the actual substance of the government's international and domestic propaganda. The end result offers a greater comprehension of the interrelationship between propaganda and the rhetorical presidency. Certainly, the actions of these two presidents helped shape the future of foreign policy activities, especially in relation to propaganda production, the rhetorical presidency, and covert actions.

NOTES

1. Fred I. Greenstein, *The Hidden-Hand Presidency: Eisenhower as Leader* (New York: Basic Books, 1982), 58–59.

2. As Stephen F. Knott explains, the Office of Strategic Services (OSS), which was created on June 13, 1942, preceded the CIA, and "served as a hatchery for a score of future CIA figures." See Stephen F. Knott, *Secret and Sanctioned: Covert Operations and the American Presidency* (New York: Oxford University Press, 1996), 157. For secondary accounts concerning the activities of the Psychological Strategy Board (PSB) and psychological warfare strategies, see Stephen E. Pease, *Psywar: Psychological Warfare in Korea, 1950–1953* (Harrisburg, PA: Stackpole Books, 1992), 16–18; John Prados, *Presidents' Secret Wars: CIA and Pentagon Covert Operations since World War II* (New York: William Morrow 1986), 28–29; and Christopher Simpson, *Science of Coercion: Communication Research and Psychological Warfare, 1945–1960* (New York: Oxford University Press, 1994), 75.

3. See Holly Cowan Shulman, *The Voice of America: Propaganda and Democracy, 1941–1945* (Madison: University of Wisconsin Press, 1990), 3–12; J. Michael Sproule, *Propaganda and Democracy: The American Experience of Media and Mass Persuasion* (New York: Cambridge University Press, 1997), 4–21, 188–193; and Stephen Vaughn, *Holding Fast the Inner Lines: Democracy, Nationalism, and the Committee on Public Information* (Chapel Hill: University of North Carolina Press, 1980), ix, 4.

4. See Walter L. Hixson, *Parting the Curtain: Propaganda, Culture, and the Cold War, 1945–1961* (New York: St. Martin's Griffin, 1998), 4–27.

5. Simpson, *Science of Coercion*, 115.

6. See Sproule, *Propaganda and Democracy,* 9–13; and Jeffrey K. Tulis, *The Rhetorical Presidency* (Princeton, NJ: Princeton University Press, 1987), 4–6.

7. See Terri Bimes and Stephen Skowronek, "Woodrow Wilson's Critique of Popular Leadership: Reassessing the Modern-Traditional Divide in Presidential History," in *Speaking to the People: The Rhetorical Presidency in Historical Perspective,* ed. Richard J. Ellis (Amherst: University of Massachusetts Press, 1998), 134–161; Daniel Stid, "Rhetorical Leadership and 'Common Counsel' in the Presidency of Woodrow Wilson," in *Speaking to the People: The Rhetorical Presidency in Historical Perspective,* ed. Richard J. Ellis (Amherst: University of Massachusetts Press, 1998), 161–181; Glen E. Thurow, "Dimensions of Presidential Character," in *Beyond the Rhetorical Presidency,* ed. Martin J. Medhurst (College Station: Texas A&M University Press, 1996), 15–29.

8. See David F. Krugler, *The Voice of America and the Domestic Propaganda Battles, 1945–1953* (Columbia: University of Missouri Press, 2000); J. Michael Sproule, "Social Responses to Twentieth Century Propaganda," in *Propaganda: A Pluralistic Perspective,* ed. Ted. J. Smith, III (New York: Praeger, 1989), 5–22; and Vaughn, *Holding Fast the Inner Lines.*

9. Most scholars who write about the rhetorical presidency center their attention on Presidents Theodore Roosevelt, Woodrow Wilson, Franklin Roosevelt, John F. Kennedy, Richard Nixon, Jimmy Carter, Ronald Reagan, and/or Bill Clinton. Truman and Eisenhower are rarely mentioned in studies involving the rhetorical presidency. See Philip Abbott, *Strong Presidents: A Theory of Leadership* (Knoxville: University of Tennessee Press, 1996); James W. Ceaser, Glen E. Thurow, Jeffrey Tulis, and Joseph M. Bessette, "The Rise of the Rhetorical Presidency," *Presidential Studies Quarterly* 11 (1981): 158–171; Richard J. Ellis, ed., *Speaking to the People: The Rhetorical Presidency in Historical Perspective* (Amherst: University of Massachusetts Press, 1998); Martin J. Medhurst, ed., *Beyond the Rhetorical Presidency* (College Station: Texas A&M Press, 1996); William Ker Muir, Jr., *The Bully Pulpit: The Presidential Leadership of Ronald Reagan* (San Francisco: Institute for Contemporary Studies, 1992); Jeffrey K. Tulis, *The Rhetorical Presidency* (Princeton, NJ: Princeton University Press, 1987); Jeffrey K. Tulis, "Revising the Rhetorical Presidency," in *Beyond the Rhetorical Presidency,* ed. Martin J. Medhurst (College Station: Texas A&M University Press, 1996), 3–14. J. Michael Hogan refers to Eisenhower's administration as a "rhetorical presidency," noting the president's interest in persuasion. Hogan, though, links the rhetorical presidency to traditional conceptions of the bully pulpit—a conception that I seek to expand. See J. Michael Hogan, "Eisenhower and Open Skies: A Case Study in 'Psychological Warfare,'" in *Eisenhower's War of Words: Rhetoric and Leadership,* ed. Martin J. Medhurst (East Lansing: Michigan State University Press, 1994), 137–155.

10. For the purposes of this book, "propaganda" is conceived of as strategically devised messages that are disseminated to masses of people by an institution for the purpose of generating action benefiting its source. The sole source of interest in this book is the U.S. government's official and unofficial propaganda ("information") channels that eventually fell under the direction of the presidential administration by the time of the Eisenhower presidency. Even though both the Truman and Eisenhower administrations referred to their "propaganda" programs as "information" agencies, I use the term "propaganda" throughout the book to refer to such programs. The term "information" represented a euphemism for the practice of propaganda, which assumed negative connotations in the aftermath of World War I and World War II. Nevertheless, privately, members of both administrations frequently talked about the role that "propaganda" and "psychological warfare" played within their foreign policy operations. Thus, practitioners used the term "propaganda" in planning sessions and internal documents.

11. In addition to using various government-sponsored media outlets (e.g., Voice of America, Radio Free Europe), the U.S. government likewise sought to influence the domestic coverage of administrative actions and aims. Certainly, Truman and Eisenhower were not the first presidents to extend the bully pulpit by relying on the U.S. news media to promulgate their messages. See Mel Laracey, "The Presidential Newspaper: The Forgotten Way of Going Public," in *Speaking to the People: The Rhetorical Presidency in Historical Perspective,* ed. Richard J.

Ellis (Amherst: University of Massachusetts Press, 1998), 66–86. The Truman and Eisenhower administrations though, used the official channels of their propaganda agencies to influence the U.S. news media, a practice that many in Congress sought to prevent in debates over peacetime propaganda. In fact, the Smith-Mundt Act (1948) stipulated that the U.S. government was prevented from propagandizing the American people. The agency was to promulgate instead internationally directed messages. See Gil Cranberg, "Propaganda and the United States," *Etc.* 41 (1984): 184–186; and House Committee on Foreign Affairs, *United States Information and Educational Exchange Act of 1948,* 80th Cong., 2d sess., 1948, H.R. 3342.

12. Muir, *The Bully Pulpit,* 1–2, 189.

13. David Zarefsky, *President Johnson's War on Poverty: Rhetoric and History* (University: University of Alabama Press, 1986), 8.

14. Ceaser et al., "The Rise of the Rhetorical Presidency," 164.

15. Barbara Hinckley, *The Symbolic Presidency: How Presidents Portray Themselves* (New York: Routledge, 1990), 16–17.

16. Bruce E. Gronbeck asserts that the "idea of discourse, if understood as acts granted political meaningfulness, has exploded" through electronic means. The proliferation of presidential policies so vital to the rhetorical effectiveness of a presidential administration could now be conducted by multiple individuals and institutions through a "multimediated rhetoric, allowing for more narrative repetition and the illusion of widespread consensus." See Bruce E. Gronbeck, "The Presidency in the Age of Second Orality," in *Beyond the Rhetorical Presidency,* ed. Martin J. Medhurst (College Station: Texas A&M University Press, 1996), 41, 45.

17. See Jacques Ellul, *Propaganda: The Formation of Men's Attitudes* (New York: Vintage Books, 1965), 52; and Sproule, "Social Responses to Twentieth-Century Propaganda," 9.

18. See Krugler, *The Voice of America.* Krugler offers a detailed examination of the congressional wranglings over the Voice of America (VOA). While contributing to our understanding of the debate surrounding VOA during the early Cold War years, Krugler does not examine the actual propaganda that was disseminated by the agency. This study seeks to offer a more complete analysis of the strategizing sessions, the debates surrounding the propaganda program, as well as the propaganda that was produced.

19. Francis A. Beer and Robert Hariman, "Realism and Rhetoric in International Relations," in *Post-Realism: The Rhetorical Turn in International Relations,* ed. Francis A. Beer and Robert Hariman (East Lansing: Michigan State University Press, 1996), 24, 11, 21.

20. Lawrence C. Soley, *Radio Warfare: OSS and CIA Subversive Propaganda* (New York: Praeger, 1989), 222–223.

21. Martin J. Medhurst contends that those who study the "rhetorical presidency" from a political perspective often place the emphasis on the institution of the presidency and tend to de-legitimize the rhetorical aspects of the executive

branch. Rhetoricians, conversely, are attuned to "what to say, how to say it, to whom, under what conditions, and with what apparent outcome." See Martin J. Medhurst, "A Tale of Two Constructs: The Rhetorical Presidency versus Presidential Rhetoric," in *Beyond the Rhetorical Presidency,* ed. Martin J. Medhurst (College Station: Texas A&M University Press, 1996), xii–xvii. Mary E. Stuckey and Frederick J. Antczak also assert that the problem with most studies on the rhetorical presidency is that they center attention on either the individual rhetorical influences of presidents or on the institutional role of the presidency. See Mary E. Stuckey and Frederick J. Antczak, "The Rhetorical Presidency: Deepening Vision, Widening Change," *Communication Yearbook* 21 (1998): 424. This study attempts to balance both approaches by recognizing the important role of rhetoric to public policy and the institutional nature of the presidency. Although Truman and Eisenhower were instrumental in exacting changes to presidential-rhetorical leadership within their administrations, their strategies were implemented by presidential groups and individuals working on behalf of the presidents and their Cabinet officials.

22. For more information on the overt and covert nature of the Eisenhower administration's propaganda program, see Shawn J. Parry-Giles, "The Eisenhower Administration's Conceptualization of the USIA: The Development of Overt and Covert Propaganda Strategies," *Presidential Studies Quarterly* 24 (1994): 263–276.

23. The term "metonymy" represents "a situation in which some subcategory or member or submodel is used . . . to comprehend the category as a whole." See George Lakoff, *Women, Fire, and Dangerous Things: What Categories Reveal about the Mind* (Chicago: University of Chicago Press, 1987), 79.

24. By naturalization, I mean that the human qualities are "removed" and the entity seemingly embodies characteristics found only in nature. The politicization of the entity is masked by its construction in more natural terms. See Roland Barthes, *Mythologies* (New York: Hill and Wang, 1972), 142–143. For the purposes of this study, I define ideology "in practice" as "a political language, preserved in rhetorical documents, with the capacity to dictate decision and control public belief and behavior." See Michael Calvin McGee, "The 'Ideograph': A Link Between Rhetoric and Ideology," *Quarterly Journal of Speech,* 66 (1980): 1–16. I am equating the term "paradigm" with perspective. Like Klaus Krippendorff, I view "dialogue" or discourse as foundational to any paradigm, particularly one involving the study of communication. Language, thus, designates paradigmatic distinctions that work then to construct reality. See Klaus Krippendorff, "On the Ethics of Constructing Communication," in *Rethinking Communication: Paradigm Issues,* eds. Brenda Dervin, Lawrence Grossberg, Barbara J. O'Keefe, and Ellen Wartella (Newbury Park, CA: Sage, 1989), 67–68.

25. For Eisenhower, 1955 represented the point where his administration cemented the propaganda structure that remained in place until the end of his presidency. Although minor changes were made to the structure in the aftermath of 1955, the militarized operations continued as designed in 1953 and beyond,

which is the reason for ending the study in 1955. From 1955 through 1960, Eisenhower continued to rely on propaganda and psychological warfare strategies as integral measures in his foreign policy operations.

26. Fred I. Greenstein, *The Presidential Difference: Leadership Style from FDR to Clinton* (New York: Martin Kessler Books, 2000), 39–40, 54–55.

27. Theodore C. Streibert to Dwight D. Eisenhower, February, 1954, Eisenhower, Dwight D: Papers as President of the United States, 1953–1961 (Ann Whitman File), Administration Series, Box 37, Dwight D. Eisenhower Presidential Library, 1.

I

The Period of Propaganda
and News

1

The Truman Administration's Legalization of Peacetime Propaganda

To understand the changes that the Truman administration exacted to the practice of propaganda from 1945 to 1949 necessitates a brief summary of the presidential propaganda activities leading up to 1945. Propaganda's *official* history is linked to President Woodrow Wilson's Committee on Public Information (CPI), which was established in April 1917 to convince the U.S. public to support the Great War effort. Intended to aid America's war efforts at home and abroad, the CPI promoted the foreign policies of the Wilson administration. As Stephen Vaughn argues, the CPI established a structure that "allowed the federal government to communicate with virtually every citizen" in an attempt to promote "nationalism," particularly "American democracy," during wartime.[1] Because CPI's output centered largely on domestic propaganda, it acted primarily as a publicity agent for Wilson's international policies.[2] According to J. Michael Sproule, the CPI centralized all material "around the official ideology of . . . the presidential administration,"[3] giving evidence to the increased importance of rhetorical influence for the president.

Wilson staffed his propaganda program with people skilled in promoting and crafting ideas (e.g., journalists, writers, and advertisers). Journalist George Creel, an ardent Wilson supporter and director of the CPI, staffed the propaganda program with journalists and intellectuals who issued some six thousand news releases over the course of the war. This practice of influencing the dissemination of news ignited considerable criticism in the postwar years. The controversy was sparked by Creel's celebration of CPI's successes in his controversial book *How We Advertised America.* Creel's assertions led many Americans to fear that the Wilson administration monopolized the media during wartime,[4] which prompted journalists to denounce the practice of propaganda throughout the 1920s and into the 1930s. One writer of the 1930s, in particular, called "propaganda" a "menace" and equated it with such "social diseases" as murder, arson, and theft.[5]

The negative conceptions of propaganda grew even stronger during World War II as propaganda was associated mostly with Hitler's Germany. The "Big Lie" theory attributed to the Nazis heightened the perception that propaganda equaled Nazi lies; many Americans thus viewed propaganda even more suspiciously during the World War II. At the same time, political officials came to accept the necessity of influencing international and domestic public opinion during World War II, leading to the creation of a second wartime propaganda agency, the Office of War Information (OWI), six months after the United States entered World War II.[6]

Like the CPI, the OWI housed a domestic and international branch and existed to coordinate government-sponsored information. Elmer Davis, OWI's director, also used a journalistic model in constructing his wartime propaganda agency. Davis, a veteran journalist, sought to capitalize on his media connections in his wartime propaganda post. Like Creel, Davis conceived of the OWI as a news agency, leading him to fill OWI's vacancies with journalists.[7]

Differences, though, existed between the CPI and OWI. CPI worked to convince the U.S. public that the war should be fought; OWI's mission focused more on winning the war. A second change conversely resulted from the turmoil surrounding CPI's focus on domestic propaganda. The Roosevelt administration reacted to the controversy by emphasizing OWI's international functions. By 1944, 90 percent of OWI's budget serviced the international propaganda activities; 10 percent centered on domestic operations.[8]

This shift of OWI to a more international orientation was significant. It created a controversy over who controlled international propaganda—the OWI or the military—with the latter directing much of the overseas propaganda during World War I.[9] As in the case of the CPI, personnel from the departments of state, war, and the navy were influential in OWI's operations, with military leaders paying little attention to civilian activities. OWI also competed with the Office of Strategic Services (OSS), the predecessor to the Central Intelligence Agency (CIA), for leadership over governmental propaganda operations. For the most part, OWI's staff was excluded from policy decisions and given only limited control over propaganda activities.[10]

Members of Congress, the State Department, and the domestic news media also voiced concern over the wartime propaganda program. Because of its international focus, Congress exerted considerable control over OWI's operations, constantly questioning its budget and serving a watch dog role over its activities. Many within the Department of State felt that the propaganda program countered diplomatic efforts—a view that generated hostility toward the program. The OWI also lost favor with the press[11]—a group that undoubtedly viewed the wartime propaganda program as a rival news agency.

Because of the hostility projected toward the U.S. propaganda program, including the critique that such programs were "wartime relics,"[12] the Truman administration deliberated over the need to dismantle governmental propaganda activities in the postwar years. As a temporary solution, President Truman abolished the OWI and transferred propaganda operations to a reluctant Department of State on August 31, 1945.[13] Propaganda officials applauded the move, assuming that in peacetime, Congress would be hesitant to withdraw funding if such practices were vested in a standing and credible department. Many State Department officials believed, however, that locating the propaganda program in their department could actually prove embarrassing for U.S. diplomatic efforts.[14]

Truman appointed William Benton, former advertiser,[15] to direct the interim program as Assistant Secretary of State for Public Affairs. Secretary of State James Byrnes extended the activities of the interim propaganda program through January 1, 1946, and congressional appropriations kept it operational through the 1947 fiscal year. The congressional debate over the permanence of a propaganda program lasted through January 1948,[16] as Benton sought to convince skeptical journalists and congressional leaders of propaganda's peacetime promise.

The wranglings over peacetime propaganda from 1945 through the passage of the Smith-Mundt Act on January 27, 1948, reveal just how the Truman administration utilized a journalistic paradigm to assuage media and congressional reservations over the need for a peacetime propaganda program. Such an approach equated propaganda with news and required the testimony of leading editors and journalists to testify to propaganda's utility and constitutionality. Rather than promoting the legalization of propaganda from the bully pulpit, though, Truman instead relied on State Department officials and members of Congress to achieve the legislative feat. The campaign that William Benton spearheaded as the director of the interim program reflected his own rhetorical acumen domestically; members of the media and Congress became convinced of a governmental "news" agency's necessity in this new kind of war—a "war of words." As Benton and his congressional supporters urged, this word "war" promised to forestall more war, promote peace, and fulfill the country's international responsibility in the postwar world.

THE TRUMAN ADMINISTRATION'S USE OF A JOURNALISTIC PARADIGM

Benton faced two major obstacles in the Smith-Mundt debates, with "resistance" emanating from "commercial broadcast interests and the wire services" and from a Congress concerned with the cost and "worth of such programs."[17] Benton first sought to convince the private media of a peacetime propaganda program's importance—a strategy that proved integral to the congressional debate. Before Congress could support a government-sponsored news agency, the U.S. press corps had to reconcile any constitutional tension. Such rhetorical efforts included an orchestrated and secretive campaign of influence. In the process of lobbying the media and Congress, Benton and other Smith-Mundt supporters redefined the new Cold War enemy and repackaged propaganda as a democratic activity integral to the preservation of peace.

The connection between the private news media and the OWI played a significant role in the media's attitude toward a peacetime propaganda program. When OWI began its operations, many of the country's news organizations (e.g., CBS and NBC) leased short-wave transmitters to the government in order to support the country's propaganda efforts. Such support was essential since the Federal Communications Commission (FCC) only granted licenses to private organizations.[18] The Associated Press (AP) and the United Press (UP) even supplied news scripts to the OWI for dissemination over the government's international news channels.[19]

The OWI also hired journalists to conduct its operations, creating a group of loyal propaganda employees who returned to private news positions after the war.[20] Although examples of journalists using their writing and broadcasting talents in support of the war effort are numerous,[21] Elmer Davis served as a typical example. Davis, OWI's director, worked for the *New York Times* in the 1920s and later acted as a news analyst for CBS, becoming one of the country's most notable radio commentators before assuming his directorship of the OWI.[22] Davis's appointment enhanced OWI's credibility for many news personnel who viewed him as "one of them."[23] World War II propagandist Charles A. H. Thomson contends that because of the shared personnel between OWI and the private news industry, journalists, "who in their earlier role would have been horrified at the idea of government intervention into the field, found their views changed by their experience in the managing of world communications for national purposes." As a result, many of OWI's personnel, in returning to the private sector after the war, "carried with them more favorable and concrete ideas about government information overseas."[24]

The Truman administration through Benton, in seeking to legalize a peacetime propaganda program after the war, used these media connections to gain legislative favor in both overt and covert ways.[25] The administration equated propaganda with news, articulating a language that media personnel and eventually members of Congress could reconcile with a democratic government. The following section demonstrates just how Assistant Secretary of State Benton, acting on behalf of the Truman administration, legitimized a U.S. propaganda program in the face of considerable journalistic and congressional opposition.

Benton's Media Campaign

When Secretary of State Byrnes approached William Benton about becoming the director of the interim propaganda program, he offered Benton advice on how to obtain the controversial legislation. The secretary of state recommended that Benton identify a "good newspaperman" to help him achieve the passage of the Smith-Mundt bill because "newspapermen have standing up on the Hill."[26] Benton heeded Byrnes's advice and also moved to construct multifaceted strategies to secure the news industry's support of an international propaganda program.

To begin with, Benton sought the aid of many journalists by tapping into the OWI alumni network for editorial favors. During a 1968 interview with the Columbia University oral history project, Benton referred to these OWI alums as his "under-cover workers . . . [who were] of great help" in advertising the necessity of a peacetime propaganda program. In order to woo OWI alums into supporting the program, Benton used his own money to purchase framed certificates of merit for former OWI employees. He also tried, though apparently unsuccessfully, to award OWI propagandists with commendation medals. Clearly, Benton felt such recognition would produce more favorable coverage of the Smith-Mundt bill by those he identified as "back at their jobs on the newspapers and magazines, often writing editorials."[27]

In another strategic move aimed at attracting the news media's favor, Benton lobbied media moguls and formed special committees composed of media personnel to recommend changes in propaganda operations. In a press release from the Department of State in May 1946, Benton publicized the statements of five radio executives broadcasting under contract with that department and acting on Benton's behalf to denounce congressional bud-

get cuts. Several prominent media executives provided supportive apprais-
als of the government's propaganda efforts: David Sarnoff, RCA chair;
Philip D. Reed, GE chair; and Frank Stanton, CBS president. As Stanton asserted, "the dangers incident to even a temporary interruption of international short-wave broadcasting are so great that we feel it both proper and
necessary for us to make this recommendation to you."[28] The following
year, Benton teamed radio executives with members of congressional appropriations' committees to discuss the "future of international broadcasting."[29] Not surprisingly, these media executives supported the continued
funding of a propaganda program that leased their company's short-wave
radio equipment. Ignoring the financial gains these executives stood to accrue for their corporations,[30] Benton argued that "these are the people . . .
who are in the best position to judge its [international information] value."[31]

Benton also grouped publishers, educators, and radio officials into what
he dubbed the Radio Advisory Committee—a committee empowered to determined "the effectiveness of the State Department's [propaganda] efforts."[32] The committee assembled such notable individuals as scholar
Harold Lasswell and broadcaster Edward R. Murrow, in addition to Gardner
Cowles, Jr., publisher of the *Des Moines Register and Tribune.*[33] The eight-
member committee concluded that the available funds for "international
broadcasting" were necessary "to avoid a serious set-back in the development of its proper relations with the rest of the world."[34]

In addition to these two committees, Benton also lobbied the American
Society of Newspaper Editors (ASNE) to aid in the promotion of the Smith-
Mundt Act. While members of the ASNE were initially hostile toward the
propaganda program,[35] the board appointed a committee to examine the
"problem of world dissemination of news" during its 1946 convention. This
eight-member group included editors from the *New York Times, St. Louis
Post-Dispatch,* and the *Baltimore Sun.* The ASNE ultimately concluded
that "the present uncertainties in international relations justify an effort by
the United States Government to make its activities and its policies clear to
the people of the world through the agency set up in the State Department."
Even with the charges of mismanagement and ineffectiveness in the interim
program, and despite strong opposition against the government's dissemination of news, committee members supported an increase in propaganda expenditures and called on the ASNE to continue oversight of propaganda
developments.[36] Benton, not surprisingly, highlighted this committee's conclusions publicly in order to bolster his own lobbying efforts.[37]

While the activities and recommendations of these three committees
were made public, the actions and even the existence of a separate committee remained hidden. In order to achieve the passage of the Smith-Mundt

Act, Benton formed a secret advising committee. While the operating costs were covered by Benton personally, he received additional funding from two major contributors to the Republican Party (Henry Luce of *Time,* and Gardiner "Mike" Cowles of Cowles publications), who also served on Benton's Radio Advisory Committee. The committee reportedly used the OWI alumni network to solicit favorable coverage; speeches were also prepared for supportive congressional leaders as they spoke in favor of the Smith-Mundt bill.[38]

Beyond grouping media elites and political officials, attempts were also made by the Truman administration to soften journalistic opposition to the propaganda program and to improve media relations. As part of the plan, U.S. correspondents were granted prompt passport and visa services and were offered help in obtaining adequate housing, food, and reasonable rates of exchange when traveling abroad on assignment.[39] On a more interpersonal level, Benton sponsored a lavish dinner for some forty members of the press corps in 1946 so as to seek their input on propaganda practices.[40] Benton also sought advice on issues pertaining to press relations from news leaders like Arthur Krock (*New York Times*), Edward Barrett (*Newsweek*), and C. D. Jackson (*Time*).[41]

Beyond that, members of the State Department strategized ways in which to encourage more favorable press coverage by inviting journalists to serve as departmental advisors. Two major State Department presumptions prompted this move. The first was that poor relations existed between the department and the press. The second assumption was that the department needed to take a more active role in "initiat[ing] the news."[42] M. J. McDermott, special assistant to the secretary of state, urged, for example, that only through more "intimate" contact could press relations be improved.[43] Edward G. Miller, Jr., staff member of the assistant secretary of state, concluded that a confidential and "an informal advisory committee of members of the press [be] . . . constituted to advise on matters of press policy." Miller argued that improving press relations was essential to "maintain[ing] a consistent foreign policy."[44]

Members of the press corps who were consulted seemed more than willing to comply. Garnett D. Horner of the *Washington Star,* recommended, for example, that "periodic intimate and confidential meetings . . . [between] the Secretary [and] a restricted group of American correspondents" occur to "give the men who have the job of interpreting what the State Department is doing the benefit of the 'high policy' guidance." Such meetings were to take place "outside the Department,"[45] according to Horner, whose willingness to join in such clandestine meetings was not unexpected. As Miller predicted, "the more information we [give] out the more sympathetic the press [becomes] to our total aims."[46]

News practitioners, though, sought their own *quid pro quo* if they were to support the goals of the administration's international broadcasting initiatives. As part of the debate over international propaganda, administrative officials insisted that the U.S. news media distribute newspapers and magazines abroad so as to educate the world about the country's ideals and initiatives. In response to this call, industry leaders claimed that the distribution of news abroad was too expensive for them because of exchange rate losses.[47] For several years, the State Department and media leaders discussed ways to rectify the financial question. The debate was finally resolved in 1948 with the passage of an "information media guarantee" (IMG), which subsidized exchange rate deficits for news organizations disseminating their messages internationally. Although State Department officials stressed that news organizations benefiting from the IMG program would be free to print what they wished, an internal document of the State Department indicated that those "information products [which] most successfully present[ed] a true picture of the United States abroad" would benefit most from the IMG program.[48] In the end, the news organizations that distributed news products abroad under the IMG initiative included the *New York Times*—a paper that Truman believed was too critical of his policies[49]—the *New York Herald Tribune*—an organization that voiced strong opposition to the IMG initially—as well as *Life, Time,* and *Newsweek* magazines. The Truman administration arguably influenced the coverage of America's domestic press through services like the IMG, which earmarked some $15,000,000 for exchange rate compensation.[50]

The Truman administration still faced obstacles even with Benton's widespread successes in persuading many leading editors and journalists of propaganda's legitimacy. As mentioned earlier, the AP and the UP supplied news to OWI during World War II. Following OWI's termination, however, both the AP and the UP withdrew their services. This move upset Benton tremendously, and he commenced an extensive publicity campaign to regain their services and support.[51]

Part of the Benton's strategy involved a public attack against the AP and UP for refusing to contribute their services. According to Benton, AP's board of directors terminated services because they believed that the government should not "engage in newscasting without creating the fear of propaganda which necessarily would reflect upon the objectivity of the news services from which such newscasts are prepared." In response to such claims, Benton tapped into the First Amendment ideology, arguing that the State Department's policy was to "advance the cause of press freedom everywhere" by getting "reliable and objective American news into vast areas of the world."[52] Questioning their loyalty, Benton charged that while the AP and UP were "willing to sell their news to foreign agencies" (e.g., the Soviet government), they were unwilling to offer such services to their own government.[53] Stepping up the pressure even further, Benton resorted to the use of fear appeals, implying that without support from organizations like the wire services, the results could be catastrophic: "Where the alternatives are, on the one hand, the greatest threat of mass obliteration the world has ever known, and on the other the necessity for the greatest and quickest spread of understanding among the peoples of the world . . . can this action be called living up to the responsibility of a free press in the post-war world?"[54] Benton's efforts nevertheless failed, and he viewed that failure as a major setback.[55] In describing the strained relationship, Benton's hostility was still evident some twenty years later: "The Associated Press had jerked wires out of the State Department, causing me to attack in headlong fashion the great sacrosanct Associated Press."[56] In spite of this defeat, Benton experienced other victories among media elites.

Benton actively worked to thwart allegations that the government's propaganda program undermined a U.S. commitment to a free press. He articulated a commitment to an international freedom of the press in 1946, asserting that the "government will play a leading role in the fight against restrictions of all sorts on international communications."[57] Toward that end, Benton asked interested media publishers to draft an international freedom of information agreement that could eventually become part of the United Nations's provisions. The *Chicago Times* assumed the task, with staff members consulting some seventy-five newspaper, magazine, radio, and motion-picture representatives for suggestions on the content of what became known as the "Treaty on Freedom of Information."[58] In the end, a U.N. conference on freedom of information was held between March 23 and April 21, 1948, featuring the leaders of the newly legalized propaganda program. In spite of their efforts to export America's free speech commitments, those attending the conference concluded that little possibility existed in getting totalitarian regimes to alter their press and speech practices.[59] Even though the conference planners failed to achieve their stated goals abroad, the State Department's leadership role proved significant. Rather than violating a foundational democratic philosophy, Benton and the Department of State actively pursued the exportation of a U.S. free press ideology, which simultaneously answered questions about the presidential administration's commitment to the First Amendment at home.

Overall, Benton's rhetorical campaign to gain the media's support for a governmental peacetime propaganda program was quite effective.[60] His use of a journalistic paradigm as well as his own "persuasiveness, pertinacity, and acumen,"[61] contributed to his ability to garner sufficient journalistic support for the extension of wartime propaganda into peacetime. His campaign also demonstrates the symbiotic relationship between the executive branch and the press in the early Cold War years. While victorious in the private sector among media elites, the Truman administration through the Department of State and interested congressional leaders had one additional hurdle facing them. They had to convince Congress that the U.S. government should initiate and fund a peacetime propaganda program at a time when much of the country wanted a return to normalcy.

THE JOURNALISTIC PARADIGM AND CONGRESS

The legalization of the first peacetime propaganda program in the United States grew out of a combined effort between the Truman administration and Congress. In May 1947, Republican Congressman Karl E. Mundt of South Dakota introduced H.R. 3342 in the House of Representatives.[62] Senator H. Alexander Smith, Republican of New Jersey, co-sponsored the Smith-Mundt bill, which was introduced during the first session of the 80th Congress. According to its framers, the bill was designed to "enable the Government of the United States to promote a better understanding of the United States in other countries, and to increase mutual understanding between the people of the United States and the people of other countries."[63]

From May 13 through May 20, 1947, Mundt chaired a subcommittee of the House Committee on Foreign Affairs, which investigated H.R. 3342. The committee consisted of three other Republicans along with three Democrats: Donald L. Jackson (R-CA), Walter H. Judd (R-MN), John Davis Lodge (R-CT), Pete Jarman (D-AL), Mike Mansfield (D-MT), and James P. Richards (D-SC). After receiving a two-thirds majority vote in the House, the bill went before a subcommittee of the Senate Committee on Foreign Relations. Senator Alexander Smith served as this subcommittee's chair, and Democratic Senator Carl A. Hatch of New Mexico acted as the other official member of the subcommittee. Other senators joined the proceedings periodically while they were in session on July 2, 3, and 5, 1947. Even though the Senate subcommittee reported the bill favorably to the floor of the Senate, it failed to come to a vote before the close of the session.[64]

Because of the controversy surrounding peacetime propaganda, Congress formed a special subcommittee in July 1947 for the purpose of conducting on-the-spot investigations of the U.S. propaganda program abroad.[65] This joint committee traveled to twenty-two European countries in September and October 1947.[66] After their return, congressional members recommitted H.R. 3342 to the Senate Committee on Foreign Relations on December 8, 1947. The committee reported the bill favorably to the Senate and recommended its passage on January 7, with the Smith-Mundt bill passing through the Senate unanimously on January 19, 1948. Public Law 402 was enacted on January 27, 1948, with the signature of President Harry S. Truman.[67]

The ease with which the Smith-Mundt bill eventually passed through Congress was surprising considering the negative connotations associated with propaganda, particularly in peacetime. Such success cannot be understood apart from the economic conditions in postwar Europe and the progression of the Cold War by 1947. Because of the devastating impact of World War II in Europe, colonial powers were weakened, which left the door open to communist expansion. Concern over the spread of communism to China, Soviet activities in Iran that became worrisome as early as World War II, and the financial exigencies in Europe, worried the Truman administration in 1946 and 1947. On March 12, 1947, Truman addressed the European and Middle Eastern crisis in his notable Truman Doctrine, which helped define his administration's parameters for fighting the Cold War; this Doctrine followed Britain's announcement that it could no longer offer financial aid to Greece. Fears of European and Middle Eastern vulnerabilities brought on by the protracted war against the Nazis, inspired Undersecretary of State Dean Acheson to articulate the domino theory that Truman furthered in his Doctrine. The financial burdens in Europe were accentuated within the Marshall Plan of June 5. Although centered on economic concerns, the Marshall Plan, like the Truman Doctrine, was inspired by fears over communist expansion.[68] These Soviet actions combined with the Truman administration's Cold War doctrines to form a backdrop for the Smith-Mundt debate.

The strength of the arguments marshaled by the bill's supporters also helped determine its fate. Smith-Mundt proponents, still under the leadership of William Benton, managed to create a new vision for U.S. foreign policy in the postwar years by calling for the country to enter a new kind of worldwide conflict that pitted one country's words against another's. Drawing on the same journalistic paradigm that Benton used to gain the news media's favor, Smith-Mundt supporters created alternative conceptions of propaganda for members of Congress. Relying on a language of news, propaganda proponents promised the creation of a new peacetime operation that could forestall yet another full-scale world war.

The Pro-Propaganda Press

Predictably, much of the congressional opposition to the legalization of peacetime propaganda was grounded in the assumption that such an organization threatened the U.S. free press system. Representative William Lemke (D-CT) questioned any governmental attempt to "compete" with private news stations, calling for financial support of short-wave stations and "those who blazed the trail with their own funds." According to Lemke, "Any other procedure would be the rankest kind of injustice."[69] Congressman Hale Boggs (D-LA) also questioned the practice of placing the government in "competition with a free press," reflecting the Russian practice of control[ling] the "radio and the press."[70] Some congressional leaders like Republican Congressman J. Edgar Chenoweth (CO), used the conflict between the State Department and the AP as evidence that a constitutional exigency existed over the government's intrusion into the news business. Referring to the goals of the Smith-Mundt bill as "novel and extraordinary," Chenoweth cited Kent Cooper, executive director of the AP, emphasizing the "abhorrence of the Government going into the news business," an act that Cooper equated with "amending the Constitution.[71]

Benton, though, was prepared for such constitutional claims and the backlash caused by the AP and UP refusals. Not surprisingly, he relied on testimonies from his special media committees to silence opposition over the government's involvement in international broadcasting. Cited most extensively was the ASNE study, the results of which were placed in the *Congressional Record* in February 1947,[72] and the subcommittee hearings of the House Committee on Foreign Affairs in May 1947.[73] As Benton claimed, "If we did not play the news straight, as the ASNE agreed in their study, in my opinion we would not have such press support for this program."[74] Employing the testimonials of ASNE members, Benton also associated propaganda with news.

Moreover, Benton evinced the media's support by excerpting statements from U.S. correspondents working abroad and passages from the Radio Advisory Committee's report. In the same May 1947 House subcommittee hearings, Benton inserted over seven pages of editorial passages from newspapers and magazines across the country (e.g., *Life* and the *New York Times*) and from business leaders (e.g., David Sarnoff, RCA, and Philip D. Reed, GE) into the hearing transcripts.[75] Reed even testified on behalf of the Smith-Mundt bill before the Senate Subcommittee of the Committee on Foreign Relations in July 1947. Reed claimed that "the simple truth about the United States . . . widely told throughout the world, will do more to reduce the risk of war, and thus to reduce the need for a multibillion dollar military force, than any other single factor."[76] This philosophy construed propaganda as a substitute for military involvement, elevating the importance of a government-sponsored news agency.

Despite concerns that the AP and the UP refused to offer their support, Benton emphasized that the third wire service, the International News Service (INS), was "selling its services to the State Department."[77] Marshaling large amounts of support from the private news community for the Smith-Mundt bill, Benton thwarted attempts to denounce the bill on First Amendment grounds. Smith-Mundt supporters, however, also looked to the Cold War context as another means to justify its new program.

Redefinition of a Wartime Ally

Connecting propaganda to the Cold War battle, Smith-Mundt proponents cultivated a postwar view of the Soviet government and called for a U.S. response to the Soviets' propaganda offensive. The Soviet government, they argued, launched a new kind of war—a "war of words"—that threatened the U.S. government and the future of democracy. Proponents of the Smith-Mundt bill now talked of a new kind of international context, where propaganda served as the primary means by which to compete against this new formidable foe.

When depicting the country's newest international enemy in the postwar years, Smith-Mundt supporters repeatedly stressed the imperialist aims of the Soviet Union. Congressman Judd maintained that "Russia herself is forcing on all her neighbors as cruel and ruthless and utterly despotic an imperialism as any the world has ever known."[78] Representative Mundt constructed a metaphorical image of a Russian bear systematically taking over weaker countries. "While we with the dove of peace were cooing to ourselves," Mundt proclaimed, "the Russian bear was moving out pulling into its bosom a swarm of little countries . . . making them part of its domain."[79] Senator Alexander Smith depicted a slightly different image of Russian imperialism for his congressional peers, alleging that the communists conspired to "divide" and then "absorb" smaller countries; communism thrived "only on chaos and human misery."[80]

Smith-Mundt supporters also spoke of a Soviet conspiracy designed to ruin U.S. credibility abroad. Proponents stressed throughout the debate that the Russian propaganda machine threatened to undermine the country's new leadership role in the world community. Representative Everett M. Dirksen (R-IL) showcased what he identified as "falsehoods" communicated by the Russian media. Dirksen concluded that the Soviet's goal involved destroying the "integrity" and the "greatness of the American system."[81] Democratic Congressman Harold D. Cooley of North Carolina claimed that the communists wanted to vilify "American democracy" while defaming its "institutions in the eyes of the people of the world."[82] Representative Mundt associated the Smith-Mundt bill with the Russian conspiracy against the United States: "The forces of aggression are moving rapidly and we must step up our action and increase our efforts in the field of information abroad if we are to prevent the eventuality of confronting a world which has been either coerced or corrupted against us."[83]

As supporters of the Smith-Mundt bill sought to redefine its new Cold War enemy, they simultaneously talked of the need for a new kind of peacetime practice—one that could aid the United States in a competition of ideas. This most recent "war," however, proved just as threatening, they argued, as any other battle the United States could face, requiring the country to take immediate action by legalizing the first U.S. peacetime propaganda agency.[84]

Propaganda Redefined

One of the primary obstacles for Smith-Mundt supporters involved separating U.S. propaganda from its traditional pejorative connotations and molding it into a journalistic framework. Throughout the debate, some proponents of the Smith-Mundt bill insisted upon the label "information" when referencing this new program. Other supporters of the program distinguished between "good" and "bad" propaganda, declaring the more honest propaganda of the United States superior to the vicious lies spread by the Soviet Union. As the debate progressed, however, Smith-Mundt supporters were forced to devise new distinctions between "good" and "bad" sources of propaganda because some political leaders objected to information about America that was too honest. These new distinctions between "good" and "bad" propaganda were linked to prevailing images of democracy and communism. Thus, while Smith-Mundt advocates wanted to alter the prevailing view of propaganda, they also sought to reconcile the establishment of a propaganda agency with a democratic government by relying on arguments grounded in a journalistic paradigm.

Assistant Secretary of State Benton and Congressman Mundt argued that the United States would not engage in the deceitful activity often associated with the practice of propaganda. Toward that end, they explained the difference between "good" and "bad" propaganda in terms of the contrasting metaphors of a "mirror" and "showcase." Benton alleged that the United States used a "mirror" approach when disseminating information, while the Soviet Union used a "showcase" method.[85] Benton explained that "in holding up a mirror, [it] shows . . . the basic goals and attitudes of this country," with the "real image . . . reflected,"[86] including the bad as well as the good.[87] In contrast, Mundt argued, the "showcase" approach resembled a "department store," which placed the "best items" in the front window that would have "the biggest appeal to the passers-by."[88] According to Benton and Mundt, this was the method employed by most other countries, including the Soviet Union.

Benton maintained further that U.S. democratic principles necessitated the "mirror" approach to overseas information, evidencing an entrenched journalistic axiom in the early Cold War years.[89] Benton maintained that his program did not "depend on misrepresentation and propaganda but . . . on a straight statement of the facts" when disseminating information. "Any other way to handle this broadcasting," Benton professed, was "so foreign to the . . . attitude of the American press," that people could not "be found to run it." "Propaganda," Benton suggested, was "out of character with the American people."[90] Only those countries "ashamed to let the people see [their] real . . . image,"[91] Benton concluded, needed to use the "showcase" approach.

While the mirror metaphor may have helped overcome some objections to propaganda, other congressional critics objected to the dissemination of negative news about the United States. Congressman Ellsworth B. Buck (R-NY) wanted assurance that the propaganda program would "sell the fine things" of the United States and "not the seamy things" like "lynchings, strikes, crime, and riots."[92] Iowa Congressman Ben F. Jensen (R) also questioned the logic of spending "millions of dollars . . . to tell the world . . . a lot of bad things" about the United States.[93] Supporters of the Smith-Mundt bill, such as Senator Lodge, assured the critics that America's "public relations program" would "never flood the world with material [that was] bad" or that was "not in the right language."[94] Like Lodge, Mundt also referred to the propaganda activities in the United States as a "public relations" effort;[95] Benton even admitted that "in activities other than those dealing with straight news . . . there would always be a strong element of the 'showcase.'"[96] Such a conception began to blend the practice of journalism with a public relations paradigm. News in the form of international propaganda had to assume a public relations form according to members of Congress in order to achieve its full impact.

Eventually, Smith-Mundt supporters grounded conceptions of propaganda in the values of democracy and communism. They juxtaposed "good" and "bad" propaganda, not so much in terms of a mirror-showcase metaphor, but in terms of the source of the information: the United States disseminated "truth" while the Soviet Union espoused "lies." Mundt maintained that the U.S. program presented "information" and "facts," arguments linked to the discourse of news. The Russians, conversely, Mundt charged, spread "propaganda" that involved "maligning," "slandering," and "lying" to its audience,[97] arguments dependent upon pejorative and historical constructions of the practice. Similarly, Representative J. Vaughan Gary (D-VA) spoke of the United States distributing "the true facts about its people . . . policies . . . and purposes," while the Russians spread "false propaganda."[98]

Even though supporters of the Smith-Mundt bill did not define propaganda clearly, they did attempt to associate most of its negative connotations with the Soviet program. With the mirror/showcase distinction, they suggested that Russian propaganda at least distorted the truth by highlighting positive information while concealing the negative. When critics objected to a "mirror" approach that might produce negative material about the United States, supporters of the program went further, suggesting that the Soviet Union dispersed "propaganda" and "lies" while the United States broadcast "information" and "truth." These claims of objectivity certainly reflected a journalistic paradigm. Such a perspective helped assuage partisan concerns and proved credible in the context of the new portrait of the Soviet Union in the postwar years. As part of their revisioning effort, Smith-Mundt supporters also had to recontextualize propaganda as a peacetime practice.

Propaganda's Promise of Peace

For many congressional leaders, foreign propaganda was a necessary evil in wartime but unnecessary in times of peace. Propaganda proponents attempted to combat that construction, urging that propaganda actually promised to promote peace. For many, the nation's active role in the preservation of peace represented perhaps the country's leading responsibility in the postwar world.

Smith-Mundt sponsors spoke of the country's new responsibilities in the earliest days of the Cold War. Democratic Congressman E. C. Gathings of Arkansas urged that "America has assumed a prominent place among the nations of the world," and "with such a distinction there goes with it responsibilities which we should not look lightly upon."[99] Assistant Secretary of State Benton detailed the role of a propaganda program for the country's new international position, claiming that the responsibility was "far too large for us to remain tongue-tied in the concert of nations."[100] In a separate address, Benton added: "The world, due to our strength, looks at us with fear and with hope. This is a new role for the United States [since] we have never before . . . been the leading world power."[101] In the same spirit, Mundt urged members of Congress to "face up to [their] responsibilities" and to determine whether they were going "to sell the voice of America, or strait-jacket [their] hands and feet, and blind [their] eyes and ears to what is taking place all around [them]."[102]

Beyond any moral responsibility to defend democracy against the newest totalitarian threat, advocates of the Smith-Mundt bill defended a propaganda system as an effective and inexpensive tool for preserving world peace. As Secretary of State George C. Marshall argued: "One effective way to promote peace is to dispel misunderstanding, fear, and ignorance."[103] Similarly, General Dwight D. Eisenhower argued that an information program would "go a long way toward establishing a firm base for preserving permanent peace."[104] As Mundt explained, "through H.R. 3342 we establish for the first time in history the machinery . . . by which this country can really do something effective in helping to create in the minds of people everywhere the attitudes . . . essential . . . [for] peace in our time."[105] Republican Congressman Dewey Short of Missouri contended that without an information program, the United States could be facing yet another war: "Unless we are willing to declare war and go in with our armies and drop our bombs," we must use the "radio, the newspaper and the psychological warfare that saved the lives of hundreds of thousands of soldiers both in the First and the Second World Wars."[106] Still for their case to prove persuasive, supporters of the program needed to convince the skeptics that foreign audiences desired news from the United States.

Portrait of a Foreign Public

In furthering the need for peacetime propaganda, Truman administration officials offered a construction of the program's intended audiences and its potential effects. A common theme in interventionist rhetoric is that foreign countries "invite" or "request" the help of the United States. A similar theme helped justify a U.S. "war of words," as supporters of the Smith-Mundt bill argued that foreign publics hungered for information from the United States and were also poised to act upon what they learned. Such arguments fashioned U.S. news/propaganda as a mandatory and ethical practice in the arena of international human rights.

Attempting to obtain financial backing for the information program before the House subcommittee on appropriations, Benton maintained it would be difficult to overemphasize "the hunger for information about America that existed within the foreign countries."[107] Similarly, former Russian ambassador W. Averell Harriman determined: "The Russian people were avidly interested in facts and news about America." Such interest stemmed "from a general knowledge that America is a great country."[108] Congressman Jarman likewise testified to the desire among the Soviet people for American information. Noting the importance of U.S. news for international audiences, Jarman argued: "We have witnesses who have seen" the State Department's magazine, *Amerika,* "dog eared, just worn to a frazzle by being used by the Russian people, and we have some fantastic testimony . . . of how much a page in the black market the Russian people would pay for this magazine."[109] Committee members who traveled to Europe reinforced such views in their final report. "On both sides of the 'curtain,' " they argued, "there are already many people who yearn for information about and inspiration from America." The congressional leaders maintained that many looked to the United States as "their last mundane ray of hope," attached "importance to what [Americans] say and print," and devoured "American books and magazines."[110] Such arguments reflected Benton's earlier claims that the U.S. news media were obliged to share the nation's story with the world community.

Smith-Mundt supporters also insisted that foreign people could distinguish the lies of Soviet propaganda from the truths of U.S. information. Mundt, for example, stated that "efforts to present a pretty picture of America and the American way of life would destroy [its] credibility on the part of listeners."[111] Congressman Mansfield argued similarly that the United States should resist misleading foreign audience because "only in telling them the truth [could] we overcome the suspicions which have been generated into their minds by a system which is wholly foreign to us."[112] Smith-Mundt proponents even maintained that the Soviet people would reject their own government's news because they would be able to sense the inherent truthfulness of U.S. news. When asked whether Soviet people swallowed "all of the propaganda of their government," Harriman responded that they were "conscious of the fact that all information is controlled and slanted," with a "great desire for the other side."[113]

In addressing the perceived effectiveness of the U.S. propaganda program, advocates of the Smith-Mundt bill suggested that once foreign audiences received the "truth" about democracy, they would rise up to reject communism. Benton justified the existence of the propaganda program on the grounds that "even in dictatorships . . . the peoples of the world . . . ultimately determine the foreign policies of their governments." He spoke of "foreign government officials, editors, journalists, radio commentators, readers, listeners," and others "who influence and decide the policies of foreign governments." He, thus, called on Congress to consider the program as an essential element of U.S. foreign policy—an international obligation. The situation required the U.S. government "to communicate not only with governments of foreign countries, but with the people who determine the actions of their governments."[114] Before the subcommittee of the House Committee on Foreign Affairs, Representative Jarman urged that the program be directed toward the peoples of these nations, "the rank and file . . .

the fellow out in the little mud hut, and his wife and children," since they were the ones that needed to understand democratic principles.[115] Such understanding, Mundt concluded, would allow these people to "become strong enough and well enough organized to resist and repel communism."[116]

Supporters of the Smith-Mundt bill essentially implied that foreign audiences would *naturally* believe the "truth" disseminated by the United States and *naturally* reject Russian falsehoods. As Congressman Charles Kersten (R-WI) argued, "the Government of the United States is based upon the true nature of man."[117] Similarly, Democratic Representative Adolph J. Sabath of Illinois maintained that "the dream of freedom is common to all men; and America is the tangible form of that dream everywhere."[118] At bottom, the whole rationale for the propaganda program rested upon this premise: that people would naturally prefer the U.S. system if only they knew more about it. Arguing in 1947, General Eisenhower's statement typified this sentiment: "The more the advantages of [our] government are spread throughout the world, the more likely it will be that that system is followed by other countries."[119]

In speaking of democracy as a natural form of government, any practice connected to democracy would likewise assume such natural qualities, even a government-sponsored news agency. Such a portrait also accorded foreign publics with considerable wisdom and power. Supporters of the Smith-Mundt bill argued that foreign peoples sensed that they had not been hearing the truth about the United States or about world affairs in general. Somehow they would recognize the truth when they heard it, and they would act on that truth to reshape the foreign policies of their governments, despite their totalitarian nature.[120] Such a construction clearly elevated propaganda's role in international relations. Providing such news, supporters of the program insisted, was a responsibility of the United States in the postwar world, and constituted the most reasonable path for preserving peace.

Thus, Smith-Mundt supporters argued not only that the United States had an obligation to promote democracy in the competition with the Soviet Union, but also that propaganda was an effective and cost-efficient guarantor of peace. In the final analysis, such an appeal proved to be an effective strategy; supporters of the Smith-Mundt bill portrayed propaganda as a necessary means for fulfilling an international duty short of expensive and dangerous military commitments overseas. To that end, policy officials characterized propaganda as a preventative measure that could exist apart from the practice of war.

Conceiving of propaganda as a peacetime instrument was necessary given that the practice was previously associated with wartime in the United States. The placement of the propaganda program in the State Department also perpetuated its peacetime imperatives. By adopting a rhetoric of news in the process of acquiring propaganda's legalized status, political officials further enhanced the program's perceived peaceful contributions. The involvement of journalists in the lobbying effort also logically led to the use of a journalistic paradigm of rhetorical influence. In the end, viewing propaganda as news and "truth" helped refashion propaganda as a democratic practice, evidencing Benton's rhetorical successes with the media and members of Congress. It was Benton's secret advising committee after all that helped craft a media campaign and prepared speeches for certain members of Congress to deliver in support of the bill. This chapter also revealed the integral role that Congress played in formalizing the peacetime propaganda agency. The length, complexity, and substance of the debates give evidence to the multitude of congressional views on how best to formulate and institute the practice of democratic propaganda—contributions the Truman administration used to advance its propaganda mission early on.

As the next chapter reveals, the Truman administration's successful strategies aided in creating a supportive environment for the practice of peacetime propaganda at home. The ideologies that the U.S. propaganda program attempted to export, however, achieved different results. In fact, as the propaganda program began exporting some of the ideas expressed in the Smith-Mundt debates, officials learned just how naïve some of their propaganda assumptions were. Such startling revelations spawned a congressional critique of the newly legalized propaganda program, which eventually led to a reassessment of the journalistic paradigm for the practice of propaganda in a heightened Cold War context.

NOTES

1. Stephen Vaughn, *Holding Fast the Inner Lines: Democracy, Nationalism, and the Committee on Public Information* (Chapel Hill: University of North Carolina Press, 1980), xi, 4.

2. See Garth S. Jowett and Victoria O'Donnell, *Propaganda and Persuasion,* 2d ed. (Newbury Park, CA: Sage Publications, 1992), 166; and Vaughn, *Holding Fast,* 235.

3. J. Michael Sproule, "Propaganda: The Ideological Rhetoric," in *Rhetoric and Ideology: Compositions and Criticisms of Power,* ed. Charles W. Kneupper (Arlington, TX: Rhetoric Society of America, 1989), 91.

4. For a discussion of the reactions to the CPI, see George Creel, *How We Advertised America* (1920; reprint, New York: Arno Press, 1972), 3; Jacques Ellul, *Propaganda: The Formation of Men's Attitudes* (New York: Vintage Books, 1965), x, 61; John W. Henderson, *The United States Information Agency* (New York: Praeger, 1969), 28; Erika G. King, "Exposing the 'Age of Lies': The

Propaganda Menace as Portrayed in American Magazines in the Aftermath of World War I," *Journal of American Culture* 12 (1989): 37; Frederick Lumley, *The Propaganda Menace* (New York: The Century Co., 1933), 415; J. Michael Sproule, "Social Responses to Twentieth-Century Propaganda," in *Propaganda: A Pluralistic Perspective,* ed. Ted J. Smith, III (New York: Praeger, 1989), 7–9; J. Michael Sproule, "Propaganda Studies in American Social Science: The Rise and Fall of the Critical Paradigm," *Quarterly Journal of Speech* 73 (1987): 63; and Vaughn, *Holding Fast,* 4, 14–18, 32–38, 141.

    5. Lumley, *The Propaganda Menace,* 415.

    6. For background information on Nazi propaganda and the Office of War Information, see Ellul, *Propaganda,* 52; J. Fred MacDonald, *Don't Touch that Dial!: Radio Programming in American Life, 1920–1960* (Chicago: Nelson-Hall, 1979), 61–81; Holly Cowan Shulman, *The Voice of America: Propaganda and Democracy, 1941–1945* (Madison: University of Wisconsin Press, 1990), 13–52; Sproule, "Social Responses," 9; Oren Stephens, *Facts to a Candid World: America's Overseas Information Program* (Stanford, CA: Stanford University Press, 1955), 1.

    7. Edwin Emery, *The Press and America: An Interpretive History of the Mass Media,* 3d ed. (Englewood Cliffs, NJ: Prentice-Hall, 1972), 525–527; Bernard Roshco, *Newsmaking* (Chicago: University of Chicago Press, 1975), 51–54; and Shulman, *The Voice of America,* 36.

    8. Shulman, *The Voice of America,* 33. Much of the domestic propaganda activities during World War II were handled by the Roosevelt administration's Treasury Department and its war bonds program. See James Jerry Kimble, "Mobilizing the Home Front: War Bonds, Morale, and the U.S. Treasury's Domestic Propaganda Campaign, 1942–1945" (Ph.D. diss., University of Maryland, 2001).

    9. Charles A. H. Thomson, *Overseas Information Service of the United States Government* (Washington, D.C.: The Brookings Institution, 1948), 27–28.

    10. Allan M. Winkler, *The Politics of Propaganda: The Office of War Information, 1942–1945* (New Haven, CT: Yale University Press, 1978), 51.

    11. Shulman, *The Voice of America,* 184.

    12. Paul P. Blackburn, "The Post-Cold War Public Diplomacy of the United States," *The Washington Quarterly* 15 (1992): 75.

    13. Henderson, *The United States Information Agency,* 35–38.

    14. Senate Committee on Foreign Relation, *Overseas Information Programs of the United States,* 83rd Cong., 1st sess., 1953. See also Senate Committee on Foreign Relations, *Overseas Information Programs of the United States,* 83rd Cong., 1st sess., 1953, S. Rept. 406.

    15. See Guide to the William Benton Papers, "William Benton: A Biographical Sketch," n.d., Department of Special Collections, The University of Chicago Library, Chicago, Illinois. Benton also served as vice-president of the University of Chicago and owner/publisher of *Encyclopaedia Britannica.*

    16. For additional information on the debate surrounding the Smith-Mundt Act, see David F. Krugler, *The Voice of America and the Domestic Propaganda*

Battles, 1945–1953 (Columbia: University of Missouri Press, 2000), 52–72; Robert William Pirsein, *The Voice of America: An History of the International Broadcasting Activities of the United States Government, 1940–1962* (New York: Arno Press, 1979), 114–116, 122–123.

17. William Benton, "My Overview of the Nineteen Forties," *The Times in Review: 1940–1949* (New York: Arno Press, 1973), n.p.

18. See Elmer Davis, "The Government's News Service: Shall It Be Continued?" *Journalism Quarterly* 23 (1946): 147; Senate Committee on Foreign Relations, *Investigation of "Voice of America" and "Know North America" Series of Broadcasts,* 80th Cong., 2d sess., 1948, 153–154; and Philo C. Wasburn, *Broadcasting Propaganda: International Radio Broadcasting and the Construction of Political Reality* (Westport, CT: Praeger, 1992), xviii.

19. Thomson, *Overseas Information Service*, 305–306.

20. Stephen Vaughn illustrates how the relationship between the media and government regarding the latter's propaganda operations can be traced to World War I and the CPI. Vaughn also notes that the U.S. government influenced the content of the news. See Vaughn, *Holding Fast*, 5–8, 32.

21. OWI's director of domestic operations previously served as publisher for the *Des Moines Register* and *Look* magazine; Joseph Barnes, the former foreign editor of the *New York Herald Times,* served as OWI's deputy director of the Atlantic area; George H. Lyon, staff member of the OWI, previously served as editor of the *Buffalo Times;* and Herbert Agar, the former editor of the *Louisville Courier-Journal,* served as the head of the British division of OWI. See Emery, *The Press and America*, 526–527.

22. See Emery, *The Press and America,* 525; and Roshco, *Newsmaking* 51.

23. Winkler, *The Politics of Propaganda,* 52.

24. Thomson, *Overseas Information Service,* 30, 86.

25. Stephen F. Knott alleges that U.S. history is replete with examples of presidential administrations "employing journalists . . . for intelligence and propaganda purposes." See Stephen F. Knott, *Secret and Sanctioned: Covert Operations and the American Presidency* (New York: Oxford University Press, 1996), 5.

26. Transcript, William Benton Oral History Interview, 1968, by the Columbia University Oral History Collection, page 167, Columbia University, New York.

27. Transcript, William Benton Oral History Interview, 182, 176.

28. "Status of American International Broadcasting," *Department of State Bulletin* 15 (May 26, 1946): 900–904.

29. "Government Calls Conference with Radio Industries to Discuss International Broadcasting," *Department of State Bulletin* 26 (May 11, 1947): 951.

30. See Senate Committee on Foreign Relations, *Investigation of the "Voice of America" and "Know North America" Series of Broadcasts,* 80th Cong., 2d sess., June 3, 1948, 190–191. Even though Charles R. Denny, vice president and general counsel of NBC, argued that NBC did not profit from leasing short-wave transmitters to the State Department, he eventually acknowledged that before

World War II, NBC incurred close to a million dollars in losses on their short-wave radio programs until the U.S. government leased their transmitters.

31. "Status of American International Broadcasting," 900.

32. "Radio Advisory Committee Urges Strengthening of Voice of America," *Department of State Bulletin* 16 (May 25, 1947): 1038.

33. For more information on Harold Lasswell's work with government propaganda, see Christopher Simpson, *Science of Coercion: Communication Research and Psychological Warfare,* 1945–1960 (New York: Oxford University Press, 1994), 26–27, 82. For a listing of the group participants, see "Radio Advisory Committee Urges Strengthening of Voice of America," 1038.

34. "Report of Radio Advisory Committee to the Assistant Secretary of State for Public Affairs," *Department of State Bulletin* 16 (May 25, 1947): 1041.

35. Sidney Hyman, *The Lives of William Benton* (Chicago: University of Chicago Press, 1969), 354.

36. American Society of Newspaper Editors, "Proceedings: Twenty-Fifth Anniversary Convention—ASNE," April, 1947, American Society of Newspaper Editors' Archives, Reston, Virginia. See also Edward W. Barrett, *Truth Is Our Weapon* (New York: Funk & Wagnalls, 1953), 59.

37. "Radio Advisory Committee Urges Strengthening of Voice of America," 1038; See also William Benton to President Truman, May, 1947, Papers of Harry S. Truman, Official File, Harry S. Truman Presidential Library (hereafter cited as the HSTPL), 1.

38. Hyman, *The Lives of William Benton,* 383.

39. M. J. McDermott, "Mechanics of and Possible Improvement in the Department's Relations with the Press," September, 1945, The William Benton Papers, Department of Special Collections, Box 375, The University of Chicago Library, Chicago, Illinois, 10.

40. See Anonymous letter to William Benton, January, 1946, The William Benton Papers, Department of Special Collections, Box 376, The University of Chicago Library, Chicago, Illinois, 1; and William A. H. Birnie to William Benton, January, 1946, The William Benton Papers, Department of Special Collections, Box 375, The University of Chicago Library, Chicago, Illinois, 1.

41. See Garnett D. Horner to William Benton, September, 1945, The William Benton Papers, Department of Special Collections, Box 375, The University of Chicago Library, Chicago, Illinois, 1; William Benton to Dean Acheson, December, 1945, The William Benton Papers, Department of Special Collections, Box 375, The University of Chicago Library, Chicago, Illinois, 1.

42. See McDermott, "Mechanics of and Possible Improvement," 8; and Edward G. Miller, Jr. to William Benton, September, 1945, The William Benton Papers, Department of Special Collections, Box 375, The University of Chicago Library, Chicago, Illinois, 1–5.

43. McDermott, "Mechanics of and Possible Improvement," 11.

44. Miller, Jr., to William Benton, 5, 1.

45. Horner to William Benton, 3.

46. Miller, Jr., to William Benton, 4.

47. Howland Sargeant to Staff Members, December, 1947, The William Benton Papers, Department of Special Collections, Box 375, The University of Chicago Library, Chicago, Illinois, 1.

48. "Proposal in Detail," December, 1947, The William Benton Papers, Department of Special Collections, Box 375, The University of Chicago Library, Chicago, Illinois, 1.

49. Bruce J. Evensen, "The Limits of Presidential Leadership: Truman at War with Zionists, the Press, Public Opinion and His Own State Department over Palestine," *Presidential Studies Quarterly* 23 (1993): 279.

50. See *Congressional Record,* 80th Cong., 2d sess., 1948, 7198–7201. For more information on the IMG program, see Martin Merson, *The Private Diary of a Public Servant* (New York: Macmillan, 1955), 15. Note that the IMG legislation was buried in the Economic Cooperation Act (Marshall Plan).

51. William Benton, "Protest by the Department of State on AP and UP Action," *Department of State Bulletin* 14 (February 10, 1946): 217–218.

52. William Benton, "Position of Department of State on AP Action," *Department of State Bulletin* 14 (January 27, 1946): 92.

53. Benton, "Protest by the Department of State," 217.

54. William Benton, "The American Press Associations: An Opportunity and Responsibility," *Department of State Bulletin* 14 (April 7, 1946): 578.

55. Hyman, *The Lives of William Benton,* 347.

56. Transcript, William Benton Oral History Interview, 164.

57. William Benton, "Freedom of the Press—World-Wide," *Department of State Bulletin* 14 (February 3, 1946): 162.

58. See "Plan for Agreement on International Freedom of Information," *Department of State Bulletin* 17 (September 14, 1947): 527; and "Draft of a Treaty on Freedom of Information," *Department of State Bulletin* 17 (September 14, 1947): 529.

59. Thomson, *Overseas Information Service,* 214–215, 316.

60. Bernard C. Cohen, *The Press and Foreign Policy* (Princeton, NJ: Princeton University Press, 1963), 75.

61. John Gunther, "Foreword," *This Is the Challenge: The Benton Reports of 1956–1958 on the Nature of the Soviet Threat,* ed. Edward W. Barrett (New York: Associated College Presses, 1958), vi.

62. *Congressional Record,* 80th Cong., 1st sess., 1947, 4621.

63. U.S. Public Law 402, *United States Information and Educational Exchange Act of 1948*, 80th Cong., 2d sess., January 27, 1948, 1011.

64. Pirsein, *The Voice of America,* 137.

65. Pirsein, *The Voice of America,* 137.

66. See Senate Committee on Foreign Relations, *The United States Information Service in Europe,* 80th Cong., 2d sess., 1948, S. Rept. 855, iii. The congressional leaders traveling to Europe included Senators Alexander Smith (Chair), Bourke B. Hickenlooper (R-IA), Henry Cabot Lodge, Jr., (R-MA), Alben W.

Barkley (D-KY), Carl A. Hatch (D-NM), and Representatives Karl Mundt (Chair), Lawrence H. Smith (R-WI), Walter H. Judd (R-MN), John Davis Lodge (R-CT), Pete Jarman (D-AL), Thomas S. Gordon (D-IL), and Mike Mansfield (D-MT).

67. Pirsein, *The Voice of America,* 138–139.

68. See Harry S. Truman, "Special Message to the Congress on Greece and Turkey: The Truman Doctrine," HSTPL, wysiwyg://33/http://www.debateinfo. com /hall_of_fame/speeches/truman.html; and George C. Marshall, "The Marshall Plan and the Future of U.S. European Relations," HSTPL, http://lcweb.loc. gov/exhibits/marshall/m9.html. See also Robert J. Donovan, *Conflict and Crisis: The Presidency of Harry S. Truman, 1945–1948* (New York: W. W. Norton, 1977), 279–291; Robert Frazier, *Anglo-American Relations with Greece: The Coming of the Cold War, 1942–1947* (New York: St. Martin's Press, 1991); Norman Friedman, *The Fifty-Year War: Conflict and Strategy in the Cold War* (Annapolis, MD: Naval Institute Press, 2000), 1–32, 43–90; Michael J. Hogan, *The Marshall Plan: America, Britain, and the Reconstruction of Western Europe, 1947–1952* (New York: Cambridge University Press, 1987); and Zachary Karabell, *Architects of Intervention: The United States, the Third World, and the Cold War, 1946–1962* (Baton Rouge: Louisiana State University Press, 1999), 17–36.

69. *Congressional Record,* 1947, 6970.

70. *Congressional Record,* 1947, 6746.

71. *Congressional Record,* 1947, 6543.

72. *Congressional Record,* 1947, 936–939.

73. House Committee on Foreign Affairs, *United States Information and Educational Exchange Act of 1947,* 80th Cong., 1st sess., 1947, 96–102.

74. House Committee on Foreign Affairs, 104.

75. House Committee on Foreign Affairs, 105–125.

76. Senate Committee on Foreign Relations, 48.

77. House Committee on Appropriations, *Department of State Appropriation Bill for 1948,* 80th Cong., 1st sess., 1947, 389.

78. *Congressional Record,* 1947, 6554.

79. *Congressional Record,* 1947, 10689.

80. *Congressional Record,* 1947, A4226.

81. *Congressional Record,* 1947, 6560.

82. *Congressional Record,* 1947, 6564.

83. *Congressional Record,* 1948, 2160.

84. For more research on Cold War metaphors and justificatory rhetoric linked to motives of war, see Robert L. Ivie, "Presidential Motives for War," *Quarterly Journal of Speech* 60 (1974): 337–345; Robert L. Ivie, "Images of Savagery in American Justifications for War," *Communication Monographs* 47 (1980): 279–294; and Robert L. Ivie, "Metaphors and the Rhetorical Invention of Cold War 'Idealists,' " in *Cold War Rhetoric: Strategy, Metaphor, and Ideology,* ed. Martin J. Medhurst, Robert L. Ivie, Philip Wander, and Robert L. Scott (East Lansing: Michigan State University Press, 1997), 103–127.

85. House Committee on Foreign Affairs, 138.

86. *Congressional Record,* 1947, 5285.

87. House Committee on Foreign Affairs, 141.

88. *Congressional Record,* 1947, 5285.

89. For research examining the journalistic paradigm and such claims of objectivity, see Richard Davis, *The Press and American Politics: The New Mediator* (New York: Longman, 1992), 11; Robert M. Entman, *Democracy without Citizens: Media and the Decay of American Politics* (New York: Oxford University Press, 1989), 19–31; Robert A. Hackett, "Decline of a Paradigm? Bias and Objectivity in News Media Studies," *Critical Studies in Mass Communication* 1 (1984): 229–259; Stephen D. Reese "The News Paradigm and the Ideology of Objectivity: A Socialist at the *Wall Street Journal*," *Critical Studies in Mass Communication* 7 (1990): 390–409; Roshco, *Newsmaking,* 44–54; Thomas Rosteck, "Irony, Argument, and Reportage in Television Documentary: *See It Now* Versus Senator McCarthy," *Quarterly Journal of Speech* 75 (1989): 277–298; and Dan Schiller, "An Historical Approach to Objectivity and Professionalism in American News Reporting," *Journal of Communication* 29 (1979): 46–57.

90. House Committee on Foreign Affairs, 131.

91. House Committee on Foreign Affairs, 141.

92. *Congressional Record,* 1947, 6969.

93. *Congressional Record,* 1947, 5285.

94. Senate Committee on Foreign Relations, 22.

95. *Congressional Record,* 1947, A4235.

96. Senate Committee on Appropriations, *Departments of State, Justice, Commerce, and the Judiciary Appropriation Bill for 1948,* 80th Cong. 1st sess., 1947, H.R. 3311, 985.

97. *Congressional Record,* 1947, 10691.

98. *Congressional Record,* 1947, 5199.

99. *Congressional Record,* 1947, 6562.

100. Senate Committee on Appropriations, 888.

101. House Committee on Appropriations, 395.

102. Senate Committee on Foreign Relations, 15.

103. House Committee on Appropriations, 8.

104. Senate Committee on Foreign Relations, 53.

105. Senate Committee on Foreign Relations, 16.

106. *Congressional Record,* 1947, 5288.

107. House Committee on Appropriations, *Department of State Appropriation Bill for 1948,* 80th Cong., 1st sess., 1947, 381.

108. House Committee on Foreign Affairs, 31.

109. Senate Committee on Foreign Relations, 39. Note that the magazine *Amerika* was created by the State Department for citizens of the Soviet Union.

110. Senate Committee on Foreign Relations, 3.

111. House Committee on Foreign Affairs, 205.

112. House Committee on Foreign Affairs, 225.

113. House Committee on Foreign Affairs, 37.

114. House Committee on Appropriations, 375–376.

115. House Committee on Foreign Affairs, 222.

116. *Congressional Record,* 1948, 3753.

117. *Congressional Record,* 1947, 7613.

118. *Congressional Record,* 1947, 6546.

119. House Committee on Foreign Affairs, 218.

120. Such arguments also reflect the existence of the "magic bullet theory" associated with propaganda in the early-to-mid part of the twentieth century. As J. Michael Sproule defines, the "magic bullet theory" is based on the notion that "messages were received exactly as presented." See J. Michael Sproule, "Progressive Propaganda Critics and the Magic Bullet Myth," *Critical Studies in Mass Communication* 6 (1989): 234.

2

The Journalistic Paradigm: U.S. Domestic and International Propaganda, 1947–1949

The propaganda strategies devised by William Benton, acting on behalf of the Truman administration, became actualized in the messages disseminated domestically by the U.S. press. Specifically, the *New York Times'* coverage of the debate surrounding the legalization of the Smith-Mundt Act from 1947 to 1948, reflected Benton's decision to equate U.S. propaganda with news. This chapter features in part an analysis of such material, which demonstrates how America's most noted newspaper[1] refashioned propaganda in much the same way as Benton and other congressional proponents of the Smith-Mundt Act. The *New York Times*, whose stories were picked up by hundreds of other newspapers around the country,[2] engaged in a public relations campaign for the propaganda program. Such coverage worked to summon support for the State Department's so-called news agency, which promised to foster peace in the new Cold War battle.

The same propaganda strategies emanating from the journalistic paradigm, however, experienced intense scrutiny from members of Congress when applied to the practice of international propaganda. To illustrate such scrutiny, this chapter also examines a program designed to inform Latin American audiences about the United States. As part of a Latin American initiative, NBC contracted with the Department of State to write a Voice of America (VOA) radio series known as *Know North America* (KNA). Not long after the KNA series aired, State Department officials and NBC employees came under considerable attack from congressional leaders for producing what some called an embarrassing portrayal of the United States. Even though the KNA broadcasts were shortlived, they became the subject of considerable controversy in Congress, spawning congressional hearings that helped inspire the Truman administration's expansion of presidential control over propaganda activity. Thus, while Benton's propaganda strategies were persuasive at home, they were deemed inappropriate for international audiences, demonstrating the initial confusion over Cold War propaganda strategies.

THE "VOICE" OF THE *NEW YORK TIMES*

When the Smith-Mundt Act passed through Congress in January 1948, its framers prohibited the U.S. government from propagandizing the U.S. public.[3] Despite such provisions, propaganda officials found alternative ways in which to "propagandize" the citizenry. They secured, for instance, the support of newspapers such as the *New York Times*, which helped market the idea of a peacetime propaganda program to a reluctant public. The *Times'* articles reflected the arguments employed by Assistant Secretary of State William Benton, demonstrating the existence of a "camouflaged" propaganda, where the actual source and the propagandistic nature of the material was masked for the intended audiences.

Just like the Smith-Mundt supporters, writers for the *New York Times* attempted to refashion propaganda in more democratic terms. Prior to the passage of the Smith-Mundt Act, *Times* reporter Edwin L. James assured readers that "propaganda does not necessarily have to be false."[4] In an editorial on that same day,[5] the *Times* used Benton's and Mundt's binary construction of propaganda, equating U.S. propaganda with telling the "truth about the United States" and the Russian program with disseminating a "storm of lies."[6]

The *Times* also championed the propaganda program by connecting it to larger foreign policy initiatives. James, for example, linked propaganda to the Marshall Plan, asserting that "there is a job to be done in getting to a greater number of people our story of what we are attempting to do with the Marshall Plan."[7] Anne O'Hare McCormick, a well-known editorial writer for the *Times*,[8] championed an increase in propaganda funding during a speech before an audience of teachers. For this group, she equated a lack of news in Europe with a greater peril to peace than "hunger, cold or the atom bomb."[9] According to McCormick, news and "information" functioned as the "first answer to the atomic bomb," which made it of greater significance than diplomatic and military measures.[10] For the *Times*, the "information program" represented a "vital weapon in the battle for the minds of men."[11]

When covering issues only tangentially related to the Smith-Mundt debate, the *Times* still featured "friends" of Benton's propaganda program in their stories. As Russell Porter covered the semiannual meeting of the Academy of Political Science, for example, he de-emphasized other featured speakers in favor of Philip D. Reed, General Electric chairperson and outspoken supporter of the Smith-Mundt bill. Porter reported on Reed's concern that "foreigners [were] especially lacking in news about the standard of living of American workers and about the aid the United States has given other countries." The central theme that Reed promulgated was "the need for education in defense of the American way of life," according to Porter's report.[12] Thus, Reed, even when addressing the topic of free enterprise, still campaigned for the U.S. propaganda program. The *Times*, in turn, featured Reed's testimony.

The *Times* also showcased the American Society for Newspaper Editors' (ASNE) support for international propaganda and the Associated Press's (AP) decision to stop contributing news to the government's Cold War effort. Sidney Shalett, in covering ASNE's 1947 convention, reported that the organization "adopted . . . with full vigor its effort to promote peace through attainment of a free flow of information and opinion among nations."[13] During the 1948 convention, Lewis Wood accented once again ASNE's support for the "government's fight against Soviet propaganda." Addressing the conflict between the State Department and the AP, Wood ended the story with the ASNE's call for the "Associated Press and United Press [to make] their reports available to the Office of Information and Education."[14] While the views of the ASNE were featured, positions of the AP and the UP were excluded from the report, emphasizing not only the ASNE's allegiance but also the editorial position of the *Times*.

Beyond that, the *New York Times* supported Benton's attempts to develop a treaty for an international freedom of information pact. The *Times* featured a story on William Benton's speech before the Inland Daily Press Association. In this address, Benton stressed the need for "bilateral negotiations with foreign countries to implement various international declarations" so that a "firm policy of world freedom of information" functioned "as a safeguard against aggressive war."[15] Once Richard J. Finnegan of the *Chicago Times* completed the "Treaty on Free News," the *New York Times* published a full text of the treaty, emphasizing that Finnegan "spoke out strongly against any Government controls over the press."[16]

Clearly, if such a treaty were to prevail, newspapers such as the *Times* would benefit from a lessening of international restrictions in the dissemination of news. Such a view is implied in the *Times'* reporting on the Smith-Mundt Act. *Times'* journalist William S. White, for example, emphasized that the government would "depend to the greatest 'practicable' extent on the existing private news and information facilities of the United States."[17] The expansion of international markets, the reliance of the State Department on private news organizations, and the passage of the information media guarantee (IMG) all stood to enhance the potential profits of news organizations, including the *New York Times*.

Finally, the *Times* demonstrated its support for the U.S. propaganda program after the passage of the Smith-Mundt Act by featuring a four-part series on the VOA. In defining VOA's mission, Austin Stevens perpetuated the rehabilitated conception of propaganda that Smith-Mundt supporters promulgated. In a front-page story, Stevens argued that the VOA offered "facts abroad about international developments . . . setting forth the United States' position in areas where it may not be known."[18] Commenting on Stevens's feature, an unidentified *Times* editorial writer championed the VOA while highlighting the positive slant that the feature writer gave to the government's short-wave radio broadcast: "We believe that a reading of the series of articles in this newspaper by Austin Stevens . . . will convince most thoughtful persons and members of Congress that the program is at present soundly visualized and that an effort is being made to give it the best direction possible." In the end, the *Times* editors concluded that the U.S. government *reluctantly* entered the "war of words"—a contest in which the United States had to prevail: "This war was not of our making but is one we must win. In it lies a better hope for world peace than the winning of a hot war of arms could bring."[19]

Even though the Smith-Mundt Act forbade the U.S. government from propagandizing its own citizens, the *New York Times* assumed the task of convincing the American people, members of Congress, and fellow journalists of the program's necessity. To that end, the *New York Times* served the propaganda aims of the Truman administration's Department of State. As William Benton boasted, his own "propaganda" helped spawn "editorials favoring" the Smith-Mundt Act in the *New York Times*.[20] Such a practice reveals the existence of a "camouflaged" propaganda,[21] because the media seemingly functioned as a domestic arm of the U.S. propaganda program, either willingly and/or unwittingly.[22] While "black propaganda" is traditionally defined as that information where the source is concealed and appears to originate from somewhere else,[23] "camouflaged" propaganda's uniqueness derives from the fact that not only is the source concealed but so too is its propagandistic form. Propaganda practitioners such as Paul A. Smith, Jr., perpetuate the myth that "the propaganda arm, by its nature, is an overt activity,"[24] a view that is reassuring to people who fear being hoodwinked by such an activity. This clarity is lacking in the domestic/camouflaged propaganda materials from the *New York Times*. Although U.S. citizens in the post-World War II period were especially sensitized to the dangers of propaganda, camouflaged propaganda hid the government's influence and the news media's, at least, partial complicity in espousing the presidential administration's message.[25]

Because audiences were less aware of its propagandistic form, the camouflaged nature of this domestic propaganda was perhaps even more effective. As propagandist C. N. Barclay argued in 1954, "home propaganda is not usually countered by efficient, if by any, methods."[26] Thus, the existence of this camouflaged propaganda helped the Truman administration legalize a peacetime propaganda program in a country committed to a free press ideology. It also helped create the Cold War ideology that persisted over the next forty-five years and beyond. Yet, despite the legislative successes domestically, the journalistic model of propaganda failed to produce the kind of propaganda that congressional members found appropriate.

AMERICA'S INTERNATIONAL "VOICE"

By far, the most well known propaganda arm of the U.S. government during the early years of the Cold War was the State Department's Voice of America. Created in February 1942, this short-wave radio became the largest section of the State Department's propaganda program during the early years of the Cold War.[27] Because of its prominence, VOA attracted considerable attention from congressional overseers of the State Department's propaganda program. As VOA officials sought to implement a journalistic paradigm for the country's Cold War battle with the Soviet Union, congressional investigators kept a watchful eye on the propaganda disseminated abroad, intervening in the business of propaganda production.

One such inquiry centered on the controversial series, *Know North America*, a radio program that aired in Latin America between November 27, 1947, and March 8, 1948. KNA was produced by NBC under contract with the Department of State. The *Know North America's* investigation in 1948 offers insight into congressional definitions of the program's mission, as congressional leaders called for a more culturally unified propaganda. Similarly, the debate demonstrates how members of Congress worked to determine the acceptable "voice" of America and the "truth" about its past and current events. Because of the seemingly diffuse nature of a journalistic propaganda program placed in the hands of employees from both the private and public spheres, this debate helped mobilize propaganda strategy in the State Department, a significant step toward the centralization of propaganda activities in the White House.

Propaganda as Entertainment

Latin America represented a region of concern for the Truman administration, which undoubtedly encouraged the State Department to direct propaganda campaigns toward that region. Such presidential worries over
Latin America began before the end of World War II as the Russians tried to
increase their influence throughout that region in 1944 and beyond. By the
end of the Smith-Mundt debates, such exigencies in Latin America had
grown. Instability existed within the governments of Bolivia, Colombia,
Nicaragua, Peru, and Venezuela, which concerned the Truman administration greatly.[28] William Benton, like many other political officials, predicted
that Latin America would become "one of the great battlegrounds in the
nonmilitary struggle" between the United States and the Soviet Union. It
could ultimately be "as important to the U.S. and to the free world [as] any
other part of the globe," Benton believed.[29] Rather than developing this
program in the State Department, though, Benton contracted with NBC to
produce the series, a move that reflected the journalistic vision of propaganda. NBC had long contributed to the government's propaganda activity
when it leased short-wave radio equipment from the news organization in
1942. Because State Department officials did not want to appear as if they
were censoring NBC, they exerted minimal supervision over the writing of
the KNA scripts.[30]

All of *Know North America* broadcasts followed a similar format. Each
contained the travels of one individual from Venezuela and another from
Cuba as they explored the United States. The show's producers intended for
one of the travelers to raise objections that Latin Americans might have
about the United States, and the other to counter such stereotypes. The series was intended to serve the program's mission of "promot[ing] a better
understanding between people of the United States and the people of other
countries," as outlined by the Smith-Mundt Act.[31] Each broadcast was
beamed to Latin America in Spanish and was designed as an entertaining
travelogue complete with music, sound effects, and humor. Even though
NBC created the idea, the Department of State reportedly approved of the
series and the format.[32]

To make each broadcast consistent, a narrator began with a statement
similar to the following: "The National Broadcasting Company presents:
Know North America, a weekly program in which we narrate the spiritual
adventures of two travelers as they discover the numerous miracles of the
historical and present-day life of the United States."[33] The broadcasts each
focused on a particular state, providing listeners with background on that
state, its cities, and important landmarks. The broadcasts featured descrip-

tions of the state's natural resources, which highlighted U.S. wealth and riches. In the case of Colorado, for example, the natural resources were identified as "gold, silver, and beet sugar."[34] In the Texas story, "wheat, rice, fruits, cattle, gold, silver, and oil"[35] became the defining products for that state.

Yet *Know North America* was more than just a travelogue. All of the scripts drew ideological conclusions primarily from the historical background of each state, and those conclusions attracted attention from congressional overseers. Controversial issues such as race relations were deemed acceptable topics by congressional leaders, as long as the proper "lessons" were designed to counter public relations problems in the United States. During the broadcast about Colorado, for instance, the travelers discussed the conflict between Native Americans and the settlers. The first traveler stated that he "always took the side of the Indians and the buffalo." The second traveler countered: "Both suffered tremendously . . . but that's progress: it destroys in order to build."[36] For congressional leaders, at least, this represented an acceptable "lesson" to be derived from the history of Native American wars in the West.

The broadcast on Alabama likewise taught an acceptable "lesson" about the history of race relations, this time focusing on the role of African Americans in U.S. history. In this program, the narrator asserted: "In order to know the United States well . . . [we must] visit the humble dwellings where true democracy is forged and Alabama is the perfect symbol of the poor state which is becoming rich through work." The narrator explained that "wealthy families maintain intact the aristocratic spirit and the workers of the large plantations are direct descendants of the slaves who did not want to abandon their masters." The "Negroes" in Alabama "today," the narrator concluded, "are free and happy and of the tragic times only songs remain."[37]

By contrast, congressional critics clearly considered other lessons about the history of U.S. race relations inappropriate. In a broadcast concerning New York City on January 12, 1948, NBC used what members of Congress deemed were troubling comments as a way to "entertain" and "educate." While "touring" the esteemed businesses of the city and places such as Park Avenue, the travelers focused on the mansions and apartments of millionaires. In perpetuating the millionaire wealth of the city, the travelers eventually ended up in Harlem, which one traveler defined as "the Paradise of Negroes," where "colored millionaires live." The travelers also began noticing and whistling at women. Highlighting one woman's coat, one traveler commented that he thought all blacks were poor in the United States. In an attempt to dispel such a myth, the narrator responded: "There is a certain Mr. DuBois who owns half of Harlem, and at night these streets are filled with aristocrats and artists who come to the great cabarets and restaurants of the black city." Of this excerpt and others about this program, congressional evaluators concluded that "it is incredible that Federal funds should be used to broadcast [this] . . . misleading material."[38]

As KNA producers continued to feature issues of race in their broadcasts, they used Alabama as a place to "educate" Latin American listeners on the history of U.S. racial divisions. Of a street that was named "Jefferson Davis Avenue," the first traveler asked, "Wasn't that the President of the Southern Confederation?" The narrator answered affirmatively and added: "On this avenue . . . only Negroes live." The first traveler interrupted and elaborated: "And he defended slavery and was the most bitter enemy of Lincoln's ideals." The second traveler responded: "That will show you that the dead do not return, because if they did the spirit of Davis would have removed the signs of this street." The narrator then declared, "In no other part of the United States has the colored race struggled and suffered so much as here."[39] For Senator Homer E. Capehart (R-IN) at least, such a statement had no place in a program designed to promote a positive image of the United States. As Capehart sarcastically declared during the hearings on the program: "I am certain that the people of Alabama who pay State . . . and Federal taxes will appreciate the fact their money is being used to advertise them to the world in such light."[40]

Other policy makers objected to certain "facts" that they felt were inconsistent with the country's democratic image. When discussing the Mormon religion in Utah, for example, broadcasters asserted that "everyone belonging to the church donated 10 percent of their income." The money, the narrator explained, was spent on the community, hospitals, public works, charitable institutions, and schools.[41] Certain congressional leaders such as Senator Capehart, argued that this broadcast attempted "to prove that Utah is a communistic or socialistic State." Capehart called the Utah story "trash" and concluded that the script represented an "insult to the United States Senate, to the people of the Nation, and particularly to the people of Utah," whose State was the "same as . . . every other State of the Union."[42]

In addition, some features used humor, which likewise attracted criticism from members of Congress. Complete with sound effects, music, and even laugh tracks, *Know North America's* producers often resorted to jokes. In the program on Utah, which contained a sidebar on Nevada, one traveler commented that the latter's two principal cities were in direct "competition": "[in] Las Vegas people get married and in Reno they get divorced." In the same broadcast, one traveler stated that Utah is the place "where men have as many wives as they can support." The other traveler responded: "There's a gleam in your eye," which prompted a response, "But man, you can't even support one."[43] In yet another broadcast, the narrator explained that in 1869, Wyoming became the first state to allow women to vote. The traveler joked: "They had to make a mistake somewhere!"[44]

Other congressional leaders were similarly outraged by the overall content of the *Know North America* series. Senator Carl A. Hatch (D-NM), for example, stated that while he had been "one of the strong supporters" of a peacetime propaganda program, he demanded an end to the "drivel, nonsense and downright falsehoods . . . set forth" in the *Know North America* broadcasts. Senator Lister Hill (D-AL) referred to the broadcasts as "base slander," while Senator Millard E. Tydings (D-MD) went so far as to claim that the broadcasts looked like "a calculated attempt to portray the United States in the most degrading way that radio technique would allow." In illustrating another complaint about KNA's content, Senator Tom Connally (D-TX) claimed: "Our worst fears have been more than realized." Connally demanded that the program be abolished if it continued to "plaster all over the world . . . slanderous, [and] outrageous stories regarding the different States of the Union."[45]

Charles V. Denny, vice president and general counsel of NBC, justified *Know North America's* style, arguing that an earlier version of the series was too "dull" to attract listener interest.[46] But some congressional critics objected to the very idea of the VOA seeking to "entertain" its audiences. Senator John W. Bricker (R-OH), for instance, questioned whether "any good" came "from the entertainment broadcasts" like the ones under question, while Senator Edward J. Thye (R-MN) called such programming "silly."[47] Republican Senator Bourke B. Hickenlooper of Iowa summarized the sentiments of many in Congress, asserting that the VOA was created to present "honest, decent, [and] factual" programming instead of trying to be too "fancy" or "flowery."[48]

All of these complaints ultimately led to questions about who was responsible for the content of *Know North America*, reflecting the paranoia and isolationist sentiment of the period. Members of Congress were bothered by the fact that the writer of *Know North America* was Dr. Rene Borgia, an employee of NBC and a non-native-born American. Responding to questions about Borgia's past, Denny explained that Borgia worked in the international broadcasting field between 1942 and 1947, including such organizations as the State Department, the Office of War Information, and with the Coordinator of Inter-American Affairs agency before coming to NBC in September 1947.[49] According to Denny, once Borgia passed the FBI security checks, he was allowed to adapt scripts for NBC and was cleared to write the KNA series thereafter.[50]

Upon hearing of Borgia's background, congressional leaders centered on the issue of loyalty checks. Senator Ferguson, for example, requested the results of the FBI report. Once Denny indicated that the report was returned and marked, "nothing in the file," the senators assessed the obligations and abilities of private companies to obtain full FBI employee investigations. Concerns were raised because NBC did not conduct complete loyalty checks. Senator Hatch, for example, urged that "every person who has any connection with these programs, in private agencies or the Government, should be subject to check," as specified by the Smith-Mundt Act.[51]

Questions were also raised about Borgia's supervisor, Alberto Gandero, who was a naturalized U.S. citizen from Cuba.[52] According to Denny's testimony, Gandero headed the Spanish language section and assigned Borgia to the KNA series. Congressional objections about Gandero centered more on the oversight of Spanish scripts by NBC and State Department officials who were unfamiliar with the Spanish language. Congressional leaders were quite alarmed because the KNA scripts were not translated into English and checked over before being aired. Denny blamed the lack of oversight on the absence of funding to institutionalize such safeguards. As a result, Gandero, who Denny defined as "a trusted and veteran employee of NBC" since 1940, served as the primary reviewer of the scripts. Shocked that the State Department did not check the NBC scripts, Senator Ferguson and others concluded that the Department of State should review all broadcasts. As Ferguson concluded: "Congress [did] not intend that there should be divided responsibility."[53]

Borgia lost his job on March 11, 1948, and Gandero was demoted on March 18, 1948, undoubtedly because of the suspicion in Washington, D.C. about "outsiders."[54] Certainly, the fear of communists in government had historical roots in the Dies Committee (i.e., the Special House Committee on Un-American Activities).[55] William P. Rogers (chief counsel for the Investigating Subcommittee of the Senate Committee on Expenditures in the Executive Department) articulated arguments that reflected such fear of communists: "No one except foreigners knew the contents of the programs."[56] Rogers and others, of course, ignored the fact that Borgia and Gandero were U.S. citizens. Borgia defended himself and the content of the scripts, charging that up to "90 percent of the material" for KNA was derived from author John Gunther and his book *Inside the U. S. A.*[57] Gunther, a prolific U.S. author, reportedly used humor in his book, which created a lot of controversy because of the way in which he depicted American cities.[58] Despite the controversy surrounding *Inside the U.S.A.*, Borgia and Gandero were the individuals who received the majority of the blame for the content of the propaganda transcripts.

Most significantly, the KNA incident resulted in changes to the content and structure of the propaganda program. As a result of the KNA investigation, several congressional critics insisted that only "knowledgeable" Americans should write the scripts. In a 1948 report, members of the House Committee on Expenditures concluded that "only American citizens who have lived the greater part of their lives within the United States, [should] be employed to prepare [the] foreign broadcasts."[59] Democratic Senator Elbert D. Thomas of Utah called for the Voice of America to be handled only by native-born Americans who truly understood American history.[60] Such a view clearly exhibited the paranoia that gripped the country by the 1940s. By this point, Americans were more than a little suspicious of "outsiders," even those who were legal American citizens.

Throughout the debate over the *Know North America*, congressional leaders loudly articulated their opinions on what constituted the true "voice" of America. While members of Congress believed that historical and cultural "lessons" should be taught to the international public, they rebuked those "lessons" that might tarnish the U.S. image abroad. Acting as the vanguards of U.S. "truths," congressional critics concluded that any information that contradicted democratic values should be replaced by stories celebrating the country's culture and past. The message seemed clear in that members of Congress wanted the State Department to assume greater control over a program that exported a more monolithic message. Such a view stood to reduce the involvement of private media organizations and critiqued the use of a journalistic paradigm for the dissemination of propaganda.

The Truman administration also learned other lessons from U.S. propaganda during the early years of the Cold War. Just as members of Congress found the *Know North America* broadcasts troubling, many within the international community also reacted negatively to such "news." Rather than creating a greater sense of understanding and promoting the United States around the globe, the propaganda instead created hostility and instilled jealousy in the very people it was designed to persuade, furthering the association between democracy and materialism.[61] As Fitzhugh Green, explains: "Foreigners were treated to copious descriptions of America's prosperity in terms of millions of automobiles, washing machines, and bathtubs for every citizen." Intending to contrast the material benefits of democracy with the substandard living conditions under communism, the program instead created "envy" and "resentment" in many parts of the world.[62]

While State Department officials were bragging about America's wealth and prosperity in propaganda programs such as KNA, the Russians were allegedly engaged in a campaign to discredit the United States abroad, while simultaneously promoting their own foreign policy aims. The failure of the journalistic paradigm combined with heightened congressional intrusion and the new Soviet "attacks" against the United States to convince the Truman administration to rethink propaganda aims and techniques. Even Smith-Mundt proponents realized it was naïve to believe Soviet propaganda would be recognized as "lies" while U.S. propaganda would be judged as "truthful"—a contention promoted during the Smith-Mundt debates and perpetuated by *Times'* journalists. William Benton, who was serving in the Senate by 1950, admitted that not only was Soviet propaganda believed, it also had significant effects: "It was Soviet Russia that has shown the tremendous power, for good or evil, of projecting ideas in international relations."[63] Thus, while the attempts to influence the domestic news media were successful, international strategies fell short of congressional expectations and proved inappropriate for the international community—a community where certain segments were persuaded by the communist message.

In order to meet this changing propaganda environment and the new exigencies in the Cold War, the Truman administration responded with a more determined propaganda effort in April 1950, launching what it called America's new "Campaign of Truth."[64] In the process, Truman took to the bully pulpit in support of the governmental propaganda program. Even before he began his public crusade, though, he moved toward a more militaristic model of propaganda, designing more secret modes of influence that worked in tandem with the official propaganda activities.

NOTES

1. See James Aronson, *The Press and the Cold War* (New York: Monthly Review Press, 1990), 17; Bernard C. Cohen, *The Press and Foreign Policy* (Princeton, NJ: Princeton University Press, 1963), 136; Donald O. Dewey, "America and Russia, 1939–1941: The Views of the *New York Times*," *Journalism Quarterly* 44 (1967): 62.

2. Doris A. Graber, *Mass Media and American Politics*, 4th ed. (Washington, D.C.: Congressional Quarterly Press, 1993), 363; and Bernard Roshco, *Newsmaking* (Chicago: University of Chicago Press, 1975), 71.

3. See House Committee on Foreign Affairs, *United States Information and Educational Exchange Act of 1948*, 80th Cong., 2d sess., 1948, H. R. 3342, 4–12; Gil Cranberg, "Propaganda and the United States," *Etc.* 41 (1984): 185.

4. Edwin L. James, "Better Prospects Now for Voice of America," *New York Times*, January 18, 1948, 3.

5. See Edwin R. Bayley, *Joe McCarthy and the Press* (New York: Pantheon Books, 1981), 48. Bayley contends that newspaper editorials in the 1950s were a "more important part of the information process than they are now," as many

readers used them to "to make sense of the puzzling, sometimes contradictory news reports."

6. "Victory for the 'Voice,'" *New York Times*, January 18, 1948, 10.

7. James, "Better Prospects," 3.

8. Marion Turner Sheehan, ed., *The World at Home: Selections from the Writings of Anne O'Hare McCormick* (New York: Alfred A. Knopf, 1956), x–xii.

9. "Lack of News Held Danger to Europe: Anne O'Hare McCormick Tells Teachers that Information for Decisions Is Absent," *New York Times*, March 12, 1947, 6.

10. "Seminar Speakers Deplore Slash in Funds for Voice of America," *New York Times*, April 25, 1947, 4.

11. "Battle for Men's Minds," *New York Times*, April 1, 1949, 24.

12. Russell Porter, "U.S. Called to Aid of Free Economy," *New York Times* April 18, 1947, 24.

13. Sidney Shalett, "U.S. Slipping in Atomic Race, Lilenthal and Bush Reveal," *New York Times*, April 20, 1947, 1.

14. Lewis Wood, "Can't Bar Strikes, Taft Tells Editors," *New York Times*, April 16, 1948, 20.

15. "Information Pacts Being Considered," *New York Times*, February 12, 1947, 10.

16. See "Free News Treaty Bans Censorship," *New York Times*, September 8, 1947, 3; and "Draft Treaty on Free News," *New York Times*, September 8, 1947, 3.

17. William S. White, "Stronger 'Voice of America' Is Backed to Counter Soviet," *New York Times*, January 17, 1948, 1.

18. Austin Stevens, "Voice of America Girds for Battle," *New York Times*, August 11, 1948, 3.

19. "Propaganda for Freedom," *New York Times*, August 16, 1948, 18.

20. Transcript, William Benton Oral History Interview, 1968, by the Columbia University Oral History Collection, page 182, Columbia University, New York, New York.

21. For further discussion of "camouflaged" propaganda, see Shawn J. Parry-Giles, " 'Camouflaged' Propaganda: The Truman and Eisenhower Administrations' Covert Manipulation of News," *Western Journal of Communication* 60 (1996): 146–167.

22. See John Hartley, *Understanding News* (London: Methuen, 1982), 62. Hartley argues that such news practices identified do not necessarily involve a "deliberate conspiracy to 'dupe' the public, [but rather result from] a complex historical process."

23. Lawrence C. Soley, *Radio Warfare: OSS and CIA Subversive Propaganda* (New York: Praeger, 1989), 25.

24. Paul A. Smith, Jr., *On Political War* (Washington, D.C.: National Defense University Press, 1989), 5.

25. For a greater sense of the "modes of production" involved in the creation of news, see Robert A. Hackett, "Decline of a Paradigm? Bias and Objectivity in

News Media Studies," *Critical Studies in Mass Communication* 1 (1984): 229–259. For the purposes of this analysis, I include the relationships between governmental officials and the media elites as well as the strategies employed by governmental officials to influence media coverage as key components within the modes of production. See also Hanno Hardt, "Newsworkers, Technology, and Journalism History," *Critical Studies in Mass Communication* 7 (1990): 352.

26. C. N. Barclay, *The New Warfare* (New York: Philosophical Library, 1954), 21.

27. For more information on the VOA, see Cedric Larson, "Religious Freedom as a Theme of the Voice of America," *Journalism Quarterly* 29 (1952): 188; Julian Hale, *Radio Power: Propaganda and International Broadcasting* (Philadelphia, PA: Temple University Press, 1975), 32; Thomas C. Sorensen, *The Word War: The Story of American Propaganda* (New York: Harper & Row, 1968), 10; and Hans N. Tuch, *Communicating with the World: U.S. Public Diplomacy Overseas* (New York: St. Martin's Press, 1990), 87.

28. See Dean Acheson, *Present at the Creation: My Years in the State Department* (New York: W. W. Norton, 1969), 330–331; and John Lewis Gaddis, *The United States and the Origins of the Cold War, 1941–1947* (New York: Columbia University Press, 1972), 51–53.

29. William Benton, *The Voice of Latin America* (New York: Harper & Brothers, 1961), xii–xiii.

30. Senate Committee on Foreign Relations, *Investigation of "Voice of America" and "Know North America" Series of Broadcasts*, 80th Cong., 2d sess., June 2, 1948, 84–88.

31. Senate Committee on U.S. Public Law 402, *United States Information and Educational Exchange Act of 1948*, 80th Cong., 2d sess., January 27, 1948, 1011.

32. Senate Committee on Foreign Relations, June 2, 1948, 89–90.

33. *Know North America*—Colorado, February 5, 1948, Charles Hulten Papers, Box 15, Harry S. Truman Presidential Library (hereafter cited as HSTPL).

34. *Know North America*—Colorado.

35. *Know North America*—Texas, December 11, 1947, Charles Hulten Papers, Box 15, HSTPL.

36. *Know North America*—Colorado.

37. *Know North America*—Alabama, December 18, 1947, Charles Hulten Papers, Box 15, HSTPL.

38. House Committee on Expenditures in the Executive Departments, *Investigation of the State Department Voice of America Broadcasts*, 80th Cong., 2d sess., 1948, 6.

39. *Know North America*—Alabama.

40. *Congressional Record*, 80th Cong., 2d sess., 1948, 6465.

41. *Know North America*—Utah, February 2, 1948, Charles Hulten Papers, Box 15, HSTPL.

42. *Congressional Record*, 1948, 6463–6464.

43. *Know North America*—Utah.

44. *Know North America*—Wyoming, n.d., Charles Hulten Papers, Box 15, HSTPL.

45. See *Congressional Record*, 1948, 6462–6473.

46. Senate Committee on Foreign Relations, June 2, 1948, 91, 95, 135.

47. Senate Committee on Foreign Relations, *Investigation of "Voice of America" and "Know North America" Series of Broadcasts*, 80th Cong., 2d sess., June 16, 1948, 12–13, 29.

48. Senate Committee on Foreign Relations, *Investigation of the "Voice of America" and "Know North America" Series of Broadcasts*, 80th Cong., 2d sess., June 14, 1948, 319.

49. President Franklin D. Roosevelt established the Coordinator of Inter-American Affairs (CIAA) to sway public opinion in Latin America positively toward American foreign policy. The CIAA, which was initially headed by Nelson Rockefeller, emphasized "mutual respect, cultural cooperation, and inter-American friendship." See Edward W. Barrett, *Truth Is Our Weapon* (New York: Funk & Wagnalls, 1953), 22–23.

50. Senate Committee on Foreign Relations, June 2, 1948, 97–101.

51. Senate Committee on Foreign Relations, June 2, 1948, 101–105. See also Senate Committee on Foreign Relations, *United States Information and Educational Exchange Act of 1948*, 1017, for more specific information on the Smith-Mundt Act, particularly regarding FBI checks.

52. Senate Committee on Foreign Relations, *Investigation of the "Voice of America" and "Know North America" Series of Broadcasts*, 80th Cong., 2d sess., June 3, 1948, 220.

53. Senate Committee on Foreign Relations, June 2, 1948, 117–125, 161.

54. Senate Committee on Foreign Relations, June 2, 1948, 133.

55. For more information on the history of anticommunist sentiment, see Robert Griffith, *The Politics of Fear: Joseph R. McCarthy and the Senate* (Amherst: University of Massachusetts Press, 1987), 30–48.

56. Senate Committee on Foreign Relations, June 3, 1948, 220.

57. Rene Borgia to George V. Allen, May 27, 1948, Charles Hulten Papers, Box 15, HSTPL. See also John Gunther, *Inside the U.S.A.* (New York: Harper and Brothers, 1947).

58. See Jay Pridmore, *John Gunther: Inside Journalism* (Chicago: University of Chicago Press, 1990), 37, 39. For more information on Gunther's book. see Ken Cuthbertson, *Inside: The Biography of John Gunther* (Chicago: Bonus B ooks, 1992), 277.

59. House Committee on Expenditures in the Executive Departments, 1948, 15.

60. *Congressional Record*, 1948, 6468.

61. White House Office, "Study on Ideological Strategy," June 9, 1954, NSC Staff Papers, 1948–1961, OCB Central Files Series, OCB 091.4, Box 70, Dwight D. Eisenhower Presidential Library (hereafter cited as DDEPL), 4.

62. Fitzhugh Green, *American Propaganda Abroad* (New York: Hippocrene Books, 1988), 24–25.

63. Senate Committee on Foreign Relations, *Expanded International Information and Education Program*, 81st Cong., 2d sess., 1950, S. Rept. 243, 6.

64. Robert William Pirsein, *The Voice of America: An History of the International Broadcasting Activities of the United States Government, 1940–1962* (New York: Arno Press, 1979), 199.

II

The Period of Militarization

3

Creating a Militarized Propaganda Structure Through the CIA, PSB, and Campaign of Truth

The events in the Cold War began to evolve as rapidly as the Truman administration's propaganda policies. In the wake of the Truman Doctrine and the Marshall Plan, concerns grew over the communist seizure of Czechoslovakia in February 1948, the growing communist activity in Italy, and the build-up of Soviet-inspired Bulgarian, Hungarian, and Romanian armed forces. On June 11, 1948, the Soviets also stopped rail traffic between Berlin and the western regions, eventually imposing a complete blockade; in June and July, Western nations airlifted supplies to that region before West Berlin was officially formed the following year. On August 29, 1949, the Soviet Union (USSR) successfully detonated its first atomic bomb as China came under communist control only months later. By June 1950, war had broken out in Korea, which created a summer of anxious moments as the peace obstacle centered on creating a northern communist sphere and a southern democratic sphere in the Southeast Asian region.[1] The exigencies of the Cold War thus intensified during Truman's last five years in office (1948–1952) and the need for a more stepped-up propaganda program represented part of his administration's response.

The Soviet's own propaganda activities further inspired the Truman administration's propaganda readjustment. Mose Harvey of the State Department's Division of Research on the Soviet Union, indicated that the Soviet Union launched a "Hate America" campaign on January 21, 1950, which stressed its desire for "peaceful coexistence" with all countries. Such a theme challenged the Truman administration's Cold War assertions concerning the Soviet's propensity for aggression; the USSR also characterized the United States as the true cold warrior,[2] a theme perpetuated by other communist countries. According to the Truman administration, North Korea and China both charged that the United States engaged in germ or biological warfare in North Korea, which "expand[ed] the aggressive war in Korea, and instigat[ed] new wars." Any diseases, plagues, or outbreaks of insects were all blamed on "U.S. imperialist aims," illustrating to Truman officials that the "hate-America theme [would] play a major . . . role in Soviet psychological strategy."[3] The ultimate goal of the enemy's campaign, the Truman administration proclaimed, involved the spread of false information designed to convince satellite countries that communism was superior to democracy.[4] Hans N. Tuch, a career Cold War veteran of "public diplomacy," explained that such Soviet "Active Measures" campaigns spread "false information to confuse or subvert foreign publics in the interest of furthering Soviet aims and ideology."[5]

In response to increased communist activity, the new Hate America campaign, and the ineffectiveness of the State Department's journalistic propaganda paradigm, the Truman administration implemented new covert propaganda strategies in 1948 and new overt propaganda strategies beginning in 1950. The covert channels (i.e., material not attributed to the U.S. government) were invested primarily in the newly established Central Intelligence Agency (CIA) by 1947,[6] and the Psychological Strategy Board (PSB) by 1951; such actions existed apart from congressional oversight. The overt activities (i.e., material attributed to the U.S. government), however, came under the guise of Truman's Campaign of Truth, and involved intense lobbying efforts on behalf of Truman and his staff to enhance congressional propaganda expenditures.

As this chapter reveals, a militaristic paradigm began to replace the journalistic one in relation to deliberations over psychological warfare and the Campaign of Truth. When faced with opposition over the need for an enhanced governmental news agency during what seemed more like an impending military crisis, the Truman administration covertly expanded its secret psychological warfare activities, keeping such actions hidden from Congress and the American people. The archival documents concerning covert activities and the establishment of the PSB reveal a progression toward centralizing propaganda strategy in the White House, reducing congressional input, and militarizing communication strategies. As the Truman administration implemented secret psychological warfare strategies, Truman took to the bully pulpit in an attempt to garner bigger propaganda budgets for the country's overt propaganda operations. This rhetoric of crisis ultimately produced a rhetoric of war, which replaced the discourse of peace characteristic of the Smith-Mundt debates. Rather than informing the world about the United States, the new tactic became the defense of U.S. foreign policy in the face of an allegedly effective Soviet propaganda campaign.

COVERT ACTIVITIES AND PSYCHOLOGICAL WARFARE

Even before the Smith-Mundt Act passed through Congress in January 1948, the Truman administration instituted a clandestine structure that allowed for covert military and propaganda activities "designed to conceal Government interest or connection."[7] Such maneuvers established the framework for psychological warfare that addressed the increased tensions in the Cold War. Part of this new structure involved the use of CIA-sponsored radio stations and the creation of the PSB, which blended the activities of the departments of State and Defense with the CIA. Combined with a language that equated propaganda and weaponry, this new structure initiated the process whereby psychological warfare and eventually all propaganda would become instruments under the direct control of the president, warranting an expanded conception of the rhetorical presidency.

The CIA and Propaganda

Some scholars maintain that Truman reluctantly created a covert structure or that he was less interested in intelligence than either his predecessor or his successor.[8] Regardless of such questionable reluctance, the scope of Truman's covert actions dramatically changed foreign policy operations from his presidency forward. Truman, in fact, altered the nature of U.S. foreign policy operations by creating the Central Intelligence Agency through The National Security Act of 1947.[9]

Only five months after the CIA's establishment, the Truman administration expanded secret propaganda activities, which were directed by the CIA and advised by the National Security Council (NSC).[10] The mission for such covert operations was defined in the NSC-4/A document of December 9, 1947: "The National Security Council directs the Director of Central Intelligence to initiate and conduct, within the limit of available funds, covert psychological operations designed to counteract Soviet and Soviet-inspired activities which constitute a threat to world peace and security or are designed to discredit and defeat the United States in its endeavors to promote world peace and security."[11] While responsive to the NSC, this directive clearly granted the CIA unrestricted action in its psychological operations.

As NSC-4/A stipulated, "nothing contained herein shall be construed to require the Central Intelligence Agency to disclose operational details concerning its secret techniques, sources or contacts."[12]

Six months later, Truman expanded the activities of the CIA even further by adding psychological warfare and paramilitary maneuvers to its mandate. Still under the authorization of the National Security Act of 1947, document NSC-10/2 empowered the CIA to conduct "espionage and counterespionage operations abroad." These covert operations were linked to "propaganda, economic warfare, preventative direct action, including sabotage, anti-sabotage . . . subversion against hostile states . . . and support of indigenous anti-communist elements in threatened countries of the free world." NSC-10/2 also established the parameters of "covert" actions, which referenced activities conducted by the United States "against hostile foreign states . . . or in support of friendly foreign states . . . but which [were] so planned and executed that . . . if uncovered the US Government [could] plausibly disclaim any responsibility for them."[13] As John Prados explains, NSC-10/2 established for the first time "a mechanism designated by the President to approve and manage secret operations . . . [that were] responsible to him."[14]

One clear outgrowth of this covert structure involved the development of two CIA-sponsored radio stations, commonly known as Radio Free Europe (RFE) and Radio Liberty (RL). Developed under the guise of private sponsorship, the CIA's involvement with both stations was not confirmed publicly until 1971. In private presidential documents, the stations were often referred to as simply "other U.S. international broadcasting" so as to preserve the cover-up.[15] RFE was created in 1949 under the "government's intelligence apparatus" of the National Committee for a Free Europe. RL was formed in 1951 under the sponsorship of the American Committee for Freedom for the Peoples of the USSR, Inc. As the title of RL's foundation implies, it existed to beam messages to the Soviet Union, using former Soviet citizens as broadcasters. RFE targeted Eastern Europe, including Czechoslovakia, Hungary, Romania, Poland, and Bulgaria. Both radios operated without congressional authorization, and little interaction existed between the two organizations.[16]

Despite their covert structure, both radio stations received a lot of public support from political officials. President Truman and General Dwight D. Eisenhower both served as honorary chairs of RL; Eisenhower also sat on the board of RFE's National Committee for a Free Europe.[17] C. D. Jackson acted as another outspoken supporter of RFE. Jackson, a lifelong friend of propaganda activities, worked for *Time*, *Life*, and *Fortune* magazines, and served as RFE's president from 1951 to 1952 before becoming President

Eisenhower's psychological warfare assistant in 1953.[18] Clearly promulgating the myth that RFE existed as a private organization, Jackson wrote to supporters of the National Committee for a Free Europe, Inc., in 1951, that "never before . . . has the Radio Free Europe formula been attempted. This is not a transplanted American radio station using Czech and Slovak voices. . . . This is a Czechoslovak station, which happens to be physically situated in Munich, speaking to Czechoslovakia."[19]

While some similarities existed between the goals of these covert radio stations and the U.S. government's overt stations (e.g., the Voice of America [VOA]), clear differences also existed.[20] As Jackson noted, the clandestine stations helped keep "hope for liberation and freedom alive in the satellite countries."[21] Explaining the advantages of RFE over the VOA, Jackson stated: "We [RFE] can play tricks, we can denounce, we can take chances, we can act fast, all things that an official Government propaganda agency cannot do."[22] Unlike VOA, RFE and RL were defined as gray propaganda,[23] meaning that their source was concealed or attributed to a nonhostile source; even its workers often toiled without the knowledge of the CIA connection. RFE and RL also attracted a more "nationalist" audience, speaking to and as an "indigenous voice" that expressed "the aspirations of the Satellite peoples."[24]

Beyond the covert apparatus that allowed for the CIA sponsorship of RFE and RL, the Truman administration ordered the development of further psychological warfare research via NSC-59 and NSC-74. In 1949, Truman called for a comprehensive program of psychological warfare by establishing a staff devoted to research and planning with NSC-59. The following year, Truman approved "A Plan for National Psychological Warfare."[25] The NSC predicted that a war would be "forced upon the United States by the USSR," warranting a new psychological warfare strategy. Both NSC-59 and NSC-74 outlined provisions for psychological warfare in times of peace, emergency, and war.[26]

Throughout this era, political officials devoted considerable attention to defining the framework and parameters of psychological warfare. Even though Edward Lilly, a former OWI (Office of War Information) official turned PSB member, contended that the term "psychological warfare" was "dreamed-up" with "no agreed upon definition of the phrase,"[27] NCS-74 defined its parameters: "Psychological warfare is an instrument of national policy and an integral part of the national war effort. It is designed to support our political and economic measures and to render, in consonance with Joint Chiefs of Staff guidance, maximum assistance in support of military operations."[28] A more explicit definition of "psychological warfare" though was reported by the Joint Chiefs of Staff (JCS). According to the JCS, psychological warfare involved attempts by a nation "to influence the opinion, emotions, attitudes and behavior of enemy, neutral or friendly foreign groups in such a way as to support the accomplishment of its national policy and aims."[29] Such a view clearly allied psychological warfare with U.S. foreign policy initiatives.

As political officials sought to conceptualize psychological warfare activities, battles erupted among members of the CIA and the departments of Defense and State over the appropriate structure and constituency of such a program. In 1949, NSC-59 clarified the appropriate roles for each department in question. As stipulated in the NSC report, the secretary of state formulated policies for the propaganda program during times of peace, national emergency, and the initial stages of war; the secretary of state also assumed responsibility for propaganda coordination and overt psychological warfare strategy in conjunction with the Department of Defense. NSC-59 additionally called for a Department of State organization that consisted of officials from that department and the Department of Defense, the CIA, and the National Security Resources Board, to develop interdepartmental propaganda and overt psychological warfare plans.[30] While the CIA (and the NSC) controlled black propaganda (i.e., the source is concealed or attributed to a hostile source) and to a certain extent gray propaganda (i.e., the source is concealed or attributed to a nonhostile source),[31] the CIA retained the authority to label material black or gray. Thus, the CIA held the discretionary power to determine whether or not the Department of State assumed a role in the dissemination of gray propaganda.[32] The NSC, which supervised all of these operations, was granted a "statutory base for coordinated intelligence activities and for coordinated activities in the field"[33] by the National Security Act of 1947.

While all seemed to allow the Department of State control of psychological warfare during times of peace, debate centered on the locus of control during times of war. This conflict surrounded competing philosophical orientations concerning the independent branches of government. From the Department of State's perspective, psychological warfare involved overall policy planning during times of peace *and* war. The Department of Defense, conversely, believed that during a national emergency and especially during wartime, policy planning should be subjected and coordinated with military strategy. Lilly located some of the tension in assumptions made about psychological planning by both departments. According to the Department of State, "political contingencies were so variable and intangible that long range political plans were impracticable, if not impossible." Rather than conceptualize long-range plans, State Department officials generally observed the development of situations before constructing short-term plans.

Such a philosophy greatly disturbed military leaders who wanted to devise long-range psychological warfare strategies.[34] David D. Newsom, a career diplomat and a former employee of the United States Information Agency, explained part of this conflict between the diplomatic corps and the military: "The diplomat traditionally is looking at . . . the prospects for the resolution of conflict. The military officer is action oriented, trained, and committed to look at the contingencies of conflict."[35]

As the debate continued over the structure and practice of a psychological warfare operation, a separate NSC action created another Cold War precedent that impacted the creation of this psychological warfare apparatus. On September 30, 1950, Truman approved the NSC-68 measure that in essence "systematized" George Kennan's (the State Department's Soviet expert) containment theory and allowed the Truman administration to increase defense (including psychological warfare) expenses in the absence of war.[36] NSC-68 represented a more defensive action designed to combat Soviet aggression and psychological warfare activity (e.g., the Hate America campaign) through a more concerted U.S. psychological warfare counterattack.[37]

In the end, Truman created a psychological warfare structure that integrated the various views of the Defense and State Departments in his formation of the PSB. While Truman rejected the call for a single PSB director to be a "sort of 'chief of staff for the cold war'" in his directive of April 4, 1951, he did appoint some of the highest officers of government to the PSB. Those involved in such psychological planning included the undersecretary of state, the deputy secretary of defense, and the director of the CIA. In addition, a JCS representative was required to "sit with the Board as its principal military advisor." The NSC supervised PSB's activities, which made all of psychological warfare activity subject to the guidance and control of the president as commander-in-chief.[38] Any PSB activity was deemed "very highly classified" by its members because of the "sensitive subjects affecting . . . national security,"[39] which expanded covert presidential powers and lessened congressional control. According to the PSB, the "very existence" of the board was "unknown to all but a small minority of Senators and Representatives," who most likely viewed it "in terms of [the government's] . . . overt propaganda efforts." The PSB sought to continue such a low congressional profile and thus served at the pleasure of the president.[40]

The control of the executive branch over the PSB is also reflected in Truman's selection of its first director. Truman convinced Gordon Gray to assume the directorship of the PSB even though he had just accepted the presidential post at the University of North Carolina. Gray, a personal friend of Truman's, served as his assistant secretary of the army (1947–1949) and his secretary of the army (1949–1950), before beginning his duties with the PSB on July 2, 1951. [41] According to Lilly, Gray's qualifications met the ideal criteria for the director's position because "an intimate of the President . . . is always aware of what the President's wishes and reactions might be." More broadly, Lilly envisioned the director as "the President's executive agent for psychological matters."[42]

Along with the PSB's more militarized structure came directives for its operations.[43] As interpreted by PSB members, the board existed to coordinate and conduct "psychological operations within the framework of approved national policies . . . formulat[ing] and promulgat[ing] overall national psychological objectives, policies and programs."[44] Such a mission actualized the belief that the U.S. government needed "to marshal the great potential force of psychological effort in the struggle against Communist aggression" through a "unified cold war strategy."[45] Such a strategy, CIA director and PSB member Walter Bedell Smith asserted, required a "'master plan'" similar to World War II, when the United States decided to focus on Germany before Japan.[46]

While the PSB did not engage in day-to-day operations of psychological strategy, it directed "overall psychological policies, objectives, and programs, and their coordination among the various departments and agencies."[47] As the recently declassified minutes of the PSB reveal, PSB's scope was quite "broad," including any activity "except overt shooting and overt economic warfare."[48] Such a mandate meant that the PSB would not micromanage the VOA or any other State Department propaganda programs. Instead, the PSB would serve as "a high-level group working in the field of broad strategy and coordination."[49] The VOA would then receive mandates to operationalize such psychological warfare plans.

Even though the Department of State remained involved in psychological operations and maintained its directorship of the overt propaganda programs, the debate over psychological warfare strategies revealed the gradual progression to a more militarized structure of propaganda operations. In reviewing the constituency of the PSB, for example, greater representation was drawn from either CIA (covert) or military officials than from the State Department. Involving more individuals with a military background undoubtedly changed the orientation of the program away from the journalistic paradigm of early propaganda efforts. Such a militarized structure simultaneously increased presidential control over psychological warfare activities as the president now served as commander-in-chief of propaganda operations. Truman's close personal friendship with Gray ensured that the PSB would receive even greater attention from the president, elevating PSB's role to the "highest hierarch[y] . . . of the executive branch."[50]

Not only did the structure of the PSB move psychological warfare and propaganda strategy closer to a military paradigm, so too did the language employed in the conversations over such strategies. Throughout the archival documents pertaining to psychological strategy, political officials relied heavily on artillery metaphors when discussing psychological warfare, propaganda, and their appropriate structures. C. D. Jackson, for example, identified RFE as a "mighty weapon in the struggle for freedom,"[51] while the authors of a PSB draft statement not only used the term "weapon" on three separate occasions in referring to psychological strategy, but also called such strategies "indispensable *arms* of United States policy for peace."[52] Other internal documents increased the metaphorical use of weaponry images. One PSB document in particular equated psychological warfare with such weapons as "the airplane, the 155 millimeter gun, the Patton Tank, and the bazooka."[53]

Such a new construction of propaganda in the wake of the Smith-Mundt debates shifted the propaganda paradigm to a militarized framework. No longer using a language of news or conceiving of propaganda as a journalistic practice, propaganda officials now equated propaganda with military weaponry and structured the program accordingly. Such a militaristic paradigm not only pervaded the private deliberations over propaganda and psychological warfare strategizing, but also became visible during the Truman administration's public Campaign of Truth; the practice of propaganda activity and the presidential involvement in such covert and overt actions was altered from that point forward.

THE TRUMAN ADMINISTRATION'S OVERT PROPAGANDA ACTIVITIES

In the aftermath of the *Know North America* hearings, members of Congress questioned the overall effectiveness of U.S. propaganda. Before increasing propaganda budgets as requested under the Campaign of Truth, congressional leaders demanded proof that U.S. propaganda was achieving its Smith-Mundt mission of "increas[ing] mutual understanding between the people of the United States and the people of other countries."[54] In a 1950 House appropriations debate, Representative John J. Rooney (D-NY) questioned the impact of U.S. propaganda on the Cold War: "How have we changed the political complexion anywhere? What have we accomplished in the Cold War?"[55] Such issues continued to plague propaganda officials during the 1951 appropriation hearings, where Representative Cliff

Clevenger (R-OH) raised a similar concern, asking whether the government's propaganda "made any friends or kept us out of any war."[56] Senator Kenneth McKellar's (D-TN) pointed questions about the propaganda program most typified the opposition's charges: "What does it [propaganda] do? What does it accomplish? What does the document do? What do you accomplish by it?" Concluding his attack, McKellar claimed: "I don't believe you have ever influenced a single" individual.[57]

Other critics' concerns explicitly reflected the problems accentuated during the KNA debates. Many congressional leaders pointed to the ineffectiveness of the propaganda that instilled envy and jealousy around the world. Representative Katharine St. George (R-NY), for example, argued that "as for the luxuries at home, that does not appeal at all . . . it builds resentment among" the international community.[58] Similarly, Representative Clarence J. Brown (R-OH) charged that "there is entirely too much boasting about American living standards, American luxuries, and American big heartedness."[59] At bottom, many wondered like Representative George Meader (R-MI), whether "far greater benefits [could] result from action and performance than from oratory."[60]

In the face of such opposition, the Truman administration and congressional supporters refashioned their rhetorical strategies in the debates surrounding the Campaign of Truth, attempting to justify increased expenditures while simultaneously alluding to the effectiveness of its output.[61] As this next section will illustrate, Truman administration officials now had to demonstrate to members of Congress that even when faced with an impending international crisis, propaganda was just as effective as any military action might be. In adapting to the new political climate brought about by the intensification of the Cold War and the pressures of Washington politics, a language of war likewise began to emerge in the public deliberations.

The Campaign of Truth

In March 1950, former Assistant Secretary of State Senator William Benton (D-CT) and twelve of his senatorial colleagues called for an enlarged "information" program, a sort of "Marshall Plan in the field of ideas."[62] Plans for such a program were already under way in the Truman administration. When President Harry S. Truman informed his newly appointed secretary of state for public affairs, Edward W. Barrett, of his desire to launch a major propaganda offensive against the Soviet Union, Barrett convinced him to label the effort a "Campaign of Truth," so as to avoid the stigma of propaganda.[63] The campaign was intended to counter directly the communist Hate America initiative and the Soviet co-optation of peace.[64]

President Truman personally launched the Campaign of Truth from the bully pulpit during a speech to the American Society of Newspaper Editors on April 20, 1950[65] (see chapter 4). Thereafter, a subcommittee of the Senate Foreign Relations Committee investigated the need for such a program in July of that same year. Both the House and the Senate held special supplemental budget hearings in response to the Truman administration's request for $32.7 million in regular appropriations and $82 million in supplemental appropriations for fiscal year 1951. The supplemental funds were designed to target twenty-eight critical areas of the world, including Iran, South Korea, Indochina, Thailand, Greece, Afghanistan, Finland, and the Soviet satellite regions.[66]

After launching the campaign, the Truman administration engaged in a massive effort to marshal support for the Campaign of Truth in and out of Congress. Propaganda advocates in fact devised a public relations campaign to pressure Congress into increasing propaganda expenditures. From April 20, 1950, through January 16, 1951, for example, propaganda officials gave some fifty-four speeches to private groups about the campaign. Truman also continued speaking out in favor of the Campaign of Truth as well throughout 1950 and 1951.[67] The number of speeches fell off in 1951, however, primarily due to criticisms emanating from Congress that they were wasting money selling the American public on the program rather than selling democracy to foreign audiences.[68]

By far the largest effort to garner support for the Campaign of Truth, however, took place in Congress. Propaganda officials and other State Department representatives testified regularly during the hearings. Others not directly associated with the program (e.g., General Eisenhower and Lt. General Walter Bedell Smith) also offered "expert" testimony about propaganda activities, which served to heighten the operation's credibility. Barrett and Truman were also intensely involved in lobbying efforts and letter-writing campaigns; privately, Truman even pressured influential members of Congress to support the campaign.[69] The heightened Cold War exigences, the Truman administration reasoned, served as the primary justification for expanding America's voice in the "war of words."

A Rhetoric of Crisis

Even though Smith-Mundt supporters defined propaganda as a necessary peacetime element of U.S. foreign policy, they secured bigger budgets for the Campaign of Truth by talking of a stepped-up Cold War crisis. The Hate America campaign weighed heavily on the minds of Truman officials and supporters. Mose Harvey of the State Department charged that the Russian campaign was "directed toward creating hatred of the United States . . . hatred on the part of the Russian people, on the part of the people on the outside."[70] Undersecretary of State Dean Acheson argued that the Soviet efforts involved "falsification, distortion, suppression and deception" intended to "misrepresent and discredit the aims and nature of American life, and the aims and nature of American foreign policy."[71] Part of this "falsification," Senator H. Alexander Smith (R-NJ) declared, involved Soviet claims that the United States was a "capitalistic, materialistic, dollar-sign nation, competing against Russian communism." Smith explained that this U.S. image was juxtaposed against the vision of the Soviets as "the champions of the downtrodden" trying to overthrow the "domination of other powers."[72]

Supporters of the Campaign of Truth appeared most incensed, however, by Soviet attempts to portray the United States as the "warmongering" nation and the Soviet Union as the "peacemakers." John Foster Dulles, then a special consultant to the secretary of state, argued that communist leaders were trying to convince the world audience that they were "the nation that stands for peace and that we are the Nation that stands for war."[73] Democratic Senator Brien McMahon of Connecticut claimed that the Soviets had successfully "tagged America" with the "warmonger" label,[74] pointing to the communists' own propaganda victories.

Other supporters of the campaign offered empirical evidence of the Soviet's propaganda successes. Senator William Benton (D-CT) alleged that history was "replete with examples of startling victories won by the masters of the Kremlin," with the "fall" of China representing only one such example.[75] Senator John J. Sparkman (D-AL) offered Korea as another case of Soviet success, arguing that the United States "might have avoided the unhappy event in Korea with an established program of intensive efforts in counteracting the malicious falsehoods spread by Communists in North Korea."[76] The Soviet Union, Senator Homer Ferguson (D-MI) concluded, had "mastered the techniques of using words as a substitute for deeds."[77]

Such Soviet victories in the "war of words" implicitly served as the justification for the United States to step up its propaganda offensive. Certainly, the reasoning appeared, if the Soviets could achieve such rhetorical successes, an expanded U.S. effort could accrue similar results. As Assistant Secretary of State Barrett suggested, any tactic would be justified given the severity of the threat: "We simply [must do] everything possible to influence the minds of men to understand our cause for which we are fighting."[78] Thus, for propaganda supporters, Soviet actions justified a new Campaign of Truth, warranting retaliatory measures that escalated the "war of words" against the Soviet government.

In an effort to operationalize this new mission that targeted specific countries, Congress passed a resolution in April 1951 designed to reaffirm the friendship of the United States with the people of the world, specifically the citizens of the Soviet Union. The resolution called for President Truman to tell the Russian people that the American people and their representatives "do not desire war, and, though firmly determined to defend their freedom, will welcome all honorable efforts to compose the differences between the two governments." Authors of the resolution explained that the American people "deeply" regretted the "artificial barriers" that "separated them from the peoples" of the Soviet Union, and they expressed "the desire of the American people to live in friendship with all other peoples."[79]

Yet even as Congress pledged its friendly relations toward the Soviet people, members sought a second Campaign of Truth strategy, attempting to foster "a split between the Russian people and the Soviet Government . . . [by] making the Russian people develop a spirit of resistance."[80] Supporting the more aggressive propaganda tactics, some congressional leaders denounced efforts designed only to "win friends" in countries already supportive of U.S. foreign policy aims. Senator Pat McCarran (D-NV), chair of the subcommittee for the Senate Committee on Appropriations, declared: "This committee is more inclined to give . . . help . . . in combating communism and more inclined to appropriate money for that purpose than . . . for other purposes."[81] In a separate statement, McCarran asked whether information officials considered France, Sweden, Switzerland, Belgium and other Western European states as "engaged in a cold war" against the United States. When VOA Director Foy D. Kohler responded "no," McCarran questioned: "Do you think it is necessary" to try to "persuade" these countries to fight "on our side in a cold war against the Kremlin" when "we have expended and have put into them in rehabilitation of their economies some $12 billion and more?"[82]

Other congressional leaders explicitly urged the program to adopt more aggressive propaganda tactics during debates surrounding the Campaign of Truth, tactics that significantly altered the Smith-Mundt mission. Senator Joseph R. McCarthy (R-WI) argued: "The Voice of America is supposed to be an instrument to fight communism . . . that is why many people are in favor of voting money for it."[83] Senator McCarran went so far as to advocate that the United States needed "a fighting policy, aim[ed] at the soonest possible collapse of the Red hierarchy" combined with "techniques of psychological warfare to match such a policy."[84] Mose Harvey illustrated how propaganda supporters even began advocating tactics that were typically associated with Soviet propaganda. According to Harvey, if the United

States wanted to "win [the] contest" with the Soviet Union, it would "have to try to match their effort."[85]

Not surprisingly, in justifying increased funds for propaganda, wartime imagery pervaded the congressional debates over the Campaign of Truth in a manner reminiscent of the private deliberations. This war rhetoric served as a means to intensify the potential impact of propaganda, as bullets were equated with words and ideas. The U.S.-Soviet struggle had become, according to supporters of the program, a "war of words," a "war of ideologies," a "propaganda war," or a "battle for the minds of men."[86] Propaganda and the Campaign of Truth were frequently referred to as instrumental "weapons" in the Cold War.[87] Assistant Secretary of State Barrett, for instance, argued that the Campaign of Truth represented the "weapon which [possessed] the firepower to pierce the iron curtain . . . [and] the explosive force to rip the camouflage from the Soviet position."[88] Officials even talked of win-loss ratios, counting the number of "victories" of each side. In a speech entitled, "Mobilization of American Strength for World Security," Barrett argued that the "Kremlin" had "nine nations lined up on their side," to "53 nations lined up on the side of the free world,"[89] which furthered the military connotations. Unless the United States continued to deploy the "T-Bomb" aggressively,[90] as supporters referred to the Campaign of Truth, the "Big Lie"[91] of Soviet propaganda would undoubtedly lead to more Soviet victories. Not only serving to increase the crisis rhetoric in the debate, such arguments also addressed questions of effectiveness,[92] as officials emphasized the win-loss ratios in the "war of words."

In developing this militaristic paradigm further, advocates of the Campaign of Truth called for an all-out propaganda war to combat Soviet psychological warfare; in the process, they drew upon the typical wartime controversies concerning limited versus full-scale warfare efforts. General J. Lawton Collins, army chief of staff, maintained: "We cannot do a job halfway. We must go all out in the battle of ideas."[93] Democratic Congressman Daniel J. Flood of Pennsylvania likewise argued that "to fail to make an all-out effort on the truth-propaganda front is . . . to commit political hara-kiri." "By our own hand," Flood concluded, "we would be inflicting a self-invited defeat of major proportions in the cold war."[94] Some officials even talked of the sacrifices that were necessary if the United States hoped to win the "war." Senator H. Alexander Smith urged the American public "to make all sacrifices needed to win the ultimate victory for freedom," by accepting "whatever controls over [the] economy" and their "individual lives" that were "necessary in order to maintain . . . strength for the tasks . . . ahead," including additional funding for propaganda.[95]

By using the language and arguments of all-out warfare, proponents of the Campaign of Truth lobbied Congress with a rhetoric of crisis. The United States needed to take Russian propaganda seriously, they argued, studying the content of the Russian message and designing better "weapons" to counter its effects.[96] The effectiveness of this crisis rhetoric in Congress is evidenced by the increased expenditures that were granted the propaganda program from 1950 through 1953. The program received approximately $111.7 million dollars for the 1951 fiscal year;[97] for the next two fiscal years, appropriations continued to rise by similar amounts.[98] In fact, for fiscal years 1951, 1952, and 1953, propaganda expenditures increased some threefold, due at least in part to the arguments amassed by the Truman administration in tandem with the intensifying Cold War context.[99]

Yet such increases in funding also resulted from the Truman administration's revised propaganda structure. In addressing the congressional complaints about the diffuse nature of U.S. propaganda operations in the aftermath of the *Know North America* hearings, the Truman administration reorganized the program on January 16, 1952. The new agency, headed by Dr. Wilson Compton and called the International Information Administration (IIA), was granted more autonomy within the State Department, with the intent of centralizing administrative duties.[100] While addressing congressional concerns, such an action also furthered the Truman administration's covert goals of lessening congressional control and increasing presidential influence over propaganda policy.

Most significantly, members of Congress, who were inspired by the Truman administration's more strident discourse, also called for a more aggressive message that transformed the rhetoric of peace from the Smith-Mundt period. As State Department and propaganda officials used a rhetoric of crisis to justify increased expenditures, congressional leaders responded with a call for a stepped-up, anticommunist message of their own, which brought significant changes to U.S. propaganda strategy during the Campaign of Truth. By the close of 1952 and thus the end of the Campaign of Truth and the Truman presidency, Assistant Secretary of State Barrett claimed that the program's main function involved exposing "to all the world the fallacies and the phony nature of communism and communistic imperialism."[101] Members of Congress likewise demanded and supported such a tonal shift in the program's international message, illustrating the effect of the Campaign of Truth and the administration's militarized rhetoric on Congress. Administrative officials thus enacted PSB's goal of a strengthened propaganda defensive against America's Cold War enemy, which shifted the emphasis of the new program from "winning friends" to "influencing people," from "public relations" to "psychological warfare."[102]

By the time that Harry S. Truman left office, the military paradigm appeared to replace the journalistic one used to obtain the legalized structure of the first peacetime propaganda program in the United States. In addition to the structural changes, the transformation is reflected in the language used throughout the private discussions among policy planners over psychological warfare and throughout the public debates over the Campaign of Truth. Such language usage reveals the naturalized equation of weaponry images with those of propaganda/psychological "warfare."[103] Detailing the significance of metaphor systems for foreign policy rhetoric, Paul A. Chilton argues that language "constitutes [the] main evidence as to the underlying belief systems that underwrite international political discourse."[104] PSB members clearly understood the definitional power of language as the Joint Chiefs of Staff, for example, called (unsuccessfully) for the use of phrase, "theater of war" to replace the State Department's preferred "theater of operations" within the debate over the PSB Plan (of operations). Such a move, the Joint Chiefs reasoned, would award "military commanders greater control of all psychological warfare directed towards the enemy."[105] Even though officials such as Gordon Gray continued to view the foreign policy operations regarding the military, the economy, and propaganda as independent endeavors,[106] the private discourse about psychological strategy revealed that a military paradigm fused propaganda and weaponry constructions. By the time of the public debates over expanding propaganda expenditures, this fusion of propaganda/weaponry images appeared quite naturalized. The expansion of Truman's covert operations of course hastened the progress toward a militarized framework and thus the naturalization of the propaganda/weaponry characterization. As Prados maintains, the PSB became a "stimulant" for intensifying the Cold War.[107]

The Truman presidency thus transformed U.S. foreign policy. Christopher Simpson argues that "between 1946 and 1950, the Truman administration created a multimillion-dollar secret bureaucracy for conducting clandestine warfare." This secret structure, Simpson maintains, helped "preserve the myth that the United States was dealing with the world in a straightforward manner consistent with the ideals of democracy."[108] The new psychological warfare structure moved the practice of government-sponsored communication closer to a more complete militarized conception for psychological warfare and for propaganda. Congressional oversight was lessened and the executive powers were expanded.[109] Truman's covert apparatus paved the way for Eisenhower to *institutionalize* covert operations. From 1945 to 1952, Truman gradually increased his involvement in propaganda operations, championing its foreign policy necessities publicly and overseeing its activities secretly. As the next chapter shows, propaganda under a military paradigm was clearly different from journalistically conceived messages.

NOTES

1. See Dean Acheson, *Present at the Creation: My Years in the State Department* (New York: W. W. Norton & Company, 1969), 320–321, 414–425; Robert R. Bowie and Richard H. Immerman, *Waging Peace: How Eisenhower Shaped an Enduring Cold War Strategy* (New York: Oxford University Press, 1998), 11–40; Norman Friedman, *The Fifty-Year War: Conflict and Strategy in the Cold War* (Annapolis, MD: Naval Institute Press, 2000), 102–143; Michael J. Hogan, *The Marshall Plan: America, Britain, and the Reconstruction of Western Europe, 1947–1952* (Cambridge: Cambridge University Press, 1987), 43–45; Zachary Karabell, *Architects of Intervention: The United States, the Third World, and the Cold War, 1946–1962* (Baton Rouge: Louisiana State University Press, 1999), 37–49; Edward Lilly, "PSB: A Short History," December, 1951, White House Office, NSC Staff Papers, 1953–1961, PSB Central Files Series, Box 6, Dwight D. Eisenhower Presidential Library (hereafter cited as DDEPL), 31–33, 45, 85–86; Martin J. Medhurst, "Truman's Rhetorical Reticence, 1945–1947: An Interpretive Essay," *Quarterly Journal of Speech* 74 (1988): 52–70; and Harry S. Truman, *Years of Trial and Hope: Memoirs by Harry S. Truman*, vol. 2 (New York: New American Library, 1956), 263–268, 339–341, 351–252, 377–380.

2. House Committee on Appropriations, *Departments of State, Justice, Commerce, and the Judiciary Appropriations for 1953*, 82d Cong., 2d. sess., 1952, 418, 408.

3. PSB D-25a, July 24, 1952, White House Office, NSC Staff: Papers, 1948–1961, OCB Secretariat Series, Ideological Documents, Box 3, DDEPL, 2–5.

4. "Countering Stalinist Propaganda," July 29, 1952, White House Office, NSC Staff: Papers, 1948–1961, OCB Secretariat Series, Doctrinal Warfare, Box 1, DDEPL, 2. For more background information on the Hate America campaign, see Saul K. Padover, "Psychological Warfare and Foreign Policy," *American Scholar* 20 (1951): 153.

5. Hans N. Tuch, *Communicating with the World: U.S. Public Diplomacy Overseas* (New York: St. Martin's Press, 1990), 115.

6. As Stephen F. Knott explains, the OSS preceded the CIA and "served as a hatchery for a score of future CIA figures." See Stephen F. Knott, *Secret and Sanctioned: Covert Operations and the American Presidency* (New York: Oxford University Press, 1996), 157.

7. "USIE and Indigenous Operations," November, 1951, White House Office, NSC Staff: Papers, 1948–1961, OCB Central Files Series, OCB 040 USIA, Box 20, DDEPL, 2.

8. See Knott, *Secret and Sanctioned*, 157; and Christopher Andrew, *For the President's Eyes Only: Secret Intelligence and the American Presidency from Washington to Bush* (New York: HarperCollins, 1995), 3.

9. See Christopher Simpson, *Science of Coercion: Communication Research and Psychological Warfare, 1945–1960* (New York: Oxford University Press, 1994), 34–41. While many scholars assert that covert operations were a Cold War phenomenon beginning in 1947, Knott maintains that the United States possesses "a rich history of clandestine operations," with the "pinnacle" of such activity existing from 1776 to 1882. See Knott, *Secret and Sanctioned*, 3–5.

10. For further analysis of NSC-4/A, see John Prados, *Presidents' Secret Wars: CIA and Pentagon Covert Operations since World War II* (New York: William Morrow, 1986), 28–29.

11. "A Report to the National Security Council by the Executive Secretary on Psychological Operations," NSC- 4/A, December, 1947, Records of Organizations in the Executive Office of the President, Record Group 429, Harry S. Truman Presidential Library (hereafter cited as HSTPL), 3.

12. "A Report to the National Security Council by the Executive Secretary on Psychological Operations," 4.

13. "A Report to the National Security Council by the Executive Secretary on Office of Special Projects," June, 1948, Records of Organizations in the Executive Office of the President, Record Group 429, HSTPL, 1–3.

14. Prados, *Presidents' Secret Wars*, 29.

15. See "Annex to the Report of the 169 Study—Radio Free Europe," July 29, 1954, White House Office, NSC Staff: Papers, 1948–1961, OCB Central Files Series, 000.77 Radio Broadcasts, Box 3, DDEPL, 1. See also Cord Meyer, *Facing Reality: From World Federalism to the CIA* (New York: Harper & Row, 1980), 110; and David D. Newsom, *Diplomacy and the American Democracy* (Bloomington: Indiana University Press, 1988), 184; and Tuch, *Communicating with the World*, 16. Tuch explains that since 1973, RFE and RL were blended into one radio station, received congressional funding and were directed by the Board of International Broadcasting.

16. For more information on RFE and RL, see David M. Abshire, *International Broadcasting: A New Dimension in Western Diplomacy* (Beverly Hills, CA: Sage Publications, 1976); James Critchlow, *Radio Hole-In-The-Head: Radio Liberty: An Insider's Story of Cold War Broadcasting* (Washington, D.C. American University Press, 1995); Julian Hale, *Radio Power: Propaganda and International Broadcasting* (Philadelphia, PA: Temple University Press, 1975); Sig Mickelson, *America's Other Voice: The Story of Radio Free Europe and Radio Liberty* (New York: Praeger, 1983); Michael Nelson, *War of Black Heavens: The Battles of Western Broadcasting in the Cold War* (Syracuse, NY: Syracuse University Press, 1997); Arch Puddington, *Broadcasting Freedom: The Cold War Triumph of Radio Free Europe and Radio Liberty* (Lexington: University of Kentucky Press, 2000); Paul A. Smith, Jr., *On Political War* (Washington, D.C.: National Defense University Press, 1989); George R. Urban, *Radio Free Europe and the Pursuit of Democracy: My War within the Cold War* (New Haven, CT: Yale University Press, 1997); and Joseph G. Whelan, *Radio Liberty: A Study of Its Ori-*

gins, Structure, Policy, Programming, and Effectiveness (Washington, D.C.: Congressional Research Service, Library of Congress, 1972).

17. See Meyer, *Facing Reality*, 111; and Whelan, *Radio Liberty*, 17–18.

18. Rhodri Jeffreys-Jones, *The CIA and American Democracy* (New Haven, CT: Yale University Press, 1989), 86.

19. C. D. Jackson to Crusaders, May, 1951, The William Benton Papers, Department of Special Collections, Box 7, The University of Chicago Library, Chicago, Illinois, 2.

20. See Martin J. Medhurst, "Eisenhower and the Crusade for Freedom: The Rhetorical Origins of a Cold War Campaign," *Presidential Studies Quarterly* 27 (1997): 652; and Tuch, *Communicating with the World*, 15–16.

21. C. D. Jackson to Mr. Luce, June, 1955, Papers of the President of the United States, 1953–1961 (Ann Whitman File), Administrative Series, Box 22, DDEPL, 1.

22. C. D. Jackson, "An American Idea and Program Is Breaking Through the Iron Curtain," September, 1951, C. D. Jackson Papers, 1931–1967, Box 82, DDEPL, 5.

23. Smith, Jr., *On Political War*, 200. According to the PSB, "attribution is made to some other source within or outside the United States" with black propaganda. See Foreign Service Information and Education Exchange Circular No. 4, "USIE and Indigenous Operations," November, 1951, State Department File, Psychological Strategy Board, HSTPL, 1; and "A Report to the National Security Council by the Under Secretary of State on a Plan for National Psychological Warfare," July, 1950, Records of Organizations in the Executive Office of the President, Record Group 429, HSTPL, 25.

24. "Annex to Report of the 169 Study," 2–4.

25. See Prados, *Presidents' Secret Wars*, 83–84.

26. See "A Report to the National Security Council by the Under Secretary of State on a Plan for National Psychological Warfare," 1; and "A Report to the National Security Council by the Under Secretary of State on the Foreign Information Program and Psychological Warfare Planning," December, 1949, Records of Organizations in the Executive Office of the President, Record Group 429, HSTPL, 1–4. NSC-59 rescinded NSC-4 and NSC-43.

27. Lilly, "PSB: A Short History," 4. Lilly received his Ph.D. from Catholic University of America in 1936 and served as a professor of history of American thought at that same university in Washington, D.C. from 1940 to 1944. During World War II, he acted as special assistant to the director of the Office of War Information and then as historian and advisor to the Joint Chiefs of Staff on psychological warfare (1946–1952) before becoming a PSB member in 1952. See E. P. Lilly to C. Tracy Barnes, August, 11, 1952, White House Office, NSC Staff: Papers, 1948–1961, OCB Secretariat Series, Official Personnel Papers PSB Degener/Lilly, Box 5, DDEPL, 1.

28. "A Report to the National Security Council by the Under Secretary of State on a Plan for National Psychological Warfare," 2.

29. Psychological Strategy Board File, January, 1953, White House Central Files, 1953–1961, Confidential File, Box 61, DDEPL, 6.

30. "A Report to the National Security Council by the Under Secretary of State on the Foreign Information Program and Psychological Warfare Planning," 1–4.

31. See "USIE and Indigenous Operations," 2, concerning the definitions of black, gray, and white propaganda (source is identified as the U.S. government). A chart/diagram regarding the allocation of psychological warfare duties identified "belligerent" warfare as a fourth method of psychological warfare, combined with overt and covert. Like covert psychological warfare, "belligerent" was also connected to, and directed by, the CIA. According to a Psychological Warfare Research report, "belligerent" operations included "the fostering of surrender, maligning, panic, terror, revolt, confusion, non-cooperation, sabotage." See "Psychological Warfare Research: A Long-Range Program," Part One, Essential Background Information, March, 1953, U.S. President's Committee on International Information Activities (Jackson Committee): Records, 1950–1953, Box 15, DDEPL, 17.

32. Lilly, "PSB: A Short History," 70.

33. Speech Draft, n.d., Gordon Gray Papers, 1946–1976, Box 2, DDEPL, 1. This document identifies the intent and structure of the National Security Council and the Operations Coordinating Board.

34. Lilly, "PSB: Short History," 75–76.

35. Newsom, *Diplomacy and the American Democracy*, 148.

36. See NSC-68, 14 April, 1950, *Foreign Relations*, I, 237–239; Bowie and Immerman, *Waging Peace*, 17–32; and John Lewis Gaddis, *Strategies of Containment: A Critical Appraisal of Postwar American National Security Policy* (Oxford: Oxford University Press, 1982), 89–126.

37. Note that other NSC actions were also influential in the practice of psychological warfare. NSC 20/4 (November 1948) established national objectives in response to Soviet aggression early on. Objectives directed toward the satellite regions in particular were identified in NSC-58/2 (December 1949) and NSC 48/5 (May 1951). NSC-114 (1951) reaffirms NSC-68. See "National Policy Applicable to Doctrinal Warfare," November, 17, 1952, White House Office, NSC Staff: Papers, 1948–1961, OCB Secretariat Series, Doctrinal Warfare (Official), Box 2, DDEPL, 1–3.

38. Gordon Gray, "Report to the President," February, 1952, Gordon Gray Papers, 1946–1976, Box 3, DDEPL, 6–7. For the organization and personnel structure of the NSC, the PSB, the Department of Defense, the Department of State, and the CIA, see William E. Daugherty, "Post-World War II Developments," in *A Psychological Warfare Casebook*, eds. William E. Daugherty and Morris Janowitz (Baltimore, MD: Johns Hopkins University Press, 1958), 143; and Michael McClintock, *Instruments of Statecraft: U.S. Guerilla Warfare, Counter-Insurgency, and Counter-Terrorism, 1945–1990* (New York: Pantheon Books, 1992), 35–39.

39. "Handbook on Psychological Strategy Board Functions and Procedures," February, 1953, White House Office, NSC Staff: Papers, 1953–1961,
PSB Central Files Series, Box 23, DDEPL, 6.

40. Wallace Irwin, Jr., to George A. Morgan, n.d., White House Office, NSC
Staff: Papers, 1953–1961, PSB Central Files Series, PSB UN, Box 24, DDEPL,
1. For further evidence of Truman's interest and power over the PSB, see "One
Year's Development of the PSB," January, 12, 1953, White House Office, NSC
Staff: Papers, 1953–1961, PSB Central Files Series, Background Material on
PSB, Box 23, DDEPL, 24–25; and James S. Lay, Jr., to the director of the PSB,
May 29, 1952, Psychological Strategy Board, White House Office, NSC Staff:
Papers, 1948–1961, OCB Secretariat Series, Ideological Documents, Box 3,
DDEPL, 1.

41. See "One Year's Development of the PSB," 1–4. See also Prados, *Presidents' Secret Wars*, 86. Prados explains that Gordon Gray served as a North
Carolina state senator before and after World War II.

42. Edward P. Lilly to Admiral Kirk, January 12, 1953, Recommendations
Regarding PSB's Future, White House Office, NSC Staff: Papers, 1953–1961,
PSB Central Files Series, PSB 334, Box 23, DDEPL, 3.

43. For secondary accounts concerning the activities of the PSB and psychological warfare strategies, see Stephen E. Pease, *Psywar: Psychological Warfare
in Korea, 1950–1953* (Harrisburg, PA: Stackpole Books, 1992), 16–18; Prados,
Presidents' Secret Wars, 84–86; and Simpson, *Science of Coercion*, 75. It is important to understand that the militarization of propaganda activities predated the
Cold War. James Jerry Kimble's work, for example, reveals how the Treasury
Department reflected a militarized mentality in its promulgation of war bonds
during World War II. The practice of conceptualizing America's propaganda program in a militarized language is likewise traceable to World War I and the activities of the CPI. See James Jerry Kimble, "Mobilizing the Home Front: War
Bonds, Morale, and the U.S. Treasury's Domestic Propaganda Campaign, 1942–
1945" (Ph.D. diss., University of Maryland, 2001). For a comprehensive view of
the militarization of U.S. culture during the 1950s, see Laura McEnaney, *Civil
Defense Begins at Home: Militarization Meets Everyday Life in the Fifties*
(Princeton, NJ: Princeton University Press, 2000).

44. Draft of Statement for PSB Meeting, n.d., Gordon Gray Papers,
1946–1976, Box 3, DDEPL, 1–2. See also, Psychological Strategy Board Minutes, August, 1951, White House Office, NSC Staff: Papers, 1948–1961, NSC
Registry Series, 1947–1962, Box 17, DDEPL, 5. The PSB was also directed to
coordinate "psychological strategy" with "all activity in the Government" related
to its practice.

45. Robert Cutler to Gordon Gray (Special Assistant to the Director), October, 1951, Gordon Gray Papers, 1946–1976, Box 3, DDEPL, 1–2,

46. Psychological Strategy Board Minutes, July, 1951, White House Office,
NSC Staff: Papers, 1948–1961, NSC Registry Series, 1947–1962, Box 17,
DDEPL, 1–2.

47. Psychological Strategy Board, September, 1951, Gordon Gray Papers, 1946–1976, Box 3, DDEPL, 1.

48. Psychological Strategy Board Minutes, July, 1951, 2.

49. Gray, "Report to the President," 8.

50. "One Year's Development of PSB," 9.

51. Jackson to Crusaders, 2.

52. Draft of Statement for PSB Meeting, 1 (emphasis added).

53. Psychological Strategy Board File, January, 1953, 8.

54. Senate Committee on Foreign Relations, *United States Information and Educational Exchange Act of 1948*, 80th Cong., 2d sess., 1948, 1011.

55. House Committee on Appropriations, *Supplemental Appropriations Bill for 1951*, 81st Cong., 2d sess., 1950, 36.

56. House Committee on Appropriations, *Department of State Appropriations for 1952*, 82d Cong., 1st sess., 1951, 918.

57. Senate Committee on Appropriations, *Departments of State, Justice, Commerce, and the Judiciary Appropriations for 1952*, 82d Cong., 1st sess., 1951, 1808–1811.

58. *Congressional Record*, 82d Cong., 2d sess., 1952, 3530.

59. *Congressional Record*, 82d Cong., 1st sess., 1951, 8676.

60. *Congressional Record*, 1952, 3537.

61. See Martin J. Medhurst, "Rhetoric and Cold War: A Strategic Approach," in *Cold War Rhetoric: Strategy, Metaphor, and Ideology*, eds. Martin J. Medhurst, Robert L. Ivie, Philip Wander, and Robert L. Scott (East Lansing: Michigan State University Press, 1997), 19–20. The conception of strategic rhetoric that I adopt for the purposes of this analysis is drawn from Medhurst's definition, in which he claims that such strategies come "into being for the purpose of realizing a goal or goals and is shaped and executed with these goals in mind."

62. Charles A. Thomson and Walter H. C. Laves, *Cultural Relations and U.S. Foreign Policy* (Bloomington: Indiana University Press, 1963), 80.

63. Thomas C. Sorensen, *The Word War: The Story of American Propaganda* (New York: Harper & Row, 1968), 26.

64. For additional information on the Hate America campaign, see Hale, *Radio Power*, 34.

65. Harry S. Truman, "Going Forward with a Campaign of Truth," *Department of State Bulletin* 22 (May 1, 1950): 669–672.

66. Senate Committee on Appropriations, *Supplemental Appropriations for 1951*, 81st Cong., 2d sess., 1950, 308.

67. For additional speeches delivered by Truman on the Campaign of Truth, see Harry S. Truman, "The Objective Is Our Efforts in Peace, Not Conflict," *Department of State Bulletin* 22 (July 19, 1950): 996–998; Harry S. Truman, "Expanded Information Program Vital to National Security," *Department of State Bulletin* 23 (July 31, 1950): 194–195; and Harry S. Truman, "The Defense of Freedom," *Department of State Bulletin* 25 (July 16, 1951): 83–86.

68. House Committee on Appropriations, *Department of State Appropriations for 1952*, 82d Cong., lst sess., 1951, 761–762, 747–757.

69. See Edward W. Barrett, *Truth Is Our Weapon* (New York: Funk and Wagnalls, 1953), 82–83; Harry S. Truman to Senator Ralph Flanders, August 30, 1950, Papers of Harry S. Truman, Official File, Box 123, HSTPL, 1; Harry S. Truman, March 5, 1951, Letter to the Speaker of the House of Representatives, Papers of Harry S. Truman, Official File, Box 123, HSTPL, 1.

70. Senate Committee on Appropriations, *Departments of State, Justice, Commerce and the Judiciary Appropriations for 1953*, 82d Cong., 2d sess., 1952, 1084.

71. Senate Committee on Foreign Relations, *Expanded International Information and Education Program*, 81st Cong., 2d sess., 1950, S. Rept., 243, 39.

72. *Congressional Record*, 1951, 1127.

73. Senate Committee on Foreign Relations, 1950, 47.

74. *Congressional Record*, 1951, 482.

75. *Congressional Record*, 1950, 81st Cong., 2d sess., 9907.

76. Senate Committee on Foreign Relations, 1950, 141.

77. *Congressional Record*, 1950, 9909.

78. Senate Committee on Appropriations, *Supplemental Appropriations for 1951*, 1950, 316.

79. U.S. Congress, *Reaffirming the Friendship of the American People for All the Peoples of the World, Including the Soviet Union*, 82d Cong., lst sess., 1951, S. Rept. 298, 1–2.

80. Senate Committee on Appropriations, 1951, 1644.

81. Senate Committee on Appropriations, 1951, 1693.

82. Senate Committee on Appropriations, 1951, 1842.

83. Senate Committee on Appropriations, 1952, 1110.

84. Senate Committee on Appropriations, 1952, 1038.

85. Senate Committee on Appropriations, 1952, 1072.

86. See *Congressional Record*, 1950, 8624, A6730; *Congressional Record*, 1951, 8774, 10631, 8954, 10619, 10639, 10640, 10646, 10649; *Congressional Record*, 1952, 3527; Edward W. Barrett, "USIE Capitalizes on Soviet Propaganda Blunders," *Department of State Bulletin* 23 (September 11, 1950): 414; Edward W. Barrett, "The Turn of the Tide," *Department of State Bulletin* 24 (February 26, 1951): 354; John M. Begg, "The American Idea: Package It for Export," *Department of State Bulletin* 24 (March 21, 1951): 409; Thurman L. Barnard, "Truth Propaganda and the U.S. Information Program," *Department of State Bulletin* 25 (November 26, 1951): 853; Wilson Compton, "An Organization for International Information," *Department of State Bulletin* 26 (March 26, 1952): 444; Wilson Compton, "Mutual Security Requires Mutual Understanding," *Department of State Bulletin* 26 (April 28, 1952): 670; Wilson Compton, "The Voice of America at the Water's Edge," *Department of State Bulletin* 26 (June 2, 1952): 865; Wilson Compton, "Crusade of Ideas," *Department of State Bulletin* 27 (September 8,

1952): 345; and Wilson Compton, "Paving a Road to Peace," *Department of State Bulletin* 27 (October 20, 1952): 604.

87. See Senate Committee on Foreign Relations, 1950, 141; Edward W. Barrett, "U.S. Informational Aims in the Cold War," *Department of State Bulletin* 22 (June 19, 1950): 992, 995; Begg, "The American Idea," 410; and Compton, "An Organization for International Information," 444.

88. Edward W. Barrett, "Expanding Techniques for a Truth Strategy," *Department of State Bulletin* 23 (December 11, 1950): 946.

89. Edward W. Barrett, "Mobilization of American Strength for World Security," *Department of State Bulletin* 23 (November 6, 1950): 736 (emphasis added).

90. See Senate Committee on Foreign Relations, 1950, 28; *Congressional Record*, 1950, 9914, A6730.

91. See *Congressional Record*, 1950, 9908; *Congressional Record*, 1951, 7294, 8954.

92. For addition information on how propaganda officials attempted to evidence the effectiveness of their Cold War message, see Shawn J. Parry-Giles, "Propaganda, Effect, and the Cold War: Gauging the Status of America's 'War of Words,' " *Political Communication* 11 (1994): 203–213.

93. House Committee on Appropriations, *Departments of State, Justice, Commerce, and the Judiciary Appropriations for 1953*, 82d Cong., 2d sess., 1952, 401.

94. *Congressional Record,* 1951, 3547.

95. *Congressional Record*, 1950, 13936.

96. House Committee on Appropriations, *The Supplemental Appropriation Bill for 1951*, 1950, 26.

97. Ronald I. Rubin, *The Objectives of the U.S. Information Agency: Controversies and Analysis* (New York: Praeger, 1966), 113.

98. Robert William Pirsein, *The Voice of America: An History of the International Broadcasting Activities of the United States Government, 1940–1962* (New York: Arno Press, 1979), 209, 224, 227.

99. See Barrett, *Truth Is Our Weapon*, 85, 82. Barrett argues that "every dime extracted from Congress was paid for in anguish, toil, and bloody brows."

100. For additional information on Truman's Campaign of Truth, see David F. Krugler, *The Voice of America and the Domestic Propaganda Battles, 1945–1953* (Columbia: University of Missouri Press, 2000), 96–116; and Pirsein, *The Voice of America*, 220.

101. Senate Committee on Appropriations, 1951, 1641.

102. Oren Stephens, *Facts to a Candid World: America's Overseas Information Program* (Stanford, CA: Stanford University Press, 1955), 6.

103. Certainly, the decision to connect psychology, communication, and war represents further evidence of the militarization of communication strategy. McClintock explains that by the 1960s, the Army used the term "special warfare" rather than "psychological warfare" or "political warfare." Such a term combined

"special operations" and the "propaganda side" of "psychological warfare." See McClintock, *Instruments of Statecraft*, 36.

104. Paul A. Chilton, "The Meaning of Security," in *Post-Realism: The Rhetorical Turn in International Relations*, eds. Francis A. Beer and Robert Hariman (East Lansing: Michigan State University Press, 1996), 195.

105. "One Year's Development of PSB," 42.

106. Gray, "Report to the President," 9.

107. Prados, *Presidents' Secret Wars*, 86.

108. Simpson, *Science of Coercion*, 36, 39.

109. Stephen F. Knott contends that there was an agreement between the presidents and Congress during the Cold War that "the president would conduct covert operations with a prudential concern for the interests of the country," produced in part by the "level of threat at the time." Knott concludes that part of the erosion of the checks and balances was due to the bi-partisan support on Cold War matters. Knott also counters the contention that the CIA and the president operated without congressional oversight because the CIA reported to high-ranking U.S. senators. See Knott, *Secret and Sanctioned*, 163–171, 185–187. In response to Knott's contentions, I argue first that the Cold War still witnessed an expansion of the presidential powers through covert operations. Second, the bi-partisan support that Cold War presidents enjoyed was linked, in part, to the rhetorical construction of the Cold War by Truman and Eisenhower; by 1961, the Cold War ideology was naturalized, produced in part by the pervasiveness of the messages that were presidentially orchestrated by the Truman and Eisenhower administrations from 1945 to 1960. Third, because of Truman's and Eisenhower's institutionalization of the propaganda program as a presidential prerogative, their successors exerted considerable control over how to meld propaganda strategy with their foreign policy aims in a manner that would benefit their administrative goals.

4

Militarized Propaganda and the Campaign of Truth, 1950–1952

As previously detailed, President Harry S. Truman took to the bully pulpit in support of the U.S. propaganda program in 1950. Unlike the Smith-Mundt phase of the propaganda program, this militarized version lashed out against communism much more vehemently than in 1948, where democracy and the United States were showcased. Determined to step up the propaganda offensive against the Soviet Union, this chapter focuses on how Truman led his administration into a new phase of the Cold War. Within this second phase, the Psychological Strategy Board (PSB) and the CIA directed propaganda operations with guidance from Truman, while the State Department implemented the PSB's overt (and covert) strategies.

A PSB-controlled propaganda sought to incite an anticommunist revolution in the target regions and to encourage defections among Soviet and satellite elites through its newly established Escapee Program. The PSB members asserted that "the positive United States-Free World ideology must be used as a revolutionary weapon to turn the followers or captives of communism against their leaders on both sides of the Iron Curtain." Beyond inciting a revolution, though, the PSB also wanted to increase defections, especially among intellectuals. According to the PSB, communists targeted "intellectual elite[s] in critical areas."[1] Like the Soviet Union, the PSB now sought to increase the number of people fleeing communism who could, in turn, write and talk about such experiences; their messages then would be disseminated widely to those people ruled by communism. This period thus marked a time when the U.S. propaganda strategies reflected many of the same tactics used by the country's Cold War enemy—tactics that a Truman-directed PSB designed and the Department of State implemented.[2]

Just as the PSB directed, the State Department continued to rely on the Voice of America (VOA) to get its message to the iron curtain countries. The PSB, though, also called for an expanded use of books as a form of propaganda during the Campaign of Truth. As Truman's bully pulpit messages were promulgated through surrogate voices over the VOA, his Campaign of Truth message was simultaneously woven into the books that the State Department distributed internationally. Many of the books distributed during the Campaign of Truth were autobiographies of individuals, frequently "intellectuals" who experienced life in the Soviet Union or who had some former connection with communism. Regardless of the authors' backgrounds, most told of how they eventually rejected communism, especially the kind of communism practiced under Stalin. Democracy, of course, stood as the alternative. Paralleling PSB's psychological warfare themes, the authors as well as the broadcasters of the VOA subtly encouraged their readers and listeners to revolt against the evil forces of communism as part of the PSB's Escapee and Doctrinal Warfare Programs.

This chapter thus demonstrates the actualization of the militarized propaganda paradigm, complete with overt and covert strategies. Guided by the PSB strategies outlined in chapter 3, the State Department's propaganda was more regulated and synchronized with the Truman administration's public policy statements. The centralization of propaganda strategy by the PSB gave Truman more control over propaganda's content. Truman's message was also rearticulated by presidential-rhetorical surrogates, many of whom, this chapter shows, voiced such messages without a visible connection with the presidential administration; some of the "surrogates" were even unaware of the U.S. government's involvement with their Cold War work (e.g., employees of Radio Free Europe [RFE] or Radio Liberty [RL]). Thus, this chapter illustrates how visions of the rhetorical presidency should be expanded to include covert activity and presidential "stand-ins."

TRUMAN'S CAMPAIGN OF TRUTH

The PSB's plans were launched during Truman's Campaign of Truth address before the American Society of Newspaper Editors (ASNE) on April 20, 1950. Unlike the Smith-Mundt period, Truman associated himself publicly with the propaganda program during the Campaign of Truth and fought for the necessary expenditures to keep it running at a strengthened pace. Most significantly, Truman's rhetoric revealed the transformed tone of the U.S. propaganda program as well as the newly implemented militarized structure.

Truman's attack on the communist Hate America campaign during much of the Campaign of Truth address, where he exposed Soviet leaders as liars and imperialists, reflects the more defensive tone of U.S. propaganda. Referencing the Soviet's own propagandistic efforts, Truman charged that "deceit, distortion, and lies are systematically used by them as a matter of deliberate policy." Such lies were most reprehensible, Truman argued, because no one countered the Soviets' plagiarized message of peace. According to Truman, the Soviets "reach directly to the peasant or the villager in these vast areas . . . [where] he hears no voice from our side to dispute them." For Truman, the Soviet peace message represented a "cloak for imperialism" that had to be countered by a message of "truth to the millions of people who are uninformed or misinformed or unconvinced."[3]

Truman's message of truth represented a rhetoric of self-determination and revolt for those people residing in communist regions. Establishing that the "free way of life" in the United States served as a "vastly superior" system than one of communist "oppression," Truman sought to communicate to the people of the communist regions that "freedom is the way to economic and social advancement, the way to political independence, the way to strength, happiness, and peace." Truman's arguments were grounded on the assumption that "the appeal of free institutions and self-government springs from the deepest and noblest aspirations of mankind. It is based on every man's desire for liberty and opportunity. It is based on every man's wish to be self-reliant and to shape his own identity."[4] As Truman explained, the Campaign of Truth sought to empower those enslaved by communism to gain their own freedom against the despotic forces. Such a message then fused the Campaign of Truth with a rhetoric of revolt.

In the next several months, Truman continued to speak publicly in support of the Campaign of Truth. Referring to U.S. propaganda ("truth") as a "weapon" that the communists "fear[ed]" more than any other,[5] Truman urged Congress to "restore" the "adequate appropriations for the Campaign of Truth."[6] As Truman contended, a lack of support for the Campaign of Truth promised more war: "We shall never be able to remove suspicion and fear as potential causes of war until communication is permitted to flow, free and open, across international boundaries." To do otherwise in this crisis situation, Truman reasoned, would prompt a "future conflict . . . by means of the most hideous weapons in the history of mankind."[7]

As Truman heightened the stakes involved with a reduction in propaganda expenditures, he simultaneously defined the rhetorical parameters of the Campaign of Truth. These propaganda themes were now to be disseminated through a more synchronized, regulated, and thus more militarized propaganda program. The next section reveals how the Voice of America responded to the new militarized propaganda structure and actualized Truman's anticommunist message. Employees of the VOA now served as Truman's newest soldiers and gave voice to his rhetoric of self-determination and revolt.

Militarizing the VOA

Not surprisingly, many of those involved in VOA's operations during the Campaign of Truth came from the ranks of practicing journalists.[8] Such journalists-turned-propagandists quickly learned, however, that news in the service of propaganda operated under a whole different set of constraints during the Campaign of Truth—constraints now more closely regulated by the Truman administration under the direction of the PSB. While trained to be "objective," to present both sides of an issue, or to attribute their material to reliable sources,[9] the "journalists" of the VOA had to answer to different standards in the aftermath of the *Know North America* (KNA) hearings.

From the KNA hearings, the Truman administration learned that Congress wanted tighter control over the program's output. In response to such general criticisms, Assistant Secretary of State for Public Affairs Edward W. Barrett reported that the program had begun more intense training for employees in a 1951 joint committee of the Senate Committee on Foreign Relations and the House Committee on Foreign Affairs. According to Barrett, "two months of *indoctrination* by some courses in the Foreign Service Institute" were required of all field employees. These individuals studied the principles of U.S. democracy and various aspects of the nation's foreign policy. Barrett stressed that lectures and writings were offered to reinforce "the indoctrination" that was required for employment with VOA.[10]

In order to monitor the effectiveness of VOA's message, Barrett indicated that the program used "local panels of cross sections of the audience in each country" to provide feedback on their broadcasts. These groups listened to certain broadcasts, filled out questionnaires, and offered advice on the programming. Except for daily newscasts, Barrett reported, "no publication" was sent into the field "until the manuscript [had] been gone over by the Embassy Staff, tried out on a local audience, [or] edited in accordance with the Embassy's best judgment."[11]

The directives for most storylines were sent to VOA offices around the world from officials within the State Department. These guidelines detailed the content and the sources to be cited in the newscasts, which shows the enhanced control of propaganda under the Campaign of Truth. Concerning stories beamed to Russia, for example, a directive dictated that the news should "promote friendliness and interest among the widest possible audience of Soviet listeners." The directive also stipulated that "news items" should be "presented at the beginning and at the end of the program." The start of the program was to focus on world events while domestic issues were to be discussed at the end of the broadcasts. Music was to occupy only 20 percent of the broadcast, and "good American folk music such as hillybilly songs, cowboy songs, railway and other work songs" was to be aired most often. VOA reporters were also advised to highlight remarks made by the president of the United States, the secretary of state, and high-ranking officials of the U.S. government,[12] reflecting the rhetorical proliferation of the presidential administration's messages.

In a separate directive, the Department of State gave VOA administrators specific guidelines for reporting on the 1952 presidential election. The report explained that "U.S. political campaigns . . . provide[d] excellent opportunities to explain [the] free and democratic system" of the United States. The broadcasters were directed to provide an account of the campaign's progress, correct distortions or misunderstandings arising in foreign opinion, reinforce the future course of the United States in world affairs, counteract Soviet-communist manipulation of campaign developments, and utilize the presidential campaign as a tool for explaining the U.S. system of government. Field journalists were instructed *not* to draw their own conclusions about individual candidates, the outcome of the campaign, or the opinions of high-ranking officials speaking out on the campaign.[13]

In the news broadcasts of the VOA, the Soviet Union, of course, served as the evil instigator of the Cold War, reflecting PSB's goals and Truman's own public discourse. In a March 6, 1951, broadcast, the VOA reinforced this view by emphasizing the "existence of huge military forces behind the Iron Curtain." The broadcast explained that in 1945, the "U.S., Britain, and the rest of the free world disarmed drastically." At this time, the United States spent only "6 percent of its national income on armaments," while the Soviet Union reportedly devoted some "eighteen percent of [its] national income . . . [to] military spending." The report concluded with testimony from Frank Nash, U.S. delegate to the United Nations Commission on Conventional Armaments, who critiqued the Soviets' commitment to peace: "The proposal to conduct a census of armaments and armed forces and to permit verification by the UN of the facts reported is a measure of a nation's peaceful intent. The U. S. stands ready to support it. Does the Soviet Government?"[14]

In a March 23, 1951, series entitled *The Iron Curtain*, the VOA, like Truman, stressed the gravity of the new Cold War context, accenting the threat of war. This particular newscast described the views of three U.S. officials: Secretary of State Dean Acheson; Senator Brien McMahon, chair of the Congressional Atomic Energy Commission; and George Kennan, former ambassador to the Soviet Union. The broadcast closed with the following statement: "The conclusion reached by all three experts is [that] . . . the Iron Curtain is a matter of deepest concern to everyone [because] it constitutes a danger to world peace. Until it is lifted, there can be no abiding security anywhere."[15]

Other VOA broadcasts accented the dismal living conditions in the communist regions, which, of course, stood as evidence for why people trapped by communism should revolt. In a VOA series entitled, *Life Behind the Iron Curtain*, individual stories were selected that allegedly exemplified life in those areas—a concept not unlike KNA broadcasts except that the new series centered more on the USSR than the USA. All of the narratives opened with a description of the program's intent, which involved presenting "the happenings in the daily lives of men and women in the Soviet Union and the oppressed areas under communistic control." In support of this goal, the VOA, for example, blamed the USSR for shortages of "fuel and firewood" in Bulgaria as well as shortages of "vegetables and dairy foods." From Poland, according to the VOA, came "reports of widespread arrests and prison sentences up to ten years for many persons . . . who took their savings to be changed at the time of the currency reform."[16] The extent of the suppression was perhaps best explained in a broadcast entitled "Seoul under the Communists," which aired on December 11, 1950. In this feature, the VOA contended that the "three-month police state in Seoul was similar in brutality and the suppression of individual freedom to the Nazi occupation of Rome and Athens."[17]

In other broadcasts, VOA subtly contrasted life in the West with living conditions in the communist countries, allowing democracy to serve as the logical alternative. During a February 15, 1951, news feature entitled *Spotlight on Dictatorship*, VOA compared how much time a person would have to work to buy products in "Rumania," France, and the United States. To buy a loaf of bread, the VOA reported, a "Rumanian" would have to work three hours and thirty minutes, compared to only twenty-five minutes in France and fifteen minutes in the United States. To buy a pair of shoes, the "Rumanian" would have to work ten days as opposed to three and a half days for a person living in France. In the United States, it would take the worker only seven hours and fifteen minutes to earn enough money to buy the shoes. The purpose of the report, the broadcaster declared, was to dispel the myth that "dictators" have "lifted living standards higher than . . . [in] capitalistic lands." The data was attributed to the publication, *Spotlight*, a bulletin of the International Confederation of Free Trade Unions.[18] Presumably, such stark contrasts between communism and democracy would inspire individuals to reject communism—a key goal for Truman's Campaign of Truth.

Thus, because of the KNA debacle and PSB's increased interagency coordination, the VOA exacted tighter control over its "journalists" by first "indoctrinating" them into their propaganda system and then providing them with propaganda scripts. Such practices allowed little room for journalistic freedom. This lack of journalistic freedom shows the increased militarization and centralization of propaganda and psychological warfare policy by the end of the Campaign of Truth. The enhanced control under which VOA's employees/journalists now labored was reminiscent of military training and maneuvers. Propaganda practitioners by then had become more like the Truman administration's newest "soldiers" who followed PSB orders. The Campaign of Truth mission was grounded in an ability to foster a spirit of resistance, revolt, or even defection—goals promulgated further by the PSB through defector propaganda during the latter stages of the campaign.

PSB'S PROPAGANDA OF DEFECTION

Even though PSB planners argued that increased interagency coordination elevated the effectiveness of U.S. propaganda and psychological warfare efforts, significant obstacles persisted in relation to the overt and covert propaganda activities. As a PSB status report determined, America's "national psychological effort . . . [was at the] greatest disadvantage in the USSR and Communist China" because of the increased jamming against VOA broadcasts in those regions.[19] In order to infiltrate the iron curtain through alternative means, PSB planners developed new strategies that involved, among other means, the use of autobiographies to intensify the number of communist defectors and to foster an atmosphere of revolt.

The exigence surrounding defectors and escapees emerged during World War II as Europeans especially fled political and religious persecution. Many of the refugee programs during World War II were humanitarian in nature. As communism spread through Eastern Europe, though, more people fled to the West. The intent of the Cold War planners was to capitalize on such defections and actually increase the numbers from the communist regions so as to "permit exploitation of political developments favorable to the cause of the Free World." Toward that end, Congress attached the Kersten Amendment to the Mutual Security Act of 1951 in order to increase the amount of budgetary assistance for future escapees. Soviet leaders immediately and forcefully attacked the act and placed it on the agenda of the 1952 U.N. General Assembly; the Soviet's objections, however, were rejected by the U.N. president. Truman authorized the Escapee Program on March 22, 1952, and the Kersten Amendment made it budgetarily operational for fiscal years 1952 and 1953. The PSB then received authorization to establish the plan of action; the Department of State implemented the means by which to employ, resettle, and care for "all escapees from the Soviet Orbit" and to make such a program known throughout the communist regions through RFE, RL, and VOA.[20]

For the PSB, the Escapee Program represented a "gold mine" of material for the short-wave radio stations. The program thus functioned as a major means by which to combat the "Hate America" campaign "inside the Iron Curtain."[21] According to the PSB, Soviet propaganda urged that "only criminals and subversives fle[d] to escape punishment for their crimes; once there "'escapees' [were] ruthlessly exploited" by the West who offered only "inhumane" living conditions. To counter such claims, the Truman administration used the escapee stories in its radio broadcasts. In Italy alone, for example, VOA and RFE offices in that region wrote over seventy defector biographies for use in their daily broadcasts.[22]

As the Campaign of Truth entered its second and third years, the PSB sought to "increase the flow of certain types of escapees and defectors,"[23] thereby "maximizing the psychological benefits in the escapee situation." The PSB declared that the "stimulation of defection is the most crucial aspect of U.S. psychological strategy."[24] Toward that end, the PSB asked the Department of Defense to likewise consider the possible "military potential" of such escapees.[25] While the PSB did not seek "mass defections,"[26] its members targeted individuals such as "skilled workers, bureaucrats and personnel of the mechanized armed forces," "inhabitants of rural areas," "nationals of Yugoslavia," "Greek ethnics,"[27] and most importantly, "intellectual elite[s]"[28] from such regions as the Soviet Union. Such a focus, PSB members asserted, would work toward the "reversal of Russian communism"—a key U.S. foreign policy objective in the Campaign of Truth.[29] In the end, the PSB hypothesized that defection "stimulate[d] disaffection in the oppressed homeland because the departed individual is a symbol to the community as one who chose freedom."[30]

PSB's vision was that more communist defections were needed to perpetuate a revolutionary spirit. A 1953 PSB status report indicated that by December 31, 1952, "over 9,000 escapees [were] receiving direct assistance"[31] from the Escapee Program, which sponsored missions in places like Germany, Austria, Italy, Greece, Turkey, and Trieste.[32] The intent of this stepped-up effort on behalf of the United States was to offer such escapees "asylum"[33] and a "better opportunity for resettlement and a higher standard of interim care."[34] Because the PSB asserted that "no area of action in psychological warfare offer[ed] better promise of highly significant results within a relatively short time span," its members called for "bold action [to] be taken to relocate" defectors, with "covert agents . . . securing the defection of selected highly placed individuals."[35]

In order to increase defections, the PSB offered incentives for would-be escapees. The PSB wanted the propaganda programs to talk about the higher quality of food, the medical and dental care available in the United States as well as the available assistance with visas, and with educational and language training.[36] In particular, the PSB called for "public announcement[s]" to be made in Germany by the "American High Commissioner," declaring that "defectors will not be returned to the Russians," and that "more satisfactory immediate living conditions for defectors and better provisions of eventual opportunities for an independent and productive life" awaited anyone who fled.[37] To help accomplish the goals of the Escapee Program, the State Department's Division of Refugees and Displaced Persons in the Bureau of the United Nations Affairs, provided policy guidelines, complete with small country staff units. Such policies were designed to help escapees attain "self-sufficiency" and to express "goodwill and hospitality" to those "whose faith in democratic ideals . . . induced them to flee the Iron Curtain countries."[38] At bottom, the organizers of this kind of "defector propaganda" wanted to make clear that "defectors and escapees will be better off in the West than behind the Iron Curtain";[39] such themes were designed to counter the Soviet "Hate America" themes that escapees were neglected, returned, or committed suicide because of their treatment by the United States government.[40]

The PSB's masterminding became evident not only in the covert propaganda operations but also in the *seemingly* overt tactics as well. As this next section illustrates, the Truman administration's attempt to foster defections became apparent in the radio broadcasts but also in the books that were distributed as part of the State Department's propaganda operations. Such books exhibit the existence of a "personified" or "defector" propaganda that paralleled the strategies of Truman's Campaign of Truth and the VOA broadcasts of the same period.

Autobiography as Doctrinal Warfare

According to the United States Advisory Commission on Information, which evaluated the State Department's propaganda activities,[41] books, like all other propaganda mediums, helped expose "the imperialist character of

Soviet communism and the threat that it present[ed] to the individuals" in target countries identified under the campaign.[42] The decision to showcase books grew out of the move toward the development of a Doctrinal Warfare Program by the PSB.

The book program began with the Office of War Information (OWI) in 1943 and was expanded by the PSB as a means by which to address the Soviet Union's Hate America campaign. The PSB argued that because books represented "permanent literature," they were "by far the most powerful means of influencing the attitudes of intellectuals." The intent was to "balance the availability of Communist literature with objective studies which would be appealing to intellectually developed persons." The goals of the Doctrinal Warfare Program thus converged with the Escapee Program as escapees "from the Iron Curtain" were encouraged to supply doctrinal warfare material.[43]

The Doctrinal Warfare Program was inaugurated on September 11, 1952, when the PSB's Doctrinal Warfare Panel first met. Its operational authority derived from NSC 68/2 and NSC 135/3.[44] According to the PSB, Doctrinal Warfare involved the "formulation and propagation of a body of ideas representing the best in western tradition" for the purposes of engaging in an "unremitting attack on the weak points in Communist ideology."[45] "Book and periodical programs" formed the centerpiece of this plan that targeted "intelligentsia and opinion-forming groups."[46] As the PSB discerned, "the elite is the infinitely more important target" than the "herd," because "new thoughts cannot be brought directly to the masses without being filtered through, and without proving their plausibility to the elites."[47] In the end, the Doctrinal Warfare Program was designed to "supplement" rather than "supplant . . . other forms of psychological warfare."[48]

As the PSB planned, the State Department sponsored the writing, publishing, and translating of selected anticommunist books. While some of the books were written for the Campaign of Truth, others were selected because they reflected Truman's propaganda themes. The State Department would typically agree to purchase a certain quantity of the publications, cover some of the costs for translation and publication, and ensure that the books could be purchased at affordable prices in target areas.[49] The anticommunist books were translated into many different languages and disseminated or sold to people around the world. For example, over 800 copies of the book *This Is Russia Uncensored* were distributed in Korea. *One Who Survived* became the first book translated into Arabic by a Syrian publisher and was "sold out shortly after publication." Over 100,000 copies of the Spanish edition of *Capitalism in America* were published in Mexico for distribution throughout Latin America.[50] In addition, such books were placed in the Department of State's overseas libraries. Stephen J. Whitfield indicates that by 1953, some "thirty-six million people were . . . visiting about two hundred . . . libraries overseas" each year.[51]

Many of the books analyzed in this chapter are autobiographies. Writing about the rhetorical force of autobiographies, Thomas W. Benson maintains that personal narratives possess an "ability to take a reader inside the writer's experience."[52] Such a focus on an author's experience can seemingly mask the political and ideological motives buried in a text, with the emphasis placed on the so-called expert testimony rather than the ideological appeal. As planned by the PSB via its Escapee and Doctrinal Warfare Programs, the autobiographies of the Campaign of Truth targeted intellectuals in particular, and promoted the rightness of the U.S. Cold War perspective. The autobiographies presumably helped readers identify with authors who experienced the Soviet system or the Communist Party directly and eventually defected from it. The persuasive power of these propaganda texts was furthered by the inner struggle that the authors detailed as they rejected communism.

Despite the messages articulated in the autobiographies, it becomes clear through an examination of the extratextual activities of the authors that many were connected to the U.S. government—connections seemingly unbeknownst to most readers. When remembering the intent of PSB planners to increase defections as well as Truman's call for a rhetoric of revolt, this autobiographical propaganda arguably served as an example of covert psychological warfare; the ultimate aims of the propaganda and the specific role of the U.S. government was masked by the autobiographical format. These books then actually functioned as a form of black propaganda because their author/source (U.S. government) was often masked by the autobiographical design.

The Heroes of Personified Propaganda

The books sponsored by the Campaign of Truth can be divided into three categories: (1) books by former Russian citizens connected with the Soviet government; (2) books by non-Russians who joined the Communist Party; and (3) books by people who lived in the United States but who possessed knowledge about communism. All of the authors eventually rejected communism and thus supported, to differing degrees, a democratic form of governance. While some of the books were written before the Campaign of Truth, they were still distributed as propaganda during the campaign and categorized as "anti-communist materials."[53] Each promoted an author's persona designed to enhance the credibility of the book's anticommunist message. Before describing how the authors identified the process through which they resolved their internal struggle over rejecting communism, they detailed their communist past.

The first set of authors experienced communism directly by working with the Soviet government. Alexander Barmine, author of *One Who Survived*, grew up in Russia, and served as a member of both the Bolshevik Army and the Bolshevik Party. In Russia, he worked as an industrialist, a soldier, and a diplomat for the Russian government. In the spring of 1939, Barmine took refuge with his wife in the U.S. Embassy in Paris. A few months later, they were issued U.S. visas, and by 1943, Barmine was serving as a private in the U.S. Army.[54] Like Barmine, Victor Kravchenko, author of *I Chose Freedom*, joined the Communist Party as a citizen of the Soviet Union and served as a loyal Party member under Stalin. Despite his service, Kravchenko maintained that he came very close to being purged from the Party. Instead, Kravchenko explained, he was assigned to the highly sensitive position of Russia's economic emissary in Washington, D.C. While acting in this capacity, he defected from the Soviet Union and remained under the protection of the U.S. government.[55]

Other authors either were outwardly sympathetic to communism or were members of the Communist Party before denouncing it. Richard Crossman edited the book *The God That Failed*, which contained accounts of six "intellectuals" who turned to communism during the 1920s and 1930s. Arthur Koestler was born in Hungary but lived in Germany and joined the Communist Party in December 1931 before leaving it in the spring of 1938. Ignazio Silone was involved with the Italian Communist Party in 1921 but left it in 1930. He then became associated with the Foreign Center of the Italian Socialist Party. Richard Wright wrote that he became a member of the Communist Party in the United States, in part, because of the conditions affecting African Americans. André Gide, while never an official member of the Communist Party, maintained that he became a strong supporter of its goals until he visited the Soviet Union. Louis Fischer, although born in the United States, became an ally of the Soviet Union. After traveling the world as a journalist, however, he too wrote that he eventually became a critic of the Soviet government. Finally, Stephen Spender reported that he became a member of the British Communist Party in 1936 only to leave it in 1937 because of the ineffective manner in which communism was practiced in the Soviet Union.[56] The chapters of these books clearly reflected the aims of the Doctrinal Warfare Program.

Experiencing communism firsthand, Elinor Lipper identified herself as a non-Russian who became sympathetic to the communist cause in the Soviet Union. Lipper, a native of Germany, arrived in Moscow in 1937, only to be arrested two months later. She claimed to have been held in Soviet prison camps from 1937 through 1948, before being allowed to return to Germany. She wrote of her experiences and her views on communism in her book *Eleven Years in Soviet Prison Camps*.[57]

The other two authors both lived at least part of their lives in the United States and articulated anticommunist sentiments. Edmund Stevens, an American who married a Russian citizen, lived in the Soviet Union for a short time. He wrote of their experiences in the region and celebrated the virtues of the U.S. system in his book *This Is Russia, Uncensored*. Stevens's autobiography functioned as a warning to the American people that the Kremlin conspired to rewrite Soviet history."[58] Frederick Martin Stern conversely was a native of Germany, who lived in the United States at the time that he wrote the book *Capitalism in America*. His book contains a collection of published letters that he penned to a friend in France, justifying the precepts of capitalism. While Stern did not incorporate his friend's responses, he did identify the procommunist or antidemocratic arguments that his friend espoused. Stern then countered such arguments in his celebration of democratic principles.[59]

Within all of these autobiographies, the authors' personas enhanced the rhetorical appeal of their conclusions concerning the "vulnerabilities of Soviet-Communist ideology," representing a sampling of the defector propaganda used during the Campaign of Truth.[60] Because all had experienced communism to some degree, their rejection of communist ideals in the end proved perhaps more compelling than the more blatant anticommunist appeals disseminated by the overt propaganda channels like the VOA. Thus, the covert nature of the autobiographies, combined with the reluctance of the witnesses to turn their backs on communism, made for a very sinister anticommunist appeal.

In creating a portrait of Russian history, several authors portrayed the Bolsheviks as courageous revolutionaries seeking freedom not just for the Soviet people but for all the downtrodden. Alexander Barmine, for example, argued that the revolution sought to "liberate oppressed people everywhere from imperialistic exploitation," which is why he was prepared to die for the revolution.[61] Louis Fischer claimed that the Bolsheviks "glorified the common man and offered him land, bread, peace, a job, a house [and] security." They promised to champion "international brotherhood" and to "abolish racial discrimination, exploitation, inequality, the power of wealth, the rights of kings, [and] the lust for territory." "The oppressed of the world, and the friends of the oppressed," according to Fischer, "saw Soviet Russia as the herald of a new era."[62]

Lenin was the most esteemed leader of this liberation movement for several of the authors, and his death symbolized the end of the great communist experiment. According to Barmine, Lenin was a "brilliant" man of action who projected "the foundations of a new world." During the height of his popularity, Barmine maintained, Lenin "became a symbol of hope to the whole of Asia."[63] Kravchenko argued similarly that Lenin represented a "symbol of hope" to the "plain people in the collieries—even the gamblers and brawlers in the barracks, the swaggerers with shoes that creaked . . . [and] Communist youths."[64] According to Ignazio Silone, Lenin's death fundamentally and permanently changed the nature of the Communist Party.[65]

Lenin's demise, of course, allowed Stalin to assume control over the Soviet government. According to several of the authors, Stalin erased the glorious Bolshevik legacy by literally rewriting Russian history. Barmine argued that Stalin, who was "haunted by the revolutionary past in which he had played an undistinguished role," rooted out "every trace" of the movement's history by exterminating the "Old Bolsheviks" who remembered the events.[66] Richard Wright maintained that Stalin also attempted to banish intellectuals because they stood to betray the new Communist Party under Stalin by questioning his revisionist history.[67] As part of this historical revisionist process, Kravchenko claimed that Stalin went so far as to create "a commission to write a new history of the Party," which would "twist" historical events to conform to the new Party line.[68] Elinor Lipper concluded that "for thirty years the Soviet people [had] been given a totally twisted, unreal, carefully censored and distorted picture" of life within and outside the iron curtain.[69] Such a theme reflected PSB's strategy of targeting Stalin rather than Marxism; Stalin represented the most pressing enemy, the one who was "rewriting history," and the one who evidenced the monopoly of leadership in the Soviet orbit.[70]

Many of the authors attributed Stalin's successful totalitarian rule to his sophisticated propaganda machine, which allowed him to control propaganda output within the Soviet Union and beyond. Alexander Barmine argued that Stalin possessed "enormous powers of propaganda throughout the world,"[71] while Arthur Koestler maintained that "propaganda was indispensable for the survival of the Soviet Union."[72] Victor Kravchenko pointed to the effectiveness of Soviet propaganda by observing that life in the Soviet Union was glamorized even in the United States during World War II as a result of Stalin's propaganda effort. According to Kravchenko, "the prevailing American notions about the wonders of Sovietism in practice were truly extraordinary," because the conditions of "slave labor, police dictatorship, the massive periodic purges, the . . . low standards of living, the great famine of 1932–33 . . . seemed to have completely escaped American attention."

Kravchenko concluded that "the greatest Soviet triumph" during World War II occurred "in the domain of foreign propaganda."[73]

Such allegations served to support Truman's Campaign of Truth goal, which Assistant Secretary of State Edward Barrett reasserted as the need "to expose to all the world the fallacies and the phony nature of communism."[74] The authors also sought to dispel the myths of Stalin's propaganda by describing very graphically the famine and slavelike working conditions brought upon the Soviet Union by the new regime. When touring the Soviet Union as a member of the army, Kravchenko wrote that he witnessed horrid conditions in all parts of the country: "I saw people dying in solitude by slow degrees, dying hideously . . . and left to starve." "The most terrifying sights," Kravchenko explained, "were the little children with skeleton limbs dangling like balloon-like abdomens."[75] Edmund Stevens argued that these conditions were caused by the collective farms established under the communist system. He described the life of his wife's aunt, who was forced to give large portions of her crops, milk, cheese, and beef to the state.[76]

The authors depicted life in the factories as equivalent to prison work camps, where the workers received little pay for laboring long hours. Barmine argued that the workers were "badly fed, badly housed, worn out by overwork, and weakened by continuous semi-starvation." He concluded that "nobody in the outside world" knew the extent to which Russian workers lived in "abject slavery."[77] Victor Kravchenko, who claimed to have managed numerous factories, described the primitive living conditions of the workers: "Workers were packed into hastily constructed wooden barracks, with leaking roofs, moist walls and floors, lacking even the most primitive hygienic comforts."[78] As the PSB strategized, the doctrinal warfare themes needed to stress how "property owners have been replaced by the bureaucrats and exploitation has become more inhumane."[79]

Because of the overall economic and social status that existed under the Kremlin's rule, the authors concluded that the communist form of government could not work—a theme promulgated throughout PSB's working documents on Doctrinal Warfare.[80] Alexander Barmine declared that communism "as an experiment in a new form of social life . . . failed." He pointed to the economic state as the primary example of this failure: "the despotic and bureaucratic administration of Russia's economic life canceled out the benefits that we expected a collectivized economy to bring." Barmine claimed that "the Soviet bureaucracy" had become "an exploiting class," and concluded that "any scheme involving monopoly ownership of a nation's economy by the state" had proven "unattainable."[81] Even though he initially turned to communism because its leaders promised to overthrow existing power structures, Louis Fischer eventually turned away from communism because it was "itself the world's biggest agglomeration of power over man."[82]

The dire conditions in the Soviet Union that led the authors to denounce communism caused some to look toward democracy as the appropriate alternative. As the PSB directed, U.S. propaganda was to "avoid references to the alleged superiority of the American way of life" in the State Department's propaganda.[83] These books fit such propaganda and psychological prescriptions because the authors spent much more time writing about communism than democracy. But when the authors promoted democracy, they presented the United States as proof that democracy worked, just as Stalin's Russia proved that communism could not.

In promoting democracy, several authors heralded capitalism as a superior system that offered a corrective to the desperate economic conditions in the Soviet Union. Capitalism's superiority emanated from its commitment to competition. Barmine, for example, maintained that "the real cost of production of Soviet goods is higher than in any capitalist country" because of "incompetent bureaucratic" practices and the "wasting [of] labor and materials." Without competition, Barmine concluded, no "stimulus" existed for "management to use their brains . . . to produce better and cheaper goods."[84] Stevens stated similarly that without competition, innovation was rare since managers feared the production rates would decrease in the process of implementing new strategies.[85] Supporting capitalism implicitly, André Gide maintained that its "disappearance" certainly did not bring "freedom to the Soviet workers"[86] as many communists maintained.

Others argued that capitalism allowed for a much better treatment of the workers—a theme that paralleled such VOA broadcasts as *Spotlight on Dictatorship* and *Behind the Iron Curtain*. Alexander Barmine claimed that "the Russian worker received a much smaller share of the product of their toil than the workers in any capitalist country—smaller than even the workers under the czar."[87] Frederick Martin Stern contended that "capitalists don't have to starve their workers in order to make profits; nor do the workers have to dispossess the capitalists in order to provide a decent livelihood for themselves and their families." Stern argued further that capitalism "brought a high standard of living to the vast majority of the people."[88]

Within their stories, the authors championed democracy and capitalism as the preferred alternative for Russia. All of the grave conditions outlined in their books could be transformed through the implementation of a democratic form of government. Stern declared that "nothing appears impossible" in the United States because "American society generates boundless optimism." Moreover, Stern claimed that capitalism actually embodied the most attractive attributes of communism that Marx envisioned. Americans "spread welfare and happiness everywhere,"[89] which proved, for Stern at least, that the utopian goals of communism were in fact best realized through the practice of democratic principles.

Most significantly, many of the books examined met the PSB criteria of articulating a message of defection that was perpetuated throughout Truman's Campaign of Truth. In a 1952 subcommittee of the Senate Committee on Appropriations, Assistant Secretary of State Edward Barrett reinforced Truman's message by contending that the Campaign of Truth sought to foster "a split between the Russian people and the Soviet Government . . . [by] making the Russian people develop a spirit of resistance."[90] The authors of these anticommunist books did not explicitly espouse the message that those enslaved by communism should defect. But the message came across in the authors' own personal stories as they reluctantly left the Party.

Some writers recalled the loyalty that they once felt toward the Communist Party. Early on, they thought it unfathomable that they would someday reject communism. Silone typified the recollections of those who converted to communism during the 1920s and 1930s: "For me to join the Party of Proletarian Revolution was not just a simple matter of signing up with a political organization; it meant a conversion, a complete dedication." He equated his conversion to "throwing oneself to the winds," which meant "breaking with one's parents and not finding a job."[91] Victor Kravchenko's experiences likewise typified those who lived through the Revolution and served as soldiers of the Communist Party. Kravchenko explained that devout followers were taught never to forget that they were a "Comsomol first, a person second." He explained that when people joined the Party, they were "forever caught"; a person could be "expelled," but no one could ever "secede." Kravchenko concluded: "Without exception we were prepared to die for Russian victory."[92]

Several of the authors wrote of the internal conflict they felt upon leaving the Party. Richard Crossman, the editor of *The God That Failed*, indicated that "not one of the contributors to [his] book . . . deserted Communism willingly or with a clear conscience."[93] Victor Kravchenko experienced high levels of guilt, recalling that he felt there was "no joy in the departure for America—only a sharp ache, a pervasive and inexpressible sorrow." Kravchenko remembered thinking that the best thing that he could do for his "suffering people was to escape" and try "to tell the world" about the corruption existing in his homeland.[94] Barmine indicated that once he realized that "any regard for the conditions of the people was entirely subordinate to the aim of maintaining the dictatorship," he began "to wrestle with the sentiments that bound" him to the Party. Despite the fact that Barmine had "been brought up in the bosom of the Party" and had not spent "one single hour" of his adult life "outside of the Party," he knew that he could no longer take not being able to "think [his] own thoughts and draw [his] own conclusions."[95]

These writers, by recalling their own experiences of fleeing Russia or rejecting communism, personified the act of defection. Such experiences suggested that readers likewise should question their own commitments to communism. In this case, the individual authors not only personified the anticommunist ideology, they also served as the locus of struggle or the site of contestation between communism and democracy, with democracy winning out in the end.[96] The power of the autobiographical form, though, is dependent on the presumption that the authors were independent thinkers rather than propagandists who worked for a particular government. Many extratextual connections existed between the U.S. government and the authors, however, reflecting the covert nature of the autobiographies.

THE HIDDEN HAND OF THE U.S. GOVERNMENT

In many of the texts examined, the links between the authors and the U.S. government were not evident to the readers. By the time the books were used as instruments of propaganda policy, several of the authors either worked for the U.S. government or were associated with organizations sponsored by the CIA, further demonstrating the complex process of ideological control involved in propaganda production. To that end, such veiled means of production made the autobiographies part of the Truman administration's psychological warfare strategy, with certain authors aware and others unaware of the influence wielded by the U.S. government over their published works.

Some of the writers willingly and others reluctantly worked for the U.S. government by serving as expert witnesses and informants for the Federal Bureau of Investigation (FBI) and other government agencies. Richard Wright, for example, identified for embassy officials people he believed were leading communists or people with "left-leaning views" before being allowed to travel from France to Spain. He also offered similar disclosures when he wanted, for example, to prevent the communist infiltration of certain literary groups to which he belonged. The extent to which Wright served as an informant for the U.S. government is uncertain. Rumors at that time connected Wright to the CIA, a common allegation aimed at many authors in France during the 1950s. What seems certain is that Wright offered informant favors to the U.S. government willingly, even though he publicly critiqued its foreign and domestic policies. Wright's sympathies for the U.S. government were furthered by the revelation that he asked to work for the OWI during World War II—a request denied because of his communist past.[97]

Victor Kravchenko also served as an expert witness for the U.S. government. During the proceedings before the House Committee on Un-American Activities, Kravchenko provided committee members with insight into the mindset of the Communist Party. Kravchenko answered questions about the USSR, particularly in relation to the total number of communists, the necessary steps to become a communist, the status of trade unionism, the existence of forced labor camps, and Soviet spying and infiltration during his testimony on July 22, 1947. The willingness of Kravchenko to offer such testimony was illustrated by his eagerness to provide further expert advice on Soviet propaganda. Demonstrating his loyalty to the United States, Kravchenko argued, "*We* must fundamentally change the entire system of propaganda in America" and adapt America's message "on the basis of the real psychology of the Russian people, and on what they really want to know about America and the outside world."[98] After absorbing Kravchenko's testimony, Representative Karl Mundt (R-SD) was quite eager for Kravchenko to speak before the Smith-Mundt hearings. Kravchenko also offered similar testimony in 1949 regarding the shipment of atomic material to the Soviet Union during World War II,[99] demonstrating his transformation from a Soviet agent to a U.S. informant.

Unlike Wright and Kravchenko who exhibited an interest in U.S. propaganda, other authors actually worked for the propaganda program. Alexander Barmine served as an informant for Joseph McCarthy, identifying communists in the U.S. government.[100] By 1953, Barmine was working as VOA's chief of the Russian branch. In this capacity, Barmine aided McCarthy's witchhunt of the State Department, alleging that propaganda officials were soft on communism, which provided key evidence for McCarthy's raid against communists in government (see chapter 5).[101]

Richard Crossman, while never a member of the Communist Party, not only edited *The God That Failed* text, but also served in a psychological warfare branch of the British government during World War II. Anthony Howard compares Crossman to C. D. Jackson, who served as a psychological warfare expert during World War II and as president of RFE thereafter;[102] William E. Daugherty also labels Crossman a "propaganda genius."[103] During World War II, Crossman headed the German section of the Political Warfare Executive, which was often called the Psychological Warfare Executive in Britain.[104] Crossman's hero reportedly was Walter Bedell Smith, Eisenhower's chief of staff and a member of the PSB.[105] Certainly, knowing of Crossman's experience with psychological warfare and wartime propaganda contextualizes *The God That Failed* in a very different light than the one presented to unsuspecting readers: "we were not in the least interested . . . in swelling the flood of anti-Communist propaganda. . . . our concern was to study the state of mind of the Communist convert."[106]

Many of these writers were also connected to U.S. political officials. Fischer, for example, maintained contact with Dean Acheson and George Kennan, the latter of whom Fischer met while attending Princeton University. Similarly, Spender occasionally met with Washington insiders like Kennan and Robert Oppenheimer.[107] Koestler, however, appeared to be the most connected to the Washington political scene. Koestler met with General William J. Donovan who directed the Office of Strategic Services during FDR's presidency. During this meeting, Koestler reportedly lobbied for a more "intelligent, vigorous, and effective psychological warfare in defense of western values and interests, as opposed to the panicky whipping up of war hysteria." It was also not unusual to find Koestler cited in PSB materials in relation to doctrinal warfare designed to combat communism.[108] Koestler relied on such connections later as he sought congressional help to secure his U.S. citizenship. Koestler's congressional "friends" (e.g., Senators Pat McCarran and Richard Nixon) proposed a private act, entitled the bill "for relief of Arthur Koestler," which was to allow Koestler permanent residency in the United States. Those in support of this bill that was brought before the Senate Judiciary Committee in 1951, included Bertram D. Wolfe, chief of the Ideological Advisory Unit of the State Department's international broadcasting division, as well as Melvin J. Lasky, who was covertly connected to the intelligence community. Despite the strong lobbying effort, the Department of Justice opposed the bill. Later, though, the Senate passed the measure by a unanimous vote.[109]

Beyond that, other more hidden relations bound the writers together as many of the six authors named above were connected to CIA-sponsored organizations. In Europe especially, an environment of suspicion and paranoia existed because many activities and organizations were feared to be backed by the U.S. CIA.[110] One such CIA-sponsored organization was the Congress for Cultural Freedom (CCF). In 1950, Hamilton explains that a group of "writers mobilized to counter Soviet propaganda" in the western part of Berlin so as to demonstrate "solidarity with the beleaguered Berliners." During the first convention, both Koestler and Silone coordinated the presentation of speeches, the distribution of pamphlets, and the development of new publications. While the meetings were in session, Koestler worked to ensure that the press received sufficient information to enhance the proliferation of ideas produced during the conference. Koestler later convinced Fischer to serve as general secretary for the CCF,[111] and Spender became an editor for *Encounter*, a literary-political magazine issued by the

CCF. Silone also acted as editor of *Tempo Presente*, an Italian magazine likewise backed by the CCF.[112] Finally, Wright also attended the CCF conferences as a journalist; his articles were subsequently printed in several editions of CCF's publications.

The extent to which the writers knew of the CIA's involvement with the CCF and its subsidiaries is not clear.[113] Yet the CIA's involvement with the CCF is not that surprising given the Truman administration's institutionalization of a covert propaganda and psychological warfare apparatus. Such a covert structure regarding the CCF resembled the activities of Radio Free Europe and Radio Liberty. Moreover, both radio stations, the CCF, and the excommunist autobiographies used communist defectors as their expert voices. This reflected the move toward centralizing propaganda and psychological warfare strategy by the end of 1952 and the implementation of the interrelated Escapee and Doctrinal Warfare Programs.

While the books served certain "overt" propaganda goals since they were issued by the State Department,[114] the autobiographies-turned-propaganda also functioned more covertly to fulfill PSB's psychological warfare tactics. This blending of overt and covert functions reveal the complexity of propaganda production and the PSB's introduction of Doctrinal Warfare to the practice of psychological warfare. To begin with, the Cold War experts became the excommunists—a practice that dated back to the Dies Committee of 1938.[115] The U.S. government then used the ethos of these defectors not only as a way to personify and resolve the ideological tension between democracy and communism, but also as an attempt to further co-opt other intellectuals. Given the covert strategies involved with using defectors as propaganda agents and the veiled relationship between many of the "authors" and the U.S. government,[116] these texts actually possessed a layering of authorship. Such authorship, though, can be traced back to the PSB and the Truman administration; Truman officials carefully selected books and/or commissioned the authorship of such books that reflected the Campaign of Truth themes. This layering of the authorship process was masked by the alleged autobiographical form of the texts; the rhetorical motives of the multiple "authors" were similarly uncertain until contextualized in PSB's private strategizing sessions. By the end of 1952, the Truman administration's militarized propaganda program had become much more sophisticated and secretive, demonstrating the need to expand conceptions of presidential authorship beyond the bully pulpit.

But, in spite of these significant changes in the propaganda's tone, a new kind of unexpected backlash appeared that brought the mission of the propaganda program into question once again. The Soviets, for example, used the defensive tone of the U.S. propaganda for their own propaganda ends as they enhanced their Hate America campaign. For the Kremlin, U.S. "hysteria" over communism actually demonstrated communism's political virility and democracy's fragility, further empowering the Soviets.[117] The Truman administration also acknowledged their psychological warfare shortcomings before leaving office as it implemented NSC-135/3 (September 1952), which called for additional funding to fight the Cold War (supporting NSC-68) and the need for more positive themes to offset the defensive nature of its international messages. Yet NSC-135/3 also articulated a more pessimistic tone, noting that even with more "propagandistic, (para)military, political, and economic countermeasures," the Soviets would still pose a significant threat.[118] In evaluating PSB's own operations in preparation for the new presidential administration, Edward P. Lilly identified problems that the newly formed agency continued to face in relation to the ongoing interagency conflict among the Defense and State Departments and the CIA. Because such in-fighting noticeably impeded PSB's operations, at least in certain circumstances, Lilly called for greater organizational cooperation in the Eisenhower administration's PSB. Disagreement, though, also continued in Congress over the correct tenor of the country's Cold War message. Some congressional leaders supported the more hardline mission, while others wanted U.S. propaganda to focus more on the United States than the Soviet Union.[119] This conflict intensified as four congressional and presidential committees turned their attention to the propaganda program in the aftermath of Eisenhower's election. The next two chapters examine these investigations as well as Eisenhower's response to the committees' findings, beginning with an analysis of how the McCarthy committee helped inspire the Eisenhower administration's institutionalization of propaganda as a presidential prerogative.

NOTES

1. "Status Report on the National Psychological Effort as of December 31, 1952," and "Progress Report of the Psychological Strategy Board," January, 1953, White House Central Files, 1953–1961, Psychological Strategy Board File, Box 21, Dwight D. Eisenhower Presidential Library (hereafter cited as DDEPL), 12.

2. Psychological Strategy Board Minutes, August, 1951, White House Office, NSC Staff: Papers, 1948–1961, NSC Registry Series, 1947–1962, Box 17, DDEPL, 3. See also David D. Newsom, *Diplomacy and the American Democracy* (Bloomington: Indiana University Press, 1988), 184.

3. Harry S. Truman, "Going Forward with a Campaign of Truth," *Department of State Bulletin* 22 (May 1,1950): 669, 670, 672.

4. Truman, "Going Forward," 671, 672.

5. Harry S. Truman, "Expanded Information Program Vital to National Security," *Department of State Bulletin* 23 (July 31, 1950): 194.

6. Harry S. Truman, "Continued Efforts Urged Against Soviet Propaganda," *Department of State Bulletin* 25 (September 3, 1951): 381.

7. Harry S. Truman, "President Urges USSR to Inform People of U.S. Friendship," *Department of State Bulletin* 25 (July 16, 1951): 87.

8. Oren Stephens, *Facts to a Candid World: America's Overseas Information Program* (Stanford, CA: Stanford University Press, 1955), 132–135.

9. See Peter B. Clark, "The Opinion Machine: Intellectuals, the Mass Media, and American Government," in *The Mass Media and Modern Democracy*, ed. Harry M. Clor (Chicago: Rand McNally, 1974), 38, 57–58; John Corry, *TV News and the Dominant Culture* (Washington, D.C.: The Media Institute, 1986), 1; Herbert J. Gans, *Deciding What's News* (New York: Vintage Books, 1979), 41–42; Roderick P. Hart, *The Sound of Leadership: Presidential Communication in the Modern Age* (Chicago: University of Chicago Press, 1987), 121; William A. Henry, III, "News as Entertainment: The Search for Dramatic Unity," in *What's News: The Media in American Society*, ed. Elie Abel (San Francisco: Institute for Contemporary Studies, 1981), 153; and Gaye Tuchman, "Objectivity as Strategic Ritual: An Examination of Newsmen's Notions of Objectivity," *American Journal of Sociology* 77 (1972): 676.

10. Senate Committee on Foreign Relations and the House Committee on Foreign Affairs, *The Voice of America*, 82d Cong., lst sess., 1951, 13–15 (emphasis added).

11. House Committee on Foreign Affairs and the Senate Committee on Foreign Relations, *The Voice of America,* 82d Cong., lst sess., 1951, 9–10.

12. "General Policy Considerations for Initial Russian Broadcasts," n d., Charles Thayer Papers, Box 5, Harry S. Truman Presidential Library (hereafter cited as HSTPL).

13. "1952 U.S. Presidential Campaign," July 8, 1952, Howland H. Sargeant Papers, Box 5, HSTPL.

14. "Causes of International Tension: Armaments of the Paris Meeting," March 6, 1951, Charles Hulten Papers, Box 18, HSTPL.

15. *The Iron Curtain*, March 23, 1951, Charles Hulten Papers, Box 18, HSTPL.

16. *Life Behind the Iron Curtain*—#44, December 28, 1950, Charles Hulten Papers, Box 18, HSTPL.

17. "Seoul under the Communists," December 11, 1950, Charles Hulten Papers, Box 18, HSTPL.

18. *Spotlight on Dictatorship*, February 15, 1951, Charles Hulten Papers, Box 18, HSTPL.

19. "Status Report on the National Psychological Effort," 3–4. See also C. E. Johnson to Major Edmund J. Bennett, November, 1952, White House Office, NSC Staff: Papers, 1953–1961, PSB Central Files Series, Box 23, DDEPL, 4; Psychological Strategy Board, December, 1952, White House Office, NSC Staff:

Papers, 1953–1961, PSB Central Files Series, Box 23, DDEPL, 4; and Mallory
Brown to George A. Morgan, March, 1952, White House Office, NSC Staff: Papers, 1953–1961, PSB Central Files Series, DDEPL, 1.

20. See Elmer B. Staats to the Board Assistants on the Escapee Program, November 18, 1953, White House Office, NSC Staff: Papers, 1953–1961, PSB Central Files Series, PSB 383.7 Escapee Program, Box 28, DDEPL, 1–3; and "A
Report for OCB Examination on Effectiveness of the Escapee Program," December 23, 1953, White House Office, NSC Staff: Papers, 1948–1961, OCB Central
Files Series, OCB 383.7 Refugees and Interned Persons, Box 118, DDEPL, 1–4,
7–8.

21. "Status Report on the National Psychological Effort," 6–7.

22. "A Report for OCB Examination on Effectiveness of the Escapee Program," 44–50.

23. Psychological Strategy Board, December, 1952, 2.

24. Edmond L. Taylor to George Morgan and Gordon Gray, January 15,
1953, White House Office, NSC Staff: Papers, 1953–1961, PSB Central Files Series, PSB 383.7 Escapees, Box 27, DDEPL, 1.

25. Psychological Strategy Board Minutes, December, 1951, White House
Office, NSC Staff: Papers, 1948–1961, NSC Registry Series, 1947–1962, Box 17,
DDEPL, 3.

26. Psychological Strategy Board Minutes, January, 1952, White House Office, NSC Staff: Papers, 1948–1962, NSC Registry Series, 1947–1962, Box 17,
DDEPL, 5.

27. "A Report for OCB Examination on Effectiveness of the Escapee Program," 13–14.

28. See "Political Warfare," n.d., State Department File, Psychological
Strategy Board, HSTPL, 4; and "Status Report on the National Psychological Effort ," 12.

29. "Political Warfare," 8.

30. "A National Psychological Program with Respect to Escapees from the
Soviet Orbit," January 15, 1953, Psychological Strategy Board, White House Office, NSC Staff: Papers, 1953–1961, PSB Central Files Series, PSB 383.7 Escapees, Box 27, DDEPL, Annex A, 1.

31. "Status Report on the National Psychological Effort," 9.

32. Operations Coordinating Board, September, 1953, "Progress Report to
the National Security Council on the Implementation of the Recommendations of
the Jackson Committee Report," White House Office: NSC Staff: Papers,
1953–1961, PSB Central Files Series, Box 22, DDEPL, Annex D, 1.

33. Psychological Strategy Board Minutes, January, 1953, White House Office, NSC Staff: Papers, 1948–1961, NSC Registry Series, 1947–1962, Box 17,
DDEPL, 2.

34. "Status Report on the National Psychological Effort," 9.

35. "Political Warfare," 15.

36. See "Status Report on the National Psychological Effort," 9; and "A Report for OCB Examination on Effectiveness of the Escapee Program," 5–6.

37. "Political Warfare," 6–7.

38. "The Escapee Program," January, 1953, White House Office, NSC Staff: Papers, 1953–1961, PSB Central Files Series, Box 27, DDEPL, 1–6.

39. "Status Report on the National Psychological Effort," 9.

40. "A Report for OCB Examination on Effectiveness of the Escapee Program," 24–25.

41. See Edward W. Barrett, *Truth Is Our Weapon* (New York: Funk & Wagnalls, 1953), 58–59; Robert E. Summers, *America's Weapons of Psychological Warfare* (New York: H. W. Wilson, 1951), 153; and Hans N. Tuch, *Communicating with the World: U.S. Public Diplomacy Overseas* (New York: St. Martin's Press, 1990), 17–18, 87.

42. U.S. Department of State, *The International Information Administration, July–December 1952* (Washington, D.C.: Division of Publications, Office of Public Affairs, 1953), 15, 19.

43. Psychological Strategy Board, June 29, 1953, U.S. Doctrinal Program, White House Office, NSC Staff: Papers, 1948–1961, OCB Secretariat Series, Doctrinal Periodicals–Dr. Lilly, Box 1, DDEPL, 4, Annex C, 1–14.

44. Psychological Strategy Board, January 15, 1953, First Progress Report of the Panel on Doctrinal Warfare, White House Office, NSC Staff: Papers, 1948–1961, OCB Secretariat Series, Doctrinal Warfare (Official), Box 2, DDEPL, 1.

45. Stefan T. Possony to Dr. Edward P. Lilly, White House Office, November 19, 1952, NSC Staff: Papers, 1948–1961, OCB Secretariat Series, Doctrinal Warfare (Official), Box 2, DDEPL, 3–4. Stefan T. Possony served as a consultant for the PSB, Lilly, and the Doctrinal Warfare Program.

46. "First Report and the Preliminary Recommendations of the Panel on Doctrinal Warfare," n.d., White House Office, NSC Staff: Papers, 1948–1961, OCB Secretariat Series, Doctrinal Warfare (Official), Box 2, DDEPL, 2.

47. Stefan T. Possony to Dr. Edward P. Lilly, January 22, 1953, White House Office, NSC Staff: Papers, 1948–1961, OCB Secretariat Series, Doctrinal Warfare (Official), Box 2, DDEPL, 1–2.

48. "Proposed Summary Statement," April 14, 1953, White House Office, NSC Staff: Papers, 1948–1961, OCB Secretariat Series, Doctrinal Warfare (Official), Box 2, DDEPL, 2.

49. U.S. Department of State, *The International Information Administration*, 23.

50. U.S. Department of State, *The International Information Administration*, 15, 19.

51. Stephen J. Whitfield, *The Culture of the Cold War* (Baltimore, MD: Johns Hopkins University Press, 1996), 196.

52. Thomas W. Benson, "Rhetoric and Autobiography: The Case of Malcolm X," *Quarterly Journal of Speech* 60 (1974): 3.

53. "Anti-Communist Materials," n.d., White House Office, NSC Staff: Papers, 1948–1961, OCB Secretariat Series Lodge Project Essays, Box 4, DDEPL, 1.

54. Alexander Barmine, *One Who Survived: The Life Story of a Russian under the Soviets* (New York: G. P. Putnam's Sons, 1945), 25.

55. Victor Kravchenko, *I Chose Freedom: The Personal and Political Life of a Soviet Official* (New York: Scribner's Sons, 1946), 449, 297.

56. Richard Crossman, ed., *The God That Failed* (New York: Harper & Brothers, 1949).

57. Elinor Lipper, *Eleven Years in Soviet Prison Camps* (Chicago: Henry Regnery, 1951).

58. Edmund Stevens, *This Is Russia, Uncensored* (New York: Didier, 1950), 111.

59. Frederick Martin Stern, *Capitalism in America: A Classless Society* (New York: Rinehart, 1950), vi, 117.

60. T. B. Larson, "Vulnerabilities of Soviet-Communist Ideology," December 8, 1952, White House Office, NSC Staff: Papers, 1948–1961, OCB Secretariat Series, Doctrinal Warfare (Official), Box 2, DDEPL, 1. The autobiographies analyzed in this section were referenced in various State Department and PSB documents. Other books were used by the State Department but were unavailable for examination, with many out of print and/or no longer in university libraries.

61. Barmine, *One Who Survived*, 86, 60.

62. Louis Fischer, n.t., in *The God That Failed*, ed. Richard Crossman (New York: Harper & Brothers, 1949), 199.

63. Barmine, *One Who Survived*, 113, 146.

64. Kravchenko, *I Chose Freedom*, 40.

65. Ignazio Silone, n.t., in *The God That Failed*, ed. Richard Crossman (New York: Harper & Brothers, 1949), 105–106.

66. Barmine, *One Who Survived*, 6, 296.

67. Richard Wright, n.t., in *The God That Failed*, ed. Richard Crossman (New York: Harper & Brothers, 1949), 154.

68. Kravchenko, *I Chose Freedom*, 283.

69. Lipper, *Eleven Years*, 36.

70. See T. B. Larson, December, 8, 1952, 3; and Stefan T. Possony to Dr. Edward P. Lilly, November 18, 1952, White House Office, NSC Staff: Papers, 1948–1961, Doctrinal Warfare (Official), Box 2, DDEPL, 1–4.

71. Barmine, *One Who Survived*, 222.

72. Arthur Koestler, n.t., *The God That Failed*, ed. Richard Crossman (New York: Harper & Brothers, 1949), 61.

73. Kravchenko, *I Chose Freedom*, 468.

74. Senate Committee on Foreign Relations, *Expanded International Information and Education Program*, 81st Cong., 2d sess., 1950, S. Rept. 243, 44–45.

75. Kravchenko, *I Chose Freedom*, 118.

76. Stevens, *This Is Russia*, 36–39.

77. Barmine, *One Who Survived*, 313–314.

78. Kravchenko, *I Chose Freedom*, 79–80, 313.

79. Stefan T. Possony, November 18, 1952, 3.

80. Stefan T. Possony, November 18, 1952, 1–4; T. B. Larson, December 8, 1952, 1–3.

81. Barmine, *One Who Survived*, 327, 313, 318.

82. Fischer, *The God That Failed*, 226.

83. "Political Warfare," 4.

84. Barmine, *One Who Survived*, 211.

85. Stevens, *This Is Russia*, 65.

86. André Gide, n.t., in *The God That Failed*, ed. Richard Crossman (New York: Harper & Brothers, 1949), 183.

87. Barmine, *One Who Survived*, 313.

88. Stern, *Capitalism in America*, 9, 46, 81.

89. Stern, *Capitalism in America*, 47, 7.

90. Senate Committee on Appropriations, *Departments of State, Justice, Commerce, and the Judiciary Appropriations for 1952*, 82d Cong., lst sess., 1951, 1644.

91. Silone, *The God That Failed*, 98.

92. Kravchenko, *I Chose Freedom*, 38, 132, 372.

93. Crossman, *The God That Failed*, 10.

94. Kravchenko, *I Chose Freedom*, 449.

95. Barmine, *One Who Survived*, 209.

96. In part, the power of Cold War autobiography is derived from its anthropomorphizing of the anticommunist ideology. As George Lakoff and Mark Johnson argue, viewing "abstract" inanimate concepts "in human terms has an explanatory power of the only sort that makes sense to most people." Trevor Parry-Giles refers to such humanizing principles as "characterology," where the "embodiment of ideology and the commitments that constitute ideology" are represented by particular individuals. See George Lakoff and Mark Johnson, *Metaphors We Live By* (Chicago: University of Chicago Press, 1980), 34; and Trevor Parry-Giles, "Character, the Constitution, and the Ideological Embodiment of 'Civil Rights' in the 1967 Nomination of Thurgood Marshall to the Supreme Court," *Quarterly Journal of Speech* 82 (1996): 366.

97. James Campbell, *Exiled in Paris: Richard Wright, James Baldwin, Samuel Beckett, and Others on the Left Bank* (New York: Scribner, 1995), 96, 277. See also Michel Fabre, *The Unfinished Quest of Richard Wright* (Urbana: University of Illinois Press, 1993), 35.

98. House Committee on Un-American Activities, 80th Cong., 1st sess., 1947, 28 (emphasis added).

99. House Committee on Un-American Activities, 81st Cong., lst sess., 1949, 1175.

100. William. F. Buckley, Jr., and L. Brent Bozell, *McCarthy and His Enemies: The Record and Its Meaning* (Chicago: Henry Regnery, 1954), 274.

101. Senate Committee on Government Operations, *State Department Information Program—Voice of America*, 83rd Cong., lst sess., 1953, 479 (Hereafter cited as the Voice of America hearings).

102. Anthony Howard, *Crossman: The Pursuit of Power* (London: Jonathan Cape, 1990), 100–101. For more information on C. D. Jackson, see Rhodri Jeffreys-Jones, *The CIA and American Democracy* (New Haven, CT: Yale University Press, 1989), 86.

103. William E. Daugherty, "Richard H. S. Crossman," in *A Psychological Warfare Casebook*, ed. Willliam E. Daugherty and Morris Janowitz (Baltimore, MD: Johns Hopkins University Press, 1958), 246.

104. Tam Dalyell, *Dick Crossman: A Portrait* (London: Weidenfeld and Nicolson, 1989), 51.

105. Dalyell, *Dick Crossman*, 61.

106. Crossman, *The God That Failed*, 2.

107. See John Goldsmith, ed., *Stephen Spender: Journals 1939–1983* (London: Faber and Faber, 1985), 181–182; and Alan Raucher, "Beyond the God that Failed: Louis Fischer, Liberal Internationalist," *The Historian* 44 (1982): 175, 180.

108. See "Countering Stalinist Propaganda," July 29, 1952, White House Office, NSC Staff: Papers, 1948–1961, OCB Secretariat Series, Doctrinal Warfare (Misc.), Box 1, DDEPL, 5.

109. See *Congressional Record*, 81st Cong., 2d sess., 1950, 16007, 17317; and Iain Hamilton, *Koestler: A Biography* (New York: Macmillan, 1982), 174, 224.

110. Campbell, *Exiled in Paris*, 196–197.

111. Hamilton, *Koestler*, 176–178, 200, 210.

112. Hugh David, *Stephen Spender: A Portrait with Background* (London: Heinemann, 1992), 257–259. See also Goldsmith, *Stephen Spender*, 130.

113. Hamilton, for example, argues that Koestler knew that the U.S. government offered financial backing for the CCF's activities, yet Koestler denied that he knew such funding originated from the CIA. Michel Fabre contends that Wright was unconcerned about the CCF's sponsorship despite allegations that Wright was extremely paranoid about the CIA's presence throughout France. Hugh David states that Spender, conversely, was very concerned about the CIA rumors. Spender felt assured that such CIA rumors were false because he believed that *Encounter* was supported by some forty different U.S. trusts and charitable foundations. In the mid-1960s, however, a California-based magazine entitled *Ramparts* disproved such claims and determined that the CIA had been covertly funding CCF from its inception, making the CCF a covert international propaganda front. See David, *Stephen Spender*, 259–262; Fabre, *The Unfinished Quest*, 416–417; Goldsmith, *Stephen Spender*, 130, 257; and Hamilton, *Koestler*, 218–219.

114. For background information on which governmental agencies were charged with the different types of propaganda, see "A Report to the National Security Council by the Under Secretary of State on A Plan for National Psychological Warfare," July, 1950, Records of Organizations in the Executive Office of the President, Record Group 429, HSTPL, 1–4, 25; Edward Lilly, December, 1951, "PSB: A Short History," White House Office, NSC Staff: Papers, 1953–1961,

PSB Central Files Series , Box 6, DDEPL, 75–76; and Speech Draft, n.d., Gordon Gray Papers, 1946–1976, Box 2, DDEPL, 1. White propaganda involves that material with which the U.S. government wishes to accept responsibility.

115. Robert Griffith, *The Politics of Fear: Joseph R. McCarthy and the Senate* (Amherst: University of Massachusetts Press, 1987), 32.

116. I found little information on Elinor Lipper, Edmund Stevens, or Frederick Martin Stern. I do know that Elinor Lipper's autobiography was excerpted in the *New York Post*, as reported on by its editor in 1953, James Wechsler. See Senate Committee on Government Operations, *State Department Information Program—Information Centers*, 83rd Cong., lst sess., 1953, 273. In addition, Edmund Stevens received a Pulitzer Prize for his work *This Is Russia—Uncensored*. Stevens served as a career journalist, living in the United States and Russia. See Anna Rothe, ed., *Current Biography* (New York: H. W. Wilson, 1951), 546.

117. Wilson P. Dizard, *The Strategy of Truth: The Story of the U.S. Information Service* (Washington, D.C.: Public Affairs Press, 1961), 43.

118. NSC-135/3, "Reappraisal of U. S. Objectives and Strategy for National Security," September 25, 1952, 1952–1954, *Foreign Relations*, 2:142–150, 209–231. See also Robert R. Bowie and Richard H. Immerman, *Waging Peace: How Eisenhower Shaped an Enduring Cold War Strategy* (Oxford: Oxford University Press, 1998), 29–33; John Lewis Gaddis, *Strategies of Containment: A Critical Appraisal of Postwar American National Security Policy* (New York: Oxford University Press, 1982), 124–125; and "National Policy Applicable to Doctrinal Warfare," November 17, 1952, White House Office, NSC Staff: Papers, 1948–1961, OCB Secretariat Series, Doctrinal Warfare (Official), Box 2, DDEPL, 4.

119. For further deliberations over the U.S. propaganda mission, see *Congressional Record*, 8lst Cong., 2d sess., 1950, 12136; *Congressional Record*, 82th Cong., lst sess., 1951, 3534, 8676, 8749, 8752; *Congressional Record*, 82d Cong., 2d sess., 1952, 3531.

III

The Period of Institutionalization and Psychological Strategy

5

McCarthyism and the Rise and Fall of Congressional Involvement in Propaganda Operations

When Dwight D. Eisenhower won the presidency, his attention immediately turned to foreign policy exigencies. He sought to end the Korean conflict even before he was inaugurated and worked toward that end throughout the early months of his administration. The Eisenhower administration pressured China and the Soviet Union, warning the former of nuclear attacks privately if the war raged on. Eisenhower also had to contend with nationalist inclinations in the developing world (e.g., Asia, Africa, Latin America, the Middle East), which he felt invited communist expansion. Iranian nationalism attracted considerable attention from Eisenhower as well, as he feared its impact on corporate interests in the West. To lessen such possibilities, Eisenhower worked successfully with the CIA to overthrow the existing Iranian leader in 1953—a move that has attracted considerable attention in more recent years. Comparable covert attention was also given to Latin America; the CIA ousted the Arbenz government in Guatemala during 1954.[1]

For Eisenhower, these foreign policy exigencies required a strengthened propaganda program if the United States was to prevail in an expanding Cold War against communism. Soon after Eisenhower won his first presidential bid in November 1952, he attended to the governmental propaganda program; it became the object of four simultaneous investigations—two initiated by the newly elected president (e.g., Rockefeller and Jackson committees) and two staged by Congress (Senate Foreign Relations and the

McCarthy committees).[2] While three of the investigations are the subject of chapter 6, the most controversial of the investigations was the McCarthy committee, which is the centerpiece of this chapter. Because Joseph McCarthy argued that the Department of State was "thoroughly infested with Communists,"[3] he embarked on a crusade to rid that department of "un-American" activity; the State Department thus became one of McCarthy's favorite targets.[4] Many onlookers and scholars alike, however, skeptically viewed McCarthy's attack as a "partisan weapon by Republicans to end the Democratic hegemony"[5] in agencies such as the Department of State.

McCarthy's initial attempts to investigate the Department of State began in 1953 when he assumed the chairmanship of the Senate Committee on Government Operations. Typically considered a "minor committee" concerned with "dull matters" of governmental operations, it also included a Permanent Subcommittee on Investigations that possessed wide authority to investigate government policies and operations at all levels.[6] The parent committee and its subcommittee awarded McCarthy "a nearly impregnable political base from which to operate."[7]

With McCarthy as chair, the subcommittee instigated 445 inquiries, 157 investigations, and 17 public hearings.[8] While McCarthy's most memorable target was the Department of Defense in 1954, two other investigations predated the famed McCarthy-Army hearings and centered on the State Department's propaganda program, the newly labeled International Information Administration (IIA).[9] The first examined the Voice of America (VOA) from February 16, 1953, through late March.[10] As this investigation closed, McCarthy ignited yet another attack on the propaganda program that continued through August 1953 and focused on the program's overseas information libraries.[11] Even though McCarthy held only fifteen sessions addressing the activities of the overseas information centers, the investigation was spread over a three-and-a-half-month period before an attentive television audience.[12] Leslie Fiedler calls McCarthy's attacks on the U.S. propaganda program bitter "onslaughts," while Daniel Bell claims the program received a "violent clubbing" during the two public hearings.[13] Throughout these proceedings, McCarthy charged the propaganda program with "encouraging subversion," and he pledged to "investigate Communist infiltration" at all levels of the program.[14]

As this chapter shows, the investigations further elevated the hysteria surrounding communism in the early 1950s. Even though the Eisenhower administration considered McCarthy's tactics reprehensible, the president refused to condemn the committee's actions publicly.[15] This "nonresponse" helped taint the credibility of the Truman administration's State Department.[16] These public hearings, coupled with the Truman administration's move toward a more covert and militarized propaganda program, served the ends of the Eisenhower administration. Ultimately, McCarthy's actions provided yet another impetus for centralizing propaganda strategy in the Oval Office and away from congressional interference. Heightened executive control expanded the means of rhetorical influence serving the presidency. Ironically, the U.S. media, which previously helped legalize and legitimize the governmental propaganda program, now aided in weakening it, bringing McCarthyism into the nation's homes uncensored and unquestioned. By 1953, an agency designed to fight communism was charged with promoting the enemy's mission—that of infiltrating and destroying U.S. democratic ideals.

McCARTHY'S TACTICS IN THE STATE DEPARTMENT INVESTIGATIONS

The McCarthy committee directed most of its attacks against the State Department during Dean Acheson's tenure as secretary of state in the Truman administration. The primary strategy for the McCarthy committee involved attempts to portray the propaganda officials and their policies as soft on communism, proving, for the committee members, the existence of a communist conspiracy. In the process of uncovering an alleged conspiracy, McCarthy called on ex-communists to marshal evidence. In the process, these witnesses "outed" individuals with seemingly communist ties and questionable pasts. As the committee interrogated propaganda officials and authors whose works appeared in the State Department's overseas libraries, it praised the behavior of former communists.

The Voice of America Investigation

During the Voice of America hearings, committee members pointed to numerous incidents to support their allegations that Truman's State Department sabotaged or somehow impeded the program's mission. Committee members demanded, for example, that Robert B. Goldmann, copy editor for VOA, explain why he changed the words "democratic" to "anti-communist," and "citizens" to "anti-communist organizations" in Guatemalan scripts. According to McCarthy and his chief counsel, Roy M. Cohn, the words "democratic" and "citizens" referenced communist activity in Guatemala, which suggested an alliance between the Communist Party and the propaganda program.[17] The committee also condemned the VOA for spending approximately $28,000 on a radio program called "The Eye of the Eagle," which McCarthy identified as a "juvenile program" lacking in anticommunist propaganda.[18]

McCarthy even accused VOA's technical engineers of sabotaging the propaganda program by placing radio transmitters in spots designed to inhibit signals from reaching the iron curtain countries. McCarthy hypothesized: "Assume I do not want [the VOA] to reach Communist territory. Would not the best way to sabotage that voice be to place your transmitters within that magnetic storm area, so that you would have this tremendous interference?"[19] In its final report, the McCarthy committee argued that certain "transmitters were being constructed in such locations [so] that the radio waves would pass through a magnetic storm area in the authoral zone."[20] All of these examples, for the McCarthy committee at least, positively identified the communist conspiracy in the Department of State.

Evidence of such a conspiracy also came from testimony offered by VOA employees—testimony that committee members seemed to accept unconditionally. After speaking with Gerald F. P. Dooher, acting chief of VOA's Near East division, McCarthy charged that "a deliberate pattern" was uncovered "to keep the Voice from being an effective anti-Communist weapon." Dooher, in speaking out against the VOA, confirmed McCarthy's suspicion and added that "a deliberate pattern [existed] to destroy or nullify the Voice."[21] In reaction to such claims, McCarthy charged that the Voice of America might more aptly be called the "Voice of Moscow."[22] In the end, the McCarthy committee declared that "poor planning, reckless disregard for taxpayers' money, incompetence, stupidity or worse was the rule and not the exception in the operation of the Voice of America."[23] While the VOA hearings centered mostly on the analysis of scripts and the placement of equipment, the investigation into the State Department's information centers delved into library practices.

The Information Center Investigation

Throughout the hearings before the Senate Subcommittee on Permanent Investigations, McCarthy questioned the State Department's selection policy concerning books that were placed in the international libraries. As chapter 4 revealed, books were a key component of the State Department's propaganda operation that were likewise integral to the Psychological Strategy Board's (PSB) Doctrinal Warfare and Escapee Programs. While some books were distributed in the communist regions, others were placed in international libraries in allied and communist territories in offices known as the United States Information Service (USIS). First, McCarthy accused the "old Acheson State Department" of distributing the "works of Communist authors" for the "purpose of fighting communism."[24] Concerning such books, Senator Karl Mundt (R-SD) argued that "public officials under Public Law 402 [did] not have the right to spend taxpayers' money" distributing "that kind of trash" to overseas centers. Mundt, a well-known proponent of peacetime propaganda, alleged that the books distributed by the overseas libraries advocated "the overthrow of Government by force and violence," "publicly and enthusiastically applaud[ed] the Russian regime," and "repeatedly [found] fault with every phase of American life."[25] Senator John L. McClellan (D-AR) maintained that the books were "actually aiding the enemy" because they were "derogatory to the American system and favorable to the system that prevail[ed] in Russia."[26] The final report issued by the subcommittee concluded that the "old State Department's book-selecting officialdom" exhibited a "curious color blindness to anything red or pink," leaving "only one obvious inference."[27]

The McCarthy committee also devoted considerable attention to determining whether certain authors were communists at the time they wrote their books. When the investigation ended, the committee determined that the State Department had been "guilty" of sponsoring authors with clear communist sympathies. In the final report from the hearings, the committee concluded that "over 30,000 books by Communists and those who . . . aided the Communist cause were in use in the . . . libraries," with "those responsible" knowingly "using [such] works." Beyond that, the committee deemed that "the officials of the old State Department" were "grossly negligent in the execution of the congressional mandate."[28] Harvey Matusow, a prominent ex-Communist witness, who later admitted he lied on the witness stand for McCarthy, confirmed that McCarthy's plan for these hearings was "simple" and "dramatic." McCarthy sought, Matusow charged, to demonstrate the communist connections with books that "would be found in the State Department's Overseas Librar[ies]."[29]

In part, the McCarthy committee was correct in its conclusion that the libraries contained pro-communist books. The Truman administration—and more importantly, former congressional committees—encouraged propaganda officials to disseminate some of the "questionable" books on the theory that books by former communists possessed more credibility behind the iron curtain. Martin Merson, former executive officer with the IIA, identified this policy as a "balanced presentation," which began in August 1949, and "called neither for the exclusion of the works of Communists nor for undue emphasis on them."[30] A directive found in the papers of William Benton, former assistant secretary of state for public affairs, explained the process by which books and periodicals were selected for the overseas libraries. In using "bibliographic guides," "published [book] reviews," and

the "advice of specialists in particular fields," propaganda officials reportedly based their selection "on the consensus of published opinions or the
opinions obtained by consultation with specialists or by utilization of resources of foundations, national associations, and other organizations." The
books presented "the United States, through the eyes of Americans," "inter-
pret[ed] the United States and the American way of life," and "present[ed]
the whole and sometimes controversial range of American thought."[31]

In addition to dismissing the rationale for including certain communist
or antidemocratic books, the McCarthy committee ignored the fact that
many of the books also had been in the Office of War Information (OWI) libraries when the United States and the USSR were allied during World War
II. Such books simply had not been removed. Additionally, some of the
books, although criticizing certain aspects of U.S. life, did not explicitly
promote communism as an alternative. By 1953, such a practice drew sharp
criticism because of the hysteria surrounding the exacerbated fear of communist infiltration. The McCarthy committee, however, demonstrated little
interest in past congressional dictates or the justifications of such policies
by State Department officials. What earlier political officials had declared
the truth about the Cold War, the McCarthy committee labeled communist
propaganda.[32]

Finally, the committee charged the State Department with failing to follow-up on FBI security questions concerning prospective employees. Such
charges were introduced during the *Know North America* hearings and became an even larger controversy by 1953. McCarthy made sure that the
State Department, and not the FBI, received blame for the hiring: "I think
we should make it very, very clear that [the security check] is meaningless,
regardless of how good a job the FBI does, unless the Security Division of
the State Department acts upon it."[33] All of the issues regarding hiring practices, book selection processes, the content of the VOA broadcasts, and the
location of radio transmitters raised suspicions about the loyalty of certain
propaganda officials—suspicions that were heightened by McCarthy's own
"expert" witnesses.

"Reformed" Communists—McCarthy's Expert Witnesses

Throughout the hearings, the McCarthy committee, like the Dies com-
mittee some fifteen years earlier, relied heavily on former members of the
Communist Party as "expert" witnesses. One key witness for McCarthy was
Louis Budenz who was known as the "witness's witness."[34] Budenz, born in
Indianapolis, Indiana, in 1891, joined the Communist Party in 1935, ini-
tially managing the Communist Party newspaper, the *Daily Worker*;

Budenz eventually served as president of the Freedom of the Press Co., Inc., which supervised that paper.[35] Budenz also self-reportedly served as the chair of the publications commission and was a member of the trade union commission and the state committees in New York and Illinois before leaving the Communist Party in 1945. As Budenz explained in the hearings over the information libraries, he left the Party because he became "a slave intellectually and spiritually to every whim and wish and policy of the Kremlin."[36]

Once leaving the Communist Party, Budenz's primary employer became the U.S. government. David M. Oshinsky contends that Budenz spent approximately 3,000 hours explaining "the Party's inner workings to the FBI," earning some $70,000 for such testimonies. During this period, Budenz reportedly testified on some thirty-three separate occasions in congressional hearings before retiring in 1957.[37] In his service to Congress, as well as to the FBI, Herbert L. Packer claims that Budenz became the "leading interpreter of Communist theology . . . because he [had] been so prolific a source of accusations against persons prominent in American political and intellectual life." Such testimonies, Packer concludes, were quite suspect since Budenz's evidence was "almost always [grounded in] hearsay rather than direct knowledge."[38]

During the investigations concerning the information libraries, ex-communist Budenz provided damaging testimony against the State Department. He identified seventy-five communist authors on a list provided by the committee and argued that because the propaganda program used so many communist books—books he considered "a vital part" of the Kremlin's psychological warfare operation—that communists must have infiltrated the agency.[39] Several of the authors Budenz implicated were questioned during the televised investigations, which heightened the sensationalism of his charges. Budenz received significant praise from McCarthy for his testimony. In a tribute to Budenz during the information center hearings, McCarthy asserted, "I think it is a great service you have rendered to this country, Mr. Budenz, since you broke with the party."[40] As McCarthy worked to eliminate communists from the U.S. government, he endowed ex-communists with the highest levels of credibility.

When other witnesses were interrogated, they were expected to renounce their past allegiance to the Party and/or provide lists of other known communists just as Budenz had. If they complied, they were commended. When author Langston Hughes, for example, denounced communism openly to the committee, Senator McClellan declared: "I want to commend anyone who will be as frank about their errors of the past as you are being before this committee and before the public."[41] During the VOA hearings, Michael G.

Horneffer, director of VOA's French Unit, was also heralded for identifying persons he believed exhibited communist tendencies. At the end of his testimony, McCarthy praised: "You are an example of the good people we have over on the Voice. Thank God we have you and people like you over there."[42]

McCarthy maintained similar contacts with other employees from the propaganda program. Harvey Matusow, a McCarthy insider, claimed that his employer had several VOA "informers."[43] Others claimed that a group calling themselves the "loyal American Underground," served as spies for McCarthy, supplying him with insider information and testimony during the hearings.[44] As Oshinsky concludes, "internal VOA memos routinely reached his [McCarthy's] office before they got to the addressee."[45] Alexander Barmine, author of *One Who Survived: The Life Story of a Russian under the Soviets* (see chapter 4), served as another witness for McCarthy; Barmine possessed a Communist Party past and continued to work for the Voice of America in spite of that past.[46] In his testimony during the VOA hearings, Barmine, chief of the Russian branch of the VOA, critiqued State Department officials, arguing that their policies "impaired the possibility of carrying effective anti-Communist propaganda." Even though Barmine formerly served as the special assistant to the Soviet's Chief of Military Intelligence, McCarthy emphasized what a "good job" Barmine was doing at the VOA.[47]

By contrast, other individuals who either refused to denounce communism, to name names, or to provide supportive testimony were publicly accused of conspiring with the Communists Party. When author Helen Goldfrank, for example, cited the Fifth Amendment in her testimony during the McCarthy committee's information centers hearings, Senator McClellan concluded: "I just want to say to the witness that she has definitely convinced me that, if she gave truthful answers to the questions asked, she would incriminate herself."[48] Another writer, Doxey A. Wilkerson, also declined to answer many of the committee's questions based on his Fifth Amendment rights. McCarthy retorted:

The innocent do not need the protection of the fifth amendment. The fifth amendment is to protect a man who is guilty of a crime. It provides that he need not convict himself of his own testimony. . . .If you are not a Communist, you see, as of today then you would say "No" and that truthful answer could not incriminate you. When you tell this committee that the truth would incriminate you, that means . . . that you are a member of the Communist conspiracy.[49]

Yet for author and journalist James Wechsler, even a public repudiation of communism did not convince committee members that he was a loyal American. McCarthy charged: "The easiest thing in the world [is] to get up and say 'Communism is bad.' The hard thing is to do a thing like Budenz: get up and testify against your former comrades to see that they are deported or sent to jail."[50] As Wechsler later claimed in his autobiography, *The Age of Suspicion*, "The true test of an ex-communist was how many of his former associates he helped to expose." Despite Wechsler's disclosures that four former communists worked for the *New York Post*, a newspaper that he edited, McCarthy continued his attack. Wechsler reasoned later that such behavior was "manifestly intended as a harassment . . . and as a warning to other editors who have displayed inadequate respect for the committee chairman."[51]

While McCarthy's interrogation tactics have long been the subject of intense scrutiny, his approach grew out of a culture sanctioned and inspired by the Truman *and* Eisenhower administrations as well as the U.S. Congress. Apart from the Kersten Amendment and the Escapee Program (see chapter 4), the Refugee Act of 1953 was the subject of debate throughout the McCarthy period. Placed into law on August 7, 1953, the act was intended "for the relief of certain refugees, and orphans" who "fled from the Union of Soviet Socialist Republics or other Communist, Communist-dominated or Communist-occupied area of Europe."[52] In addition, the Emergency Relief Act was also passed in 1953 upon the recommendation of President Eisenhower. It was designed "to admit up to 207,000 escapees, refugees, and other selected persons, over and above the normal quota system."[53] As the PSB argued privately, "In the free world, escapees are the most articulate instruments to counter communist propaganda" and "the best sources of information and intelligence in the Soviet world."[54] Both acts were intended to support the Escapee and the Doctrinal Warfare Programs.[55] McCarthy's use of ex-communist witnesses must be contextualized within a broader context of legislative and executive actions in relation to defectors and refugees (and communist converts). What set McCarthy apart, though, was the way in which the U.S. news media showcased his actions.

The Media's Role in Perpetuating McCarthy's Tactics

One of McCarthy's key strategies involved gaining as much media exposure as possible concerning the allegations made by the McCarthy committee.[56] Stephen J. Whitfield argues that "no politician of his time was craftier at exploiting the habits of the press for his own self-aggrandizing ends."[57]

McCarthy's strategies involved not only the domestic media but the international media as well, with McCarthy taking his show "on the road."

In the middle of the McCarthy committee hearings, McCarthy sought international exposure. He sent two of his employees on a tour of the overseas information libraries in Europe. Beginning in Paris on April 4, 1953, Roy Cohn, the chief counsel to the subcommittee, and David Schine, chief consultant, toured the Department of State's overseas libraries in Berlin, Frankfurt, Munich, Bonn, Vienna, Belgrade, Athens, and Rome, ending in London on April 21. Throughout their "whirlwind tour," dozens of reporters and photographers followed Cohn and Schine, covering their brief perusal through the card catalogs at every stop.[58] While in Paris, Cohn and Schine even dropped in on exiled author Richard Wright, one of the authors highlighted in chapter 4. Cohn and Schine sought information from Wright on a newly appointed State Department official. Despite threats to force Wright to testify, Wright denied knowing the individual in question.[59]

Even though the anticommunist pair received the amount of coverage desired, the event proved counterproductive for the McCarthy committee and for the credibility of the United States as a whole. Michael Straight points out that the tour "made the United States the laughing stock of the world";[60] Robert Goldston maintains similarly that the "Cohn-Schine vaudeville junket in Europe undoubtedly did more damage to the reputation of the United States than years of Communist propaganda."[61] The duo's "pointless" trip was covered by the international press in a very "hostile and often unfair" manner, which heightened the public relations debacle for the propaganda program.[62]

In the United States, the primary media strategy for the McCarthy committee involved the prevention of State Department officials from defending their program during the televised portion of the hearings. Much of their testimony was taken behind closed doors or during nontelevised appropriation hearings for the 1954 fiscal year.[63] When State Department officials were interrogated publicly, the questioning focused more on their past political actions than on their connections to the State Department's propaganda program. When Reed Harris, IIA deputy director, testified, for example, the committee delved into his high school and college political leanings. Harris was allowed little time to defend the allegations, especially before the television cameras. As a result of the investigations, he resigned.[64]

While the media's backlash abroad may have embarrassed the McCarthy committee, the domestic news coverage aided the committee. Initially, many reporters simply covered McCarthy as "straight news," providing viewers and readers with more "factual" information. The anticommunist message that dominated the Washington political scene became the top story for the nation's journalists. Some scholars argue that the media helped create McCarthy; others refute such creative media powers. Nevertheless, many agree that McCarthyism changed news reporting considerably.[65] As Thomas C. Cochran explains, "in the calmer atmosphere of the late 1950s, network executives sought to gain greater control over the content of broadcasting,"[66] leading to "interpretive reporting,"[67] and awarding journalists the license to critique as well as report.

Certainly, the media's role in relation to the propaganda program evolved over the course of this debate. An institution that helped legalize and legitimize peacetime propaganda now aided members of Congress in almost destroying the program. Perhaps the answer to this ironic turn of events and coverage lies in the reality that the media succumbed to anticommunist political pressures of the executive and the congressional branches. By 1953, the Cold War ideology that the Truman administration espoused and the media promulgated achieved a level of naturalization and urgency as the Soviet Union continued its expansive tendencies. Given the link between the Cold War and the U.S. propaganda program, the domestic news media actually covered the Cold War consistently. This ideological mindset involved denouncing and defeating communism, even to the point of questioning the loyalty of governmental officials and their programs whose very purpose was to combat the Cold War enemy. Not only did McCarthyism bring about changes in journalistic practices, it also had a significant effect on the nation's international credibility and the future of the peacetime propaganda program.

THE AFTERMATH OF McCARTHYISM

Notably, McCarthy's investigations paralleled Eisenhower's first few months in office. Rather than comment on the investigations, however, Eisenhower remained publicly silent on the issue even though McCarthy's attacks centered on a key governmental agency. As this section suggests, Eisenhower's silence fostered a revision in the propaganda program's mission and structure, which further shifted the locus of power for propaganda operations from Congress and the State Department to the White House.

The Eisenhower Administration's "No-Response" Approach

Dwight D. Eisenhower did not welcome the McCarthy committee's investigations because he believed the administration should investigate the agency first through the Rockefeller and Jackson committees (see chapter

6).[68] While the president indeed may have resented the hearings, they ultimately promoted his political agenda. Eisenhower's refusal to respond to McCarthy was controversial, but it allowed the committee to complete its mission while simultaneously cleaning out Democratic holdovers in the State Department from the two previous administrations.

Eisenhower's decision to ignore McCarthy grew from his philosophies about the presidency. To begin with, Eisenhower believed that the president should not become involved in congressional business—a view that stemmed from Eisenhower's disdain for congressional scrutiny of the executive branch. In his memoirs, Eisenhower explained that by condemning McCarthy, he would have "greatly enhance[d] his publicity value without achieving any constructive purpose."[69] He echoed such opinions in his personal correspondence, concluding in a letter to his brother, Milton Eisenhower, that "only a short-sighted or completely inexperienced individual would urge the use of the office of the Presidency to give an opponent the publicity he so avidly desires."[70] Thus, as Eisenhower wrote: "I continued in my determination to ignore him."[71]

At the same time, Eisenhower was quite concerned about the overall domestic and international political implications of McCarthyism. Eisenhower viewed McCarthy's activities as a major public relations embarrassment and was especially alarmed by the European interest in the Republican senator from Wisconsin.[72] Despite such strong concerns, and despite pressure from presidential staffers like C. D. Jackson to engage in a more offensive attack against McCarthy, Eisenhower chose to stay above the political fray publicly. Privately, however, Eisenhower blamed Truman and the U.S. news media for the McCarthy debacle, becoming defensive against any suggestion that his own rhetorical response to McCarthy in any way contributed to the country's credibility problems.[73] In a letter dated July 27, 1953, Eisenhower wrote the following to his friend, William E. Robinson, of the *New York Herald Tribune:* "I was rather resentful of the fact that the very agencies [e.g., the media] who had made McCarthy were the ones most offended by his practices and methods, and were loudest in their demands that I be the one to cut him down to size."[74]

Even though Eisenhower deplored McCarthy's tactics, the two viewed the communist threat similarly. In his memoirs, Eisenhower complained of the "complacency or skepticism toward security risks in government," which increased the dangers posed by "international Communism." Even as he believed that "un-American activity [could] not be prevented or routed out by employing un-American methods,"[75] Eisenhower saw the need to rid the State Department of disloyal employees. In April 1953, Eisenhower signed an executive order, authorizing officials of federal agencies to fire employees if reasonable doubt existed concerning their loyalty. Eisenhower later prevented those who were under investigation for communist activity from articulating their Fifth Amendment rights.[76] In a May 1953 letter to Harry Bullis of General Mills, Eisenhower explained his executive order, commenting that "legal procedures" were necessary to help rid government of "the insecure and disloyal."[77]

Overall, few in Washington came to the defense of the State Department's propaganda program. Earlier friends such as Eisenhower and Mundt allowed the Wisconsin senator to critique the program with minimal opposition.[78] One person, though, who did stand up to McCarthy was, not surprisingly, William Benton. Prior to the VOA and information library hearings, Benton publicly attacked McCarthy in the Senate, where Benton was serving by 1951. Benton's opposition grew predominantly from McCarthy's 1950 charge that communists had infiltrated the State Department.[79] Believing that McCarthy's appeals promoted "fear and hate," which negatively affected the country's credibility internationally,[80] Benton issued a resolution in Congress to censure McCarthy in the summer of 1951. McCarthy responded by filing a libel suit against Benton in 1952 for two million dollars; McCarthy also actively campaigned against Benton in the latter's unsuccessful re-election bid to the U.S. Senate. In the end, McCarthy accused Benton of anticommunist activities, and Benton lost the senatorial election while McCarthy stayed on in the Senate. Benton took at least partial credit, though, for the eventual censuring of McCarthy in 1954.[81] McCarthy's message against him, however, undoubtedly influenced the behavior of other political officials who chose to remain silent in the midst of McCarthy's crusade.

In the end, Eisenhower's handling of the McCarthy investigation illustrated his political savvy and the covert nature of Eisenhower's rhetorical influence. McCarthy eventually destroyed himself without explicit help from the president. Most of Eisenhower's oppositional actions, in fact, took place behind the scenes. Eisenhower urged, according to Martin J. Medhurst, "friends in government, business, industry, religion, and education to oppose McCarthy and all he stood for with every means at their disposal."[82] Such knowledge then offers insight into Eisenhower's predisposition for covert means of rhetorical influence. Eisenhower's "friends" served as the president's rhetorical surrogates as they voiced his opposition to McCarthy for him.

Whether Eisenhower actually intended to use McCarthy's investigations as a means to clean out the State Department is not yet proven. Many scholars contend that such was the case.[83] Regardless of Eisenhower's intent, one cannot discount the ease with which the McCarthy committee's actions created a heightened exigence that allowed the new administration to reorganize the propaganda program and to stock it with new and more "loyal" employees. In spite of these positive outcomes for the Eisenhower administration, the committee investigations did produce additional consequences, which altered the nation's credibility abroad just as Eisenhower feared.[84]

The Fragility of Democracy, The Virility of Communism

The McCarthy committee's investigations of the propaganda program reflected a transformation in the way in which democracy and communism were articulated in political debates about propaganda. These changes subsequently affected the tone of the U.S. propaganda program. During the Smith-Mundt debates, democracy was assumed to be naturally appealing to the people of the world, with communism constructed as naturally unappealing. In only six short years, however, communism seemed more virile while democracy appeared more fragile. By 1953, policymakers were no longer so naive as to expect the values of democracy to sell themselves. Instead, they voiced the belief that communist propaganda needed to be combated aggressively. This change reflected the conspiracy logic associated with the McCarthy era. The "paranoid style" of McCarthy's rhetoric accorded the propaganda of the "enemy" with tremendous power, which required an "all out crusade" involving more extreme tactics than the typical "methods of political give-and-take."[85]

Throughout the McCarthy committee hearings, the testimony of former Communist Party members contributed greatly to a portrait of this powerful and effective communist conspiracy. According to Budenz, communist leaders sought to "establish by violence the Soviet dictatorship in every country of the world" because all Kremlin officials believed that "communism and capitalism [could] not live in the same world." Budenz accented the urgency of the situation by arguing that even the most elaborate defense system would not suffice; the United States needed an equally potent "internal security" mechanism. Budenz stated: "I think we must arm ourselves, decidedly. And then, along with armament, we must maintain our own internal security and protect our morale and have those firm policies which will make our armament also worthwhile." The committee members appeared to accept Budenz's testimony unquestionably; Senator Stuart Symington (D-MO) concluded that the United States needed to develop an "adequate national security" system, even at the expense of the country's "standard of living."[86]

Budenz and other witnesses testifying before the McCarthy committee emphasized the power of the Soviet's psychological warfare program in their portrait of a more threatening communist conspiracy. Rather than portraying communism as naturally unappealing, they portrayed Soviet propaganda as having a powerful impact on public opinion around the world. Budenz argued that the Communist Party conspired to "overthrow . . . the Government of the United States" by infiltrating "every agency of public opinion." The Kremlin believed, Budenz argued, that communist agents "must penetrate . . . all policy-making bodies in order to mold the minds of the people" in the countries they wished "to undermine." Once again, committee members appeared to accept Budenz's testimony, pointing to the use of communist books as an effort to "mold" public opinion. According to Senator McClellan, "the books and documents" that were made "available in public libraries are sources of propaganda that the Communists in Russia regard [highly]." Budenz echoed McClellan's assertion, alleging that books represented a major way of "breeding communism." McCarthy pointed to the persuasiveness of the communist philosophy by supporting the removal of the communist books and implicitly supporting the practice of burning them.[87] By acknowledging the power of Soviet propaganda, the McCarthy committee made the case for a more aggressive response by the U.S. government.

Yet, the McCarthy committee's use of conspiracy theories points to the rhetorical bind that propaganda policymakers faced. While McCarthy's witnesses constructed the seriousness of the situation in order to justify stronger countermeasures, they inadvertently conceded the vulnerability of democratic institutions.[88] In earlier years, congressional leaders believed that by simply explaining democratic principles, foreign people would naturally accept them as their own. The McCarthy committee, however, admitted that a strong case had been made for the communist way of life, which unintentionally strengthened the persuasive force of communism.

The language that McCarthy's witnesses used further perpetuated the power of this communist conspiracy. Weaponry metaphors reappeared in the McCarthy committee forum, this time as evidence for the communist conspiracy. For instance, in the oversees library hearings, Budenz linked books to the communist "psychological warfare" effort, identifying books as "a very important weapon" in the communist "campaign," turning this medium into another instrument of war similar to the short-wave radio. According to Budenz, not only could these "weapons" "infiltrate" and "penetrate," but they could also "*poison* the wells of public opinion," which made books function as an integral "method of breeding communism throughout the world."[89]

Such metaphors, while contributing to the virility of communism, also led U.S. propagandists (e.g., the PSB) to step-up their propaganda campaign against this almost unstoppable force. By speaking of communism in such terms, the McCarthy committee conceded the fragility of their own message and granted their Cold War enemy and its propaganda with immeasurable power. Richard H. Rovere alleges that the investigations, when publicized internationally, "scandalized many foreigners who had [a] habit of listening to [VOA]."[90] Benton maintained that some in Europe went so far as to equate McCarthyism with Hitlerism.[91] In addition to the inadvertent public relations debacle abroad, McCarthyism elevated the hysteria surrounding communism inside and outside of the U.S. government.

The McCarthy hearings represented yet one more congressional attempt to dictate the mission of the U.S. propaganda in reaction to a changing political scene. Even as agency officials sought to follow past congressional prescriptions, the McCarthy committee demanded that IIA officials embrace their view of propaganda or be branded as communists. The State Department and the propaganda program essentially became political pawns for the committee; they found themselves in an inescapable situation where they were targets of the McCarthy witchhunt yet received little support from the presidential administration. With no one from the Eisenhower administration coming to the aid of the agencies, the McCarthy committee was able to weaken the credibility of the propaganda program further through what even Eisenhower regarded as unfair tactics.

When the investigations finally ended, McCarthy failed to smoke out a single communist. The investigations did, however, exact a tremendous toll on the program. Hundreds of State Department employees either quit or were fired, and numerous VOA language programs and overseas libraries were shut down. As a result of the committee's actions, the propaganda program's administrator, its deputy director, and VOA's chairman all resigned. For those who stayed, morale dipped considerably. Many employees felt abandoned by Washington and their supervisors. In addition, hundreds of books allegedly sympathetic toward communism were banned from overseas libraries, and some were even burned by diligent employees.[92] While Eisenhower was widely criticized for his "no response" approach to McCarthy,[93] his strategy allowed the McCarthy committee time to engineer a major overhaul in the Department of State.

With the State Department and the propaganda program in shambles as a result of McCarthy's investigations, the Eisenhower administration was able to reorganize the program according to its own vision. By removing the propaganda program from the State Department in August 1953, a new organization, the United States Information Agency (USIA), became more directly accountable to the president. Conducting its own investigation into the U.S. propaganda program, the Eisenhower administration redefined the mission of the program, elevating the role of covert operations for the practice of propaganda and the rhetorical presidency. Interestingly, McCarthy played a major role in this metamorphosis, despite Eisenhower's behind-the-scenes actions to silence him. The next chapter reviews the conclusions of the other three congressional and presidential investigations and details how the Eisenhower administration responded by centralizing propaganda operations in the White House.

NOTES

1. Chester J. Pach, Jr., and Elmo Richardson, *The Presidency of Dwight D. Eisenhower* (1979; reprint, Lawrence: University Press of Kansas, 1991), 84–83. See also Zachary Karabell, *Architects of Intervention: The United States, the Third World, and the Cold War, 1946–1962* (Baton Rouge: Louisiana State University Press, 1999), 50–91, 92–135.

2. For more information on these committees, see Robert William Pirsein, *The Voice of America: An History of the International Broadcasting Activities of the United States Government, 1940–1962* (New York: Arno Press, 1979), 273–292, 313–326.

3. Allen J. Matusow, *Joseph R. McCarthy* (Englewood Cliffs, NJ: Prentice-Hall, 1970), 19–24.

4. Matusow, *Joseph R. McCarthy*, 65.

5. Richard M. Fried, *Men Against McCarthy* (New York: Columbia University Press, 1976), x. Other scholars and political officials offer similar claims. See Richard H. Rovere, *Senator Joe McCarthy* (New York: Harper Torchbooks, 1959), 21; and Michael Straight, *Trial by Television and Other Encounters* (New York: Devon Press, 1979), 123.

6. Robert Goldston, *The American Nightmare: Senator Joseph R. McCarthy and the Politics of Hate* (Indianapolis, IN: Bobbs-Merrill, 1973), 117; and Robert Griffith, *The Politics of Fear: Joseph R. McCarthy and the Senate* (Amherst: University of Massachusetts Press, 1987), 208.

7. Griffith, *The Politics of Fear*, 210–211. For more information on the McCarthy committee from someone who witnessed his actions, see Arthur V. Watkins, *Enough Rope: The Inside Story of the Censure of Senator Joe McCarthy by His Colleagues—The Controversial Hearings that Signaled the End of a Turbulent Career and a Fearsome Era in American Public Life* (Englewood Cliffs, NJ: Prentice-Hall, 1969), 21.

8. Other members of the subcommittee included: Republicans Everett M. Dirksen (IL); Karl E. Mundt (SD); Charles E. Potter (MI); and Democrats John L. McClellan (AR); Henry Jackson (WA); and Stuart Symington (MO). See Griffith, *The Politics of Fear*, 212.

9. For more information on the McCarthy-Army hearings, see Griffith, *The Politics of Fear*, 241–269.

10. Goldston, *The American Nightmare*, 119; and Rovere, *Senator Joe McCarthy*, 199.

11. Senate Committee on Government Operations, *State Department Information Program—Information Centers*, 83d Cong., 1st sess., 1953, 40 (Hereafter cited as Information Centers hearing).

12. David M. Oshinsky, *A Conspiracy So Immense: The World of Joe McCarthy* (New York: Free Press, 1983), 280.

13. Leslie Fiedler, "McCarthy as Populist," in *The Meaning of McCarthyism*, ed. Earl Latham (Lexington, MA: D. C. Heath, 1973), 89; Daniel Bell, "Status Politics and New Anxieties," in *The Meaning of McCarthyism*, ed. Earl Latham (Lexington, MA: D.C. Heath, 1973), 119. For more information on the McCarthy hearings, see David F. Krugler, *The Voice of America and the Domestic Propaganda Battles, 1945–1953* (Columbia: University of Missouri Press, 2000), 166–196.

14. Thomas C. Reeves, *The Life and Times of Joe McCarthy: A Biography* (New York: Stein and Day, 1982), 479; Goldston, *The American Nightmare*, 119. See Pirsein, *The Voice of America*, 276. Pirsein contends that McCarthy arranged "TV coverage and full Committee attendance for . . . particularly sensational item[s]," helping him to "keep his 'crusade' in the spotlight."

15. Stephen E. Ambrose, *Eisenhower: The President*, vol. 2 (New York: Simon and Schuster, 1984), 58.

16. See Wilson P. Dizard, *The Strategy of Truth: The Story of the U.S. Information Service* (Washington, D.C.: Public Affairs Press, 1961), 41–42. Dizard explains that the State Department's credibility faltered because the American public appeared to believe McCarthy's charges.

17. Senate Committee on Government Operations, *State Department Information Program—Voice of America*, 83rd Cong., 1st sess., 1953, 553–560. (Hereafter cited as the Voice of America hearing).

18. Voice of America hearing, 82–93.

19. Voice of America hearing, 8.

20. Senate Committee on Government Operations, *Waste and Management in Voice of America Engineering Projects*, 83rd Cong., 2d sess., 1954, S. Res. 40, 10.

21. Voice of America hearing, 443.

22. Voice of America hearing, 185.

23. Senate Committee on Permanent Investigations, *Waste and Management*, 10.

24. Information Centers hearing, 433, 485.

25. Information Centers hearing, 495.

26. Information Centers hearing, 50.

27. Senate Committee on Government Operations, *State Department Information Program—Information Centers*, 83rd Cong., 2d sess., 1954, S. Rept. 879, 10 (Hereafter cited as the Information Centers report).

28. Information Centers report, 12–13.

29. Harvey Matusow, *False Witness* (New York: Cameron & Kahn, 1955), 214–215.

30. Martin Merson, *The Private Diary of a Public Servant* (New York: Macmillan, 1955), 12. See also Reeves, *The Life and Times of Joe McCarthy*, 479.

31. "The Selection of Books, Periodicals and Documents for Libraries Overseas," March, 1947, The William Benton Papers, Department of Special Collections, Box 376, The University of Chicago Library, Chicago, Illinois, 2–4.

32. For more on the selection processes of the USIS, see the testimony of Arnaud d'Usseau in the Information Centers hearing, 464–473. d'Usseau argues that certain books were used in the OWI libraries and had not been removed from the shelves. See also the Information Centers hearing, 460–462, where Doxey A. Wilkerson's critique of race relations policies in the United States was claimed to mirror the Communist Party's philosophy by the McCarthy committee. Finally, Edward W. Barrett, another propaganda insider, provides a synthesis of the McCarthy committee's actions. See Edward W. Barrett, *Truth Is Our Weapon* (New York: Funk & Wagnalls, 1953), 129–138.

33. Voice of America hearing, 141.

34. Harvey Matusow, *False Witness*, 62, 67.

35. For background information on Budenz, see Fried, *Men Against McCarthy*, 73; Oshinsky, *A Conspiracy*, 149; Herbert L. Packer, *Ex-Communist Witnesses: Four Studies in Fact Finding* (Stanford, CA: Stanford University Press, 1962), 121–124; and Information Centers hearing, 42.

36. Information Centers hearing, 58.

37. See Oshinsky, *A Conspiracy*, 149; and Packer, *Ex-Communist*, 124.

38. Packer, *Ex-Communist*, 5–6, 175–176.

39. Information Centers hearing, 44, 48.

40. Information Centers hearing, 42.

41. Information Centers hearing, 80.

42. Voice of America hearing, 182.

43. Harvey Matusow, *False Witness*, 208.

44. Reeves, *The Life and Times*, 478.

45. Oshinsky, *A Conspiracy*, 256.

46. Barmine at least, like Budenz, identified communists that McCarthy later investigated. See William. F. Buckley, Jr., and L. Brent Bozell, *McCarthy and His Enemies: The Record and Its Meaning* (Chicago: Henry Regnery, 1954), 274.

47. Voice of America hearing, 479.

48. Information Centers hearing, 95.

49. Information Centers hearing, 446.

50. Information Centers hearing, 307.

51. James A. Wechsler, *The Age of Suspicion* (New York: Random House, 1953), 5, 7, 269, 282.

52. *The Refugee Act of 1953*, 83d Cong., lst sess., 1953, P. L. 203, 1.

53. See Robert Cutler to General Smith, April 13, 1954, White House Office, NSC Staff: Papers, 1948–1961, OCB Central Files Series, OCB 383.7, Box 118,

Dwight D. Eisenhower Presidential Library (hereafter cited as the DDEPL), 1; and Elmer B. Staats to the Board Assistants, November 18, 1953, White House Office, NSC Staff: Papers, 1953–1961, PSB Central Files Series, PSB 383.7 Escapee Program Section, Box 28, DDEPL, 3–4.

54. Psychological Strategy Board, "A National Psychological Program with Respect to Escapees from the Soviet Orbit," January 15, 1953, White House Office, NSC Staff: Papers, 1953–1961, PSB Central Files Series, PSB 383.7 Escapees, Box 27, DDEPL, Annex A, 2–4.

55. "A Report for OCB Examination on Effectiveness of the Escapee Program," December 23, 1953, White House Office, NSC Staff: Papers, 1948–1961, OCB Central Files Series, OCB 383.7 Refugees and Interned Persons, Box 118, DDEPL, 43.

56. Harvey Matusow, *False Witness*, 213.

57. Stephen J. Whitfield, *The Culture of the Cold War* (Baltimore, MD: Johns Hopkins University Press, 1996, 1991), 163.

58. See Goldston, *The American Nightmare*, 121; Oshinsky, *A Conspiracy*, 279; and Rovere, *Senator Joe McCarthy*, 190–191.

59. James Campbell, *Exiled in Paris: Richard Wright, James Baldwin, Samuel Beckett, and Others on the Left Bank* (New York: Scribner, 1995), 100–101.

60. Straight, *Trial by Television*, 134.

61. Goldston, *The American Nightmare*, 122.

62. Oshinsky, *A Conspiracy*, 279.

63. Information Centers report, 10, 14–20.

64. For more information on the testimony of State Department officials, see Voice of America hearing, 350–387; and Barrett, *Truth Is Our Weapon*, 107.

65. For more information on the media's coverage of McCarthy, see James Aronson, *The Press and the Cold War* (New York: Monthly Review Press, 1990); Edwin R. Bayley, *Joe McCarthy and the Press* (New York: Pantheon Books, 1981), 219; Daniel J. Boorstin, *The Image: A Guide to Pseudo-Events in America* (New York: Harper Colophon, 1964), 22; Jeff Broadwater, *Eisenhower and the Anti-Communist Crusade* (Chapel Hill: University of North Carolina Press, 1992); Douglass Cater, *The Fourth Branch of Government* (New York: Vintage Books, 1965), 107; Fried, *Men Against McCarthy*, 172; Griffith, *The Politics of Fear*, 142; Oshinsky, *A Conspiracy*, 189; Michael Parenti, *Inventing the Politics of News Media Reality*, 2d. ed. (New York: St. Martin's Press, 1993), 119–126; and Whitfield, *The Culture of the Cold War*, 167–169.

66. Thomas C. Cochran, "Media as Business: A Brief History," *Journal of Communication* 25 (1975): 163.

67. Bayley, *Joe McCarthy*, 219.

68. Dwight D. Eisenhower to Clifford Roberts, December 7, 1954, Dwight D. Eisenhower: Papers as President of the United States, 1953–1961 (Ann Whitman File), Name Series, Roberts, Clifford, Box 27, DDEPL, 1. See also Robert J. Donovan, *Eisenhower: The Inside Story* (New York: Harper & Brothers, 1956), 37.

69. Dwight D. Eisenhower, *Mandate for Change, 1953–1956* (Garden City, NY: Doubleday, 1963), 320. See also Broadwater, *Eisenhower and the Anti-Communist*, 157.

70. Dwight D. Eisenhower to Milton Eisenhower, October 9, 1953, Dwight D. Eisenhower: Papers as President of the United States, 1953–1961 (Ann Whitman File), Name Series, Eisenhower, Milton, 1952–1953, Box 12, DDEPL, 3. See also Dwight D. Eisenhower to William E. Robinson, March 12, 1954, Dwight D. Eisenhower: Papers as President of the United States, 1953–1961 (Ann Whitman File), Name Series, Robinson, William E., 1952–1955, Box 29, DDEPL, 1–3.

71. Eisenhower, *Mandate for Change*, 320.

72. Broadwater, *Eisenhower and the Anti-Communist*, 118–119.

73. For more information on McCarthy and Eisenhower, see Piers Brendon, *Ike: His Life and Times* (New York: Harper & Row, 1986); Broadwater, *Eisenhower and the Anti-Communist*, 119; Fried, *Men Against McCarthy*, 256; Griffith, *The Politics of Fear*, 200; Martin J. Medhurst, *Dwight D. Eisenhower: Strategic Communicator* (Westport, CT: Greenwood Press, 1993); Oshinsky, *A Conspiracy*, 260; and Thomas Rosteck, "The Case of Eisenhower Versus McCarthyism," in *Eisenhower's War of Words: Rhetoric and Leadership*, ed. Martin J. Medhurst (East Lansing: Michigan State University Press, 1994): 73–95.

74. Dwight D. Eisenhower to William E. Robinson, July 27, 1953, Dwight D. Eisenhower: Papers of the United States, 1953–1961 (Ann Whitman File), Name Series, Robinson, William E., 1952–1955, Box 29, DDEPL, 1.

75. Eisenhower, *Mandate for Change*, 308, 321.

76. Pach, Jr., and Richardson, *The Presidency of Dwight D. Eisenhower*, 64.

77. Dwight D. Eisenhower to Harry Bullis, May 18, 1953, Papers as President of the United States, 1953–1961 (Ann Whitman File), DDE Diary Series, Box 3, DDEPL.

78. See Oshinsky, *A Conspiracy*, 284–285; and Straight, *Trial by Television*, 131.

79. "Introduction," n.d., The William Benton Papers, Department of Special Collections, The University of Chicago Library, Chicago, Illinois, 15.

80. William Benton, "Europe and Senator McCarthy," *The Fortnightly Review* (reprint), April 1954, 3–4.

81. For background information on Benton's actions concerning McCarthy, see "Introduction," 15–16; Sidney Hyman, *The Lives of William Benton* (Chicago: University of Chicago Press, 1969), 456–461, 480, 484; and Transcript, William Benton Oral History Interview, 1968, by the Columbia University Oral History Collection, page 210, Columbia University, New York.

82. Medhurst, *Dwight D. Eisenhower*, 103. For additional information on Eisenhower and McCarthy's relationship, see Fred I. Greenstein, *The Hidden-Hand Presidency: Eisenhower as Leader* (New York: Basic Books, 1982), 155–227.

83. Ambrose argues that during his first Cabinet meeting, Eisenhower "urged aggressive action against Communists in government" and sought to "purge" the State Department in particular." Others, such as Robert William Pirsein, also sug-

gest that Eisenhower's approach to McCarthy enabled "the new Administration to fill the openings with its own choices," which may help explain why no administrative official came to the propaganda program's aid during the hearings. See Ambrose, *Eisenhower*, 64; and Pirsein, *The Voice of America*, 246.

84. Thomas Rosteck contends that Eisenhower's response to McCarthy "likely legitimated the Cold War paranoia of the McCarthy movement." See Rosteck, "The Case of Eisenhower," 90.

85. See Richard Hofstadter, "The Paranoid Style in American Politics," in *The Paranoid Style in American Politics and Other Essays*, ed. Richard Hofstadter (New York: Knopf, 1966), 3–6.

86. Information Centers hearing, 52, 56.

87. Information Centers hearing, 48, 50, 53.

88. See David Brion Davis, *The Slave Power Conspiracy and the Paranoid Style* (Baton Rouge: Louisiana State University Press, 1969), 29. Davis argues that the "image of an expansive, subversive force" can represent "individual and communal anxieties over being duped and slipping behind."

89. Information Centers hearing, 44, 50.

90. Rovere, *Senator Joe McCarthy*, 198.

91. Benton, "Europe and Senator McCarthy," 4.

92. For information on the effects of the McCarthy committee, see Laurien Alexandre, *The Voice of America: From Detente to the Reagan Doctrine* (Norwood, NJ: Ablex, 1988), 13; Ambrose, *Eisenhower*, 61; Dizard, *The Strategy of Truth*, 43; Fried, *Men Against McCarthy*, 258; Goldston, *The American Nightmare*, 122–123; Oshinsky, *A Conspiracy*, 278–284; Pirsein, *The Voice of America*, 246; Reeves, *The Life and Times*, 491; and Hans N. Tuch, *Communicating with the World: U.S. Public Diplomacy Overseas* (New York: St. Martin's Press, 1990), 18.

93. See Brendon, *Ike*, 276; and Griffith, *The Politics of Fear*, 196, 200.

6

Propaganda as a Presidential Tool in the Eisenhower White House

In addition to the McCarthy hearings that centered on the Voice of America and the information libraries discussed in chapter 5, there were other congressional and executive committees that investigated the U.S. government's propaganda and psychological warfare operations at the outset of the Eisenhower administration. To begin with, the Senate Foreign Relations Committee turned its attention to the propaganda program in November 1952 as well as in March and April 1953. These senators hoped to determine how best to make the peacetime propaganda program a more effective Cold War instrument.[1]

Accompanying the congressional hearings were two presidentially appointed committee investigations that greatly impacted the future of the propaganda program. While the scope of the first, the President's Advisory Committee on Government Reorganization (Rockefeller committee), extended beyond the practice of propaganda, it provided a major impetus for removing the program from the Department of State. The second, which Eisenhower called the President's Committee on International Information Activities (Jackson committee), centered exclusively on the propaganda program and suggested the most significant programmatic reforms. At the time of the investigation, the Eisenhower administration determined that "no publicity" should be given "to the [Jackson] Committee or its work,"[2] with the bulk of its recommendations remaining classified until the 1980s. Since then, however, it has become quite clear that the Jackson committee played a very significant role in the Eisenhower administration's entire approach to the Cold War. As Blanche Wiesen Cook argues, the committee's activities influenced "United States foreign policy for decades,"[3] particularly the role of propaganda in relation to U.S. foreign policy.

As this chapter shows, all of the investigations eventually helped bring about the establishment of the United States Information Agency (USIA) on August 1, 1953. This act removed the program from the Department of State and awarded propaganda a more prominent and permanent place in the foreign policy apparatus of the U.S. government. While the structure resembled its historical predecessors (e.g., the Committee for Public Information and the Office of War Information), it became much more central to the U.S. foreign policy mission during wartime *and* peacetime. Wilson P. Dizard maintains that the USIA's formation confirmed and cemented "the growing importance of popular persuasion in foreign policy."[4] As members of the Psychological Strategy Board (PSB) expressed in 1952, "nothing is more important to the President in a critical time of mounting international tensions when an accidental bombing could lead to war."[5]

It was not by accident nor is it surprising that propaganda blossomed under Eisenhower's tenure. During World War II, Eisenhower exhibited a keen interest in psychological operations—a devotion that grew out of Eisenhower's desire to avoid conventional warfare.[6] Eisenhower's commitment to propaganda extended to his appointment of career propagandist, C. D. Jackson, as special assistant to the president, as chief advisor on psychological strategy, and as presidential speech writer.[7]

While the conclusions reached by the Senate Foreign Relations Committee combined with the Rockefeller and McCarthy committees to inspire the independent status of the U.S. propaganda program, the Jackson committee encouraged the development of new *covert* Cold War strategies during the Eisenhower administration. Determined to rehabilitate the propaganda program from the attacks of the McCarthy committee and the problems of the Truman administration's propaganda tactics, this reorganization reduced the number of propaganda channels openly identified with the U.S. government and increased secret operations even beyond the clandestine actions of the Truman years. The propaganda program under Eisenhower thus became a more stable and institutionalized force in U.S. foreign policy. The USIA essentially became a "news" organization that masked the intricate and massive covert propaganda activities that were disassociated from the U.S. government. Unlike the Truman administration's use of the journalistic paradigm, the USIA sought to disseminate more straight news, devoid of the public relations tones of the Smith-Mundt years. Despite the journalistic appearance of the overt channels of propaganda, the entire program assumed a militarized structure. Such a propaganda pyramid of operations allowed Eisenhower to serve as commander-in-chief of the propaganda program, with the White House functioning as the central command post. In the end, this structure served to lessen outside congressional interference into a program that attracted so much attention during the previous six years; the restructuring likewise increased the rhetorical power of the presidency by giving the administration more control over the content of multiple media outlets.

ASSESSING THE STATUS OF THE U.S. PROPAGANDA PROGRAM

The Truman administration's propaganda program, despite its more centralized structure, continued to attract considerable criticism from members of Congress and the new executive branch for failing to achieve its high expectations. On February 19, 1951, Senators Alexander Wiley (R-WI) and William Benton (D-CT) called for yet another study of the propaganda program with Senate Resolution 74, which passed through Congress on June 30, 1952. The first of the Senate Foreign Relations' subcommittee hearings lasted only two days (November 20 and 21, 1952) under the chairmanship of Senator J. William Fulbright (D-AR), and centered on the executive branch of the program's operations. As part of its investigation, this subcommittee conducted on-the-spot examinations of certain propaganda operations abroad in a manner reminiscent of the 1947 Smith-Mundt fact-finding mission. The second phase of the Senate Foreign Relations' hearings achieved legislative authority on February 20, 1953, with the passage of Senate Resolution 44. The latter represented the Fulbright committee's recommendation to reconvene the subcommittee. Senator Bourke B. Hickenlooper (R-IA) chaired these more extended public hearings, which were designed to explore why "the program [was] not meeting the high expectations which [were] held out for it . . . [and] to recommend remedies."[8]

As the Hickenlooper committee conducted its public hearings, other political officials examined the propaganda program from behind the scenes, fulfilling Eisenhower's call for a reorganized and streamlined government. The Rockefeller committee, chaired by Nelson Rockefeller, became the first of the official committees to call for the separation of the propaganda program from the State Department. While the Rockefeller committee justified the need to separate the two programs, the actual discord over such a move was played out more publicly in the Hickenlooper committee. Some members of the Hickenlooper committee supported a separation of the two. Other committee members and witnesses, however, argued that the propaganda program be given a more independent status in the Department of State.

The Hickenlooper Committee

In its final report, the Hickenlooper committee identified the shortcomings of the propaganda program as well as potential remedies for such problems. While the committee located numerous problems, many centered around the lack of effective leadership emanating from the Department of State. Some of the problems were undoubtedly linked to the reluctance of many State Department officials to get involved in the business of propaganda in 1945 and the discord between the Departments of State and Defense that existed over the PSB's formation. According to the final report, "those who had observed the program in unofficial capacities generally expressed the view that the administrative needs of a hard-hitting, fast-moving information program could hardly be met within the confines of a cautious, tradition-bound, bureaucratic foreign office."[9] The Hickenlooper committee was supported in this conclusion by the U.S. Advisory Commission on Information, which received its authority from the Smith-Mundt Act to evaluate the propaganda program semiannually.[10] As cited in the final report of the Hickenlooper committee, the Advisory Commission argued that "too much time and effort on the part of IIA has been spent in attempting to fit the program into the structure of the Department and to convincing officials of its importance."[11] Mark A. May, chair of the Advisory Commission, testified before the Hickenlooper committee that the commission recommended taking the propaganda program out of the State Department in order to give "full recognition to . . . [the] use of propaganda as a major instrument for winning the cold war."[12]

Further critiques of the propaganda program were also offered. In a preliminary report given to members of the Jackson committee in April 1953, Carl Marcy, a staff consultant for the Hickenlooper committee, claimed that a clear consensus over the propaganda program's mission was lacking—a mission that the committee believed should center on "destroying communism." Committee members argued further that Congress directed the content of the propaganda too much, resulting in a propaganda that failed to meet the needs of targeted audiences. At that point in the committee's deliberations, members supported the split between the propaganda program and the State Department; the authors of the preliminary report asserted that the program was "too low in the Executive hierarchy . . . and lack[ed] prestige, even within the [State] Department"—a department that was "not set up to handle . . . the information program."[13]

Even though the impetus existed within the Hickenlooper committee to take the propaganda program out of the Department of State, not all concurred. William Benton, a strong advocate of the diplomatic branch, predictably supported the status quo. Benton, who testified before the Hickenlooper committee, provided an interesting twist to his justification for the existing structure, arguing that "the State Department need[ed] the information program" because of the credibility problems the former faced.[14] Senators Fulbright and Mundt also voiced their support for leaving the two programs intact, due in part to the fear that such a separation would cause the propaganda program to lose "prestige." The conflict over the issue clearly influenced the committee's final report. In the end, the Hickenlooper committee compromised and called for giving the propaganda program "greater autonomy within the Department of State for a trial period of 1 year; or establish[ing] it as a separate agency," with the "exchange of persons program" remaining in the State Department.[15] The Hickenlooper committee, however, was not the only group investigating the issue.

The Rockefeller Committee

While the Hickenlooper committee wavered on the issue of separation, the Rockefeller committee's final recommendations were much more decisive. On April 7, 1953, Rockefeller issued the final report on "foreign affairs organization" to President Eisenhower. Of the eight recommendations, two dealt exclusively with the U.S. propaganda program. The first centered on the Voice of America (VOA). Committee members called for the VOA to carry only "official United States' positions." The other recommendation concerned the establishment of a "new foreign information agency," which would "consolidate" information activities into a "new agency [that] would be established under the National Security Council." The justification of these recommendations was driven by the stated "imperative that all our material and intellectual resources and skills be harnessed to the formulation and execution of positive and effective efforts designed to achieve the National goals." The committee determined that such "foreign affairs organization" required much greater centralization and coordination; the "foreign information [propaganda] programs" were included in the charge.[16]

When the Rockefeller committee report was shared with members of the Psychological Strategy Board, they requested that the Jackson committee be fully apprised of the conclusions. Members of the PSB urged that final action of the Rockefeller report be delayed until after the Jackson committee completed its own review.[17] In the end, the conclusions reached by both the Hickenlooper and the Rockefeller committees were turned over to the

Jackson committee, whose conclusions propagandist Thomas C. Sorensen called, the most "thorough" and "perceptive" of the major committees investigating the program.[18]

The Jackson Committee

As defined by Eisenhower's presidential directive, the Jackson committee was empowered to evaluate "international information policies and activities" as they related to "international relations and the national security" of the United States. Named for its chair, New York businessman and former CIA deputy director, William Jackson,[19] the eight-member committee began its inquiry on January 26, 1953, and issued its final report on June 1.[20] During the six-month study that was financially funded by the CIA, committee members interviewed some 250 witnesses and advocated the abolition of Truman's Psychological Strategy Board. In its place, the Jackson committee called for the establishment of an Operations Coordinating Board (OCB) to coordinate national security policy and psychological operations (i.e., to continue the work of the PSB, albeit with greater coordination).[21]

As this section demonstrates, one of the Jackson committee's major conclusions was that the U.S. propaganda program under Truman suffered from a lack of centralized leadership that resulted in confusion over the program's mission. Calling on Eisenhower to take control of the nation's propaganda activities, the committee recommended that all propaganda policies originate from the White House, evidencing the committee's desire to expand presidential-rhetorical powers. Such a move would serve not only to clarify the agency's mission, but also to elevate the significance of propaganda in the government's overall foreign policy structure. For the Jackson committee, propaganda needed to be coordinated with all other governmental policies and actions, reflecting the move toward *institutionalizing* a militarized propaganda program.

Critiquing Truman's Propaganda Program

Like the PSB and, thus, the Truman administration, the Jackson committee worked from the premise that the Soviet rulers sought "world domination." But while committee members believed a threat of war existed, they predicted that "the Soviet rulers" wanted "to avoid general war" because of the threat of "atomic attack." The committee concluded that the Soviets would rely heavily on "political warfare" as their major weapon in the Cold War—a perpetuation of the Hate America campaign.[22]

Similarly to the PSB, the Jackson committee also recognized the communists' skill in political warfare and the appeal of communist ideals. Committee members maintained that the "communist ideology" possessed "significant appeal to many people," especially those who were "underprivileged, discriminated against . . . and whose religious faith or loyalty to existing institutions" was severed. Because of this appeal, members of the committee urged that the American public be braced for a "protracted conflict" since the Soviet system did not appear to be on the brink of "collapse or drastic alteration."[23]

Even though the Jackson committee recognized the power of the country's Cold War opponent, its members felt confident that the United States and the free world could, with considerable effort and time, win the Cold War. The Jackson committee called for the "free world, under the United States leadership," to band together and "agree on general objectives" to "carry out common policies." The Jackson committee considered psychological warfare to be a primary weapon for the United States in the "war of words."[24] As the Jackson committee report revealed, its members envisioned a conflict that pitted propagandist against propagandist, with the most keen strategists claiming victory in the end.

In its assessment of the Truman administration's propaganda efforts, the Jackson committee complained that the role of propaganda had been subordinated to the other arms of that administration's foreign policy apparatus. In a letter to President Eisenhower, Jackson committee members urged that "psychological activity [was] not a field . . . separable from the main body of diplomatic, economic, and military measures. . . . It [was] an ingredient of such measures."[25] This view was explained further in a White House press release on July 8, 1953, which acknowledged the receipt of the Jackson committee report. According to press secretary James C. Hagerty, former propaganda agents presumed that "'psychological strategy' somehow exist[ed] apart from official policies and actions and [could] be dealt with independently by experts in this field." Instead, Hagerty reported, the Jackson committee believed "a 'psychological' aspect or implication [existed for] every diplomatic, economic, or military policy and action."[26]

Identifying further problems with Truman's program, the Jackson committee charged that "opportunities had been missed to take the offensive in global propaganda campaigns." Many of the current and past programs, committee members believed, had been "merely defensive." Beyond that, committee members complained that "the United States [had spoken] with a multitude of voices," resulting in a "haphazard projection of too many and too diffuse propaganda themes." Still yet, the committee concluded that Truman's propaganda program suffered from a severe credibility problem because the information served "little use for . . . foreign audience[s]," who were "quick to take offense at advice and exhortation received from abroad."[27]

The Jackson committee's conclusions, of course, must be contextualized in the politics of a presidential transition of power. Although the PSB declared that greater "coordination and integration" of psychological warfare operations were needed between the "overt and covert" activities,[28] the Truman administration and the PSB undoubtedly disagreed with other claims emanating from this presidentially appointed committee—claims that served the ends of the Eisenhower administration's reorganization strategies. Despite the partisan nature of the committee, their critiques nevertheless provided the impetus for reorganizing the propaganda program.[29]

Centralizing Propaganda Strategy in the White House

The Jackson committee determined that in order to overcome the existing problems, revisions were necessitated. First, committee members concluded that U.S. propaganda needed more direction "from the President."[30] In order to achieve that end, the Jackson committee called for the program to be centralized in the White House under the direction of the presidentially controlled National Security Council (NSC): "This proposal involves the claims that the propaganda function, like the military and economic, is sufficiently different from diplomacy to warrant separate administration; propaganda should serve national policy which is made by the member departments of NSC rather than the State Department."[31] Even more than the Truman administration, the Jackson committee's philosophy furthered the militarization of the program by connecting it to the presidency rather than to the diplomatic arm of the U.S. government. The Jackson committee thus envisioned that the U.S. propaganda program would function to proliferate presidential pronouncements,[32] evidencing greater synchronization between propaganda strategy and the foreign policies of the executive branch.

Beyond centralizing propaganda strategy, the Jackson committee proposed that the U.S. propaganda program assume one central goal. This goal included the strengthening of international support for the country's foreign policy aims: "To persuade foreign peoples that it lies in their own interest to take actions which are also consistent with the national objectives of the United States. The goal should be to harmonize wherever possible the personal and national self-interest of foreigners with the national objectives of the United States."[33] C. D. Jackson, a member of the PSB, explained the need to convince "men and women throughout the world on both sides of the Iron Curtain . . . to believe that what we are, and what we stand for in the world, *is consistent with their own aspirations.*"[34]

A key ingredient of the Jackson committee's plan involved gathering information about target audiences. A Jackson committee document concerning the "Study Center for People's Psychology in the Communist Dominated Countries," called for U.S. propagandists to "watch and study the existing trends, attitudes toward various problems, and [the] morale" of foreign audiences. Similarly, the committee asked for program officials to discover the "essential needs, [and] aspirations" of international peoples as well as their "attitudes toward Communist rule . . . [and] toward the Western world." The report stipulated further that propaganda agents needed to find out "what captive people find attractive," and what they consider to be "boring," "theoretical," and "irritating."[35] Because people "resent being told what to think," a June 22, 1953, "Memorandum on Radio in Psychological Warfare" determined that U.S. propagandists needed to provide foreign audiences with the kind of information they desired. The authors of the report concluded: "The art of persuasion is to give him what he wants so truthfully and so skillfully as to influence his thinking in the process."[36]

One of the most significant changes that the Jackson committee called for involved a decrease in the use of official propaganda channels. The committee recommended "that short-wave broadcasts be discontinued" in some areas, that the wireless bulletin be continued only in areas that "express[ed] a desire for its retention," and that fewer pamphlets, magazines, and films carry the official seal of the U.S. government. Such an organizational change stemmed from the belief that "the sheer volume of material bearing the American label [was] harmful."[37]

The committee also requested that the tone of propaganda be altered. Like the political officials of the Smith-Mundt debate, the Jackson committee members maintained that the program under Eisenhower needed to disseminate "truth." According to the committee members, "To be effective, [propaganda] must be dependable, convincing, and truthful . . . [because] too much or too blatant propaganda can be harmful."[38] In order for the material to assume a more explicit aura of "truth," the Jackson committee concluded that the official channels should disseminate more "straight news," reflecting a return to a more journalistic paradigm for the overt propaganda channels. Committee members argued further that the VOA should broadcast more "objective, factual news" that served as a "source of truth and information about world events." For the committee, the defining characteristic of these channels became the distribution of material "for which the United States Government [was] prepared to accept responsibility,"[39] a criterion that relied on the ideological perception of a free and objective press.

Along with broadcasting "news," the Jackson committee called for a more positive tone in the propaganda officially identified with the U.S. government. Because the committee believed that the propaganda of Truman's Campaign of Truth had been too "defensive,"[40] committee members wanted the program to accentuate the "positive" by emphasizing how the United States was "creating conditions of freedom and happiness . . . for human beings." Yet the boastful propaganda of the Smith-Mundt era was likewise to be avoided. Such a focus, C. D. Jackson maintained, would help the United States achieve its own "interests and aspirations" as well as the interests and aspirations of "men and women everywhere." This process, though, did not preclude the program from "making dignified, forceful, and factual refutations of Soviet accusations."[41] Such propaganda, which relied on a journalistic paradigm, would become the front for the more secretive psychological warfare operations.

Even though the Jackson committee wanted the revised propaganda program to accentuate the positive aspects of democracy, committee members believed the U.S. government should still combat communist lies forcefully. The Jackson committee, though, relegated the dissemination of more polemical propaganda to the "private" agencies. Within its study, the Jackson committee advocated that "all material intended for purposes of political warfare against the Soviet regime . . . be diverted to Radio Liberation [Liberty] or other non-official stations."[42] Such a move required an increase in federal support to be diverted to the sponsors of Radio Free Europe (RFE) and Radio Liberty (RL). Such funds then would help hire "Soviet nationals" to disperse propaganda designed to "weaken the Soviet regime," a practice that reconstituted the use of defector propaganda discussed in chapter 4. The committee recommended not destroying RFE's "cover" so that it could continue taking "positions for which the United States would not desire to accept responsibility."[43]

"Exploitation" surfaced as the defining characteristic for the Jackson committee's vision of psychological warfare. First, the committee stipulated that "by helping to expose the true nature of communist activities, by penetrating, undermining, dividing . . . [and] hampering its access to funds, the basic weakness of the apparatus [could] be exploited." The committee also advised the nonofficial agencies to manipulate "the gap between communist ideology and Soviet practice" and to accentuate that the Soviet Union represented an "aggressive power seeking to dominate" all countries. Beyond that, the committee wanted these "private" agencies to emphasize "the failure of the communist regimes to live up to their promises." Such a tactic reflected the Truman administration's use of defector propaganda to inspirit insurrections. Thus, the Jackson committee wanted the Eisenhower administration to force the Soviets into "a course [of action] favorable to the United States."[44]

Although the Jackson committee focused its energies on elevating the reputation of the U.S. propaganda program abroad, committee members also concerned themselves with the program's reputation at home. Members of the committee accentuated the constraints imposed on the practice of propaganda in democratic societies. The committee reasoned that unlike the Soviet government, which could "conduct its affairs with a minimum regard for public opinion," free societies required "wide understanding and support for [their] policies."[45] Committee members thus sought to institute an astute propaganda program that would attract the domestic political support necessary for its implementation and success abroad.

The need for such domestic support mounted especially in the wake of McCarthy's investigations. In an apparent reference to McCarthy's allegations, the Jackson committee claimed that the "foreign information program" had been "harassed and assaulted by criticism . . . which [was] inaccurate, unfair and destructive." As a result, the Jackson committee maintained that "public understanding and support of the program" was even more "vital." The committee recommended the release of information to the American public about the program—a practice previously outlawed by the Smith-Mundt Act.[46] The committee justified such alterations on the grounds that "the security of the United States [could] not be achieved in isolation," and the propaganda program served as part of the government's overall international policy.[47]

The Jackson committee also called for the president to institute greater coordination and strategic planning of messages delivered to the American people in order to fulfill international propaganda aims. The committee believed the presidential administration needed to consider the "impact" of its "public statements" "upon other nations of the free world, particularly in Europe." The committee advised, for example, that a "delicate" balance be "struck between providing the American people with information that [would] permit them to grasp . . . the basic realities of the world, [while] driving more vulnerable and therefore nervous allies into neutralism."[48]

Indeed, the Jackson committee viewed propaganda as the key instrument for the United States in its battle against the Soviet Union. While committee members saw communism as a powerful threat to democratic ideals, the conflict was depicted in such a way that democracy would prevail. Like the Hickenlooper and Rockefeller committees, the Jackson committee members believed that tactically sound foreign policies supported by an effective propaganda machine, could prove the winning combination in the "war of words" with the Soviet Union. But in order for the program to achieve heightened effectiveness, such propaganda strategies needed greater synchronization from, and centralization in, the White House. Eisenhower clearly agreed with the committee's assumptions and recommendations and, in fact, began implementing them even before the United States Information Agency (USIA) was officially formed.

THE USIA AND THE "VOICE" OF THE PRESIDENCY

Like the Jackson committee members, Dwight D. Eisenhower regarded communism as a major threat and thus led his administration on an expansive and longitudinal campaign against it.[49] This section shows how the Eisenhower administration implemented the recommendations of the congressional and presidential committees. Upon the advice of the Jackson and Rockefeller committees, Eisenhower's new propaganda program, the USIA, was established on August 1, 1953, as an independent agency, separate from the propaganda operations of the State Department. Directed from the White House, with the commander-in-chief assuming more responsibility in the agency's day-to-day and long-range plans, the USIA centralized U.S. propaganda operations and cultivated the ethos of a "news" agency. The intent was for the USIA to disseminate "positive" material while relegating the more strident propaganda to the covert channels. Even though the aggressive psychological warfare materials would not bear the official seal of the U.S. government, the Eisenhower administration would strictly control and coordinate the entire propaganda program, demonstrating the institutionalization of a militarized propaganda structure, complete with overt and covert operations. As the Eisenhower administration gained control over an enhanced communication system, the rhetorical influence of the president likewise expanded to include the covert messages as well as the use of presidential-rhetorical surrogates.

When the USIA was established, agency officials were directed to "report to the President through the National Security Council."[50] The OCB was set up as an extension of the NSC and functioned to ensure that the plans developed by the NSC and the president were enacted rather than filed away.[51] The mission of the OCB and the NSC was articulated publicly in a press release concerning the newly restructured propaganda program. In a July 8, 1953, memo to the press, Hagerty explained in broad terms that the OCB, which "coordinate[d] . . . national security policies," would help further what Eisenhower called the "reconstitution and revitalization of the National Security Council." For the Eisenhower administration, the OCB existed to coordinate USIA plans with those of the Departments of State and Defense as well as the CIA.[52] Membership of the OCB consisted of the undersecretary of state (chair), the deputy secretary of defense, the deputy director for Mutual Security, the director of the CIA, and a special assistant to the president, an integrated constituency that reflected, in part, the design of the PSB. The president, of course, was empowered to appoint a chief executive officer of the OCB.[53] In order to enhance complete coordination, the secretary of state was required to provide "full guidance" to USIA's director on issues of "foreign policy."[54]

Under Eisenhower's organizational design, the president served as the commander-in-chief and the secretary of state was designated as Eisenhower's "channel of authority within the executive branch on matters of foreign policy."[55] The NSC and the OCB served as Eisenhower's liaison with the USIA, which continued to receive directives concerning propaganda's content from the Department of State. Despite its independent structure, the USIA was answerable to the president and the Department of State. The president now assumed more authority over the program than during the Truman years, and congressional oversight was likewise lessened.

Even though many of these recommendations originated from the Rockefeller and Jackson committees, Eisenhower clearly advocated such a militarized apparatus—a view that undoubtedly influenced the mindset of both committees. In a preliminary document on the reorganization of government, Eisenhower advocated that "a clear line of responsibility" be established with "adequate authority . . . for all operations, so [that] the people will always know who is responsible for carrying out any particular job." Eisenhower also threatened to replace any administrator who "fail[ed] to perform" his grand plans.[56] With reference to foreign policy planning, Eisenhower especially wanted to ensure secrecy among his executive departments (e.g., the OCB and the NSC), and to mask his involvement with the OCB. His influence was to be preserved through his trusted advisor, C. D. Jackson, who functioned as Eisenhower's "Gordan Gray."[57] To that end, Eisenhower structured issues of foreign policy in such a way so as to heighten executive power and to lessen congressional control. Stephen F. Knott maintains that this action did not really disturb members of Congress. As Knott asserts, "America's Cold War legislators let the executive branch do its job" because of the "bipartisan support for the Cold War."[58]

Despite Knott's contentions, the degree of congressional support for the executive-controlled foreign policy apparatus must be questioned, especially given the minimal knowledge Congress had of Eisenhower's covert actions. The structure that Eisenhower established under NSC-5412/1–2 gave his administration full license to conduct foreign policy with little congressional oversight. With NSC-5412, Eisenhower called for "the overt foreign activities of the U.S. Government" to be "supplemented by covert operations," which NSC-5412 defined as: "propaganda, political action; economic warfare; preventive direct action, including sabotage, anti-sabotage, demolition; escape and evasion and evacuation measures; subversion against hostile states or groups . . . support of anti-communist elements . . . ; deception plans and operations; and all activities compatible with this directive necessary to accomplish the foregoing." Grounded in the legislative authority of the National Security Act of 1947, NSC-5412 empowered the CIA to conduct these covert operations according to NSC guidance. Eisenhower also involved the OCB by making this group the "normal channel for securing coordination of support among the Departments of State and Defense and the Central Intelligence Agency."[59] As Elmer B. Staats, OCB's first executive officer, declared, OCB existed to ensure the "coordinated implementation of national security policies approved by the President." Its executive status led the OCB to determine that "there [was] no need for . . . publiciz[ing] the OCB outside of the executive branch" because of the "many difficulties [that] could arise." [60]

Through the NSC, Eisenhower enhanced presidential involvement in psychological warfare planning.[61] NSC-5412 designated a planning group to oversee such CIA-initiated operations, which included presidentially appointed individuals from the Departments of State and Defense and other presidentially selected representatives.[62] As John Prados asserts, NSC-5412 awarded these "secret warriors with the broadest possible charter." While Eisenhower maintained close contact with the "5412 group," he also wanted to preserve his "deniability" by not participating with the group's activities directly.[63] The term deniability epitomized this 5412 group. Eisenhower wanted the U.S. government to "plausibly disclaim any responsibility" for such covert actions just as the Jackson committee recommended.[64]

The Eisenhower administration's reorganization plan also brought changes to the overt aspects of the propaganda program. To begin with, the VOA's headquarters moved from New York to Washington, D.C. so as to ensure tighter coordination of its operations. The USIA's new director, Theodore S. Streibert, cut positions as part of the president's "reduction-in-force" efforts, which meant the departure of some employees who were viewed as security risks—a legacy of McCarthy's investigations (chapter 5). In the first year, the USIA experienced a 36 percent reduction in total operating funds and a 25 percent reduction in personnel.[65]

Even though the overt activities were streamlined, the USIA's role in the overall stature of U.S. foreign policy was elevated. Such an enhanced position led to a marked change in the tone of the overt broadcasts. According to a "Progress Report" by the OCB dated September 30, 1953, USIA's broadcasts were to "present a full exposition of the United States actions and policies."[66] The OCB determined that while "the tone and content should be forceful and direct," a "propagandist note should be avoided." In order to cultivate the credibility of a "news" agency, the OCB determined that the VOA should "consist of factual news reporting supplemented by commentaries designed to provide sober and responsible interpretations of events . . . policies . . . and actions of the United States."[67] In a letter to William Benton on May 1, 1953, Eisenhower explained that this more "careful regard for the truth" would result in the USIA becoming more "respected and trusted throughout the world."[68]

In furthering its reorganizational efforts, the Eisenhower administration expanded the polemical, psychological warfare materials just as the Jackson committee prescribed. These more secretive operations were also keenly coordinated with the overt actions. As Eisenhower directed, "clandestine arrangements" needed to be made with "magazines, newspapers . . . and book publishers in some countries" to supplant official propaganda operations.[69] According to the PSB, which existed for some seven months under Eisenhower before being transformed into the OCB, the USIA was to attribute propaganda to the United States only when "such attribution" functioned as an "asset." At the same time, more "private American organizations" (e.g., RFE and RL) were to be used for the advancement of U.S. "objectives."[70] Eisenhower thus diverted part of his administration's propaganda efforts from the VOA to the "covert" mediums that were not publicly connected to the USIA.

Yet before the VOA, RFE, and RL could compete effectively within the word war against communism, the Eisenhower administration had to contend with the effects of Soviet jamming operations. Before 1951, the only radio signals that were disrupted by the Soviets included those sent out by the BBC and the VOA in the Russian language. By 1952, Soviet jamming efforts were so widespread that much of the material beamed from the West to the iron curtain region met with significant radio interference. Throughout the early part of 1953, the NSC studied the jamming issue, which produced NSC-169 of October 27, 1953. To begin with, the NSC recommended that the OCB coordinate the phases of NSC-169 through the establishment of the Technical Panel on International Broadcasting (TPIB). The TPIB's mission involved the implementation of "policies, programs or activities intended to improve the technical management and over-all effectiveness of American official or unofficial broadcasting operations."[71]

Problematizing Soviet jamming operations was integral to the Jackson committee's mission of developing global propaganda campaigns that promulgated the discourse of the president. Such campaigns were to be directed toward those persons capable of effecting change, centering on presidential addresses delivered from the bully pulpit. The PSB also called for a major effort to force Soviet leaders into "difficult decisions of policy," and recommended that the propaganda program "press a clear and fresh vision of American purposes on the Soviet and satellite peoples" so they would "associate their aspirations" with those of the United States. In addition to the anticommunist strategies, the PSB sought to unify "the Free World around positive and sustained efforts to seek the peace," while providing "a new and more firm base within the United States for the pursuit of American interests and objectives." In the end, the U.S. propaganda program was to become the center for a "psychological warfare offensive" against the Soviet Union. This move would involve the exploitation of all available propaganda channels in the process of explicating the "meaning and purposes" of presidential "initiatives" and "objectives."[72] Such directives would be developed and orchestrated by the PSB-turned-OCB and represented a notable expansion of the rhetorical presidency.

Such strategies were to be integrated with an expansion of the PSB/OCB's Doctrinal Warfare Program. Initiated by the Truman administration in 1952 (see chapter 4), the PSB studied the prospects of doctrinal warfare and issued its report in March 1953. The PSB, and especially Edward P. Lilly who chaired the investigation, called for the expansion of the Doctrinal Warfare Program so as to promulgate "systematic, analytical attacks on the doctrinal bases of communism, objectively exposing its contradictions and vagaries" while accentuating "the spirit and philosophy of American and Western life." As part of the mission for the Doctrinal Warfare Program, Lilly and the PSB called for a small group to be formed that would work closely with the PSB/OCB and the president's assistant for psychological operations in order to implement doctrinal warfare policies reliant on books and periodicals.[73]

In the final analysis, then, when the Eisenhower administration created the USIA and the OCB, it centralized all propaganda and psychological warfare activities in a manner characteristic of military operations. While granting the agency its independence from the State Department, Eisenhower assumed more control over its activities—implanting his military structure on the executive branch. To that end, to call the USIA an independent agency is somewhat of a misnomer, given the control exerted over it by Eisenhower through his presidentially directed groups such as the PSB/OCB. This centralization process resulted in increased direction from the White House over the U.S. message, making the USIA and the nonofficial propaganda mediums instruments of the president. Toward that end, Eisenhower's rhetorical powers and the covert channels extended beyond the bully pulpit to include messages delivered by rhetorical surrogates over overt and covert propaganda media. The overt channels were connected to the VOA and were charged with promulgating the president's voice and his foreign policy themes in an open manner. The administration, though, turned the more strident propaganda, some of which permeated the airways of the VOA under the Campaign of Truth, over to the covert agencies. As the Jackson committee recommended, the Voice of America spoke with the "authority of the United States Government," while stations such as Radio Free Europe and Radio Liberty could purport "to be the voice of the freedom forces of the respective target countries."[74] These latter stations would likewise showcase Eisenhower's propaganda campaign themes surreptitiously through surrogate voices reflective of Truman's defector propaganda; refugees and nonrecognizable government propagandists personified and proliferated the anticommunist ideology in support of the Doctrinal Warfare Program and Eisenhower's bully-pulpit messages. All of these strategies were designed to increase U.S. credibility abroad and to increase substantially the messages supporting Eisenhower's Cold War strategies.

Such overt actions masked all of the psychological warfare activities that were taking place behind the scenes. Most noticeably, the Eisenhower administration and its authorized groups managed to coordinate the overt and covert propaganda activities more completely than the Truman administration. Such processes involved the construction and synchronization of broad-based propaganda offensives that featured major presidential addresses as the centerpieces of grand and ubiquitous propaganda campaigns.

NOTES

1. See Robert William Pirsein, *The Voice of America: An History of the International Broadcasting Activities of the United States Government, 1940–1962* (New York: Arno Press, 1979), 273–292, 313–326.

2. "Appraisal Survey of Our Cold War Effort," November 26, 1952, U.S. President's Committee on International Information Activities (Jackson Committee): Records, 1950–1953, Box 1, Dwight D. Eisenhower Presidential Library (hereafter cited as DDEPL).

3. Blanche Wiesen Cook, *The Declassified Eisenhower: A Divided Legacy* (Garden City, NY: Doubleday, 1981), 176.

4. Wilson P. Dizard, *The Strategy of Truth: The Story of the U.S. Information Service* (Washington, D.C.: Public Affairs Press, 1961), 41, 44.

5. Major Bennett to Mr. Johnson, Psychological Strategy Board, November, 1952, White House Office, NSC Staff: Papers, 1953–1961, PSB Central Files Series, Box 23, DDEPL, 2.

6. For more discussion on Eisenhower's interest in propaganda, see Fitzhugh Green, *American Propaganda Abroad* (New York: Hippocrene Books, 1988), 28; and Rhodri Jeffreys-Jones, *The CIA and American Democracy* (New Haven, CT: Yale University Press, 1989), 85.

7. C. D. Jackson served as Eisenhower's psychological warfare chief in North Africa during World War II. While in this position, Jackson acted as the supreme authority over the Office of War Information in that region. From 1951 through 1952, Jackson served as president of Radio Free Europe. See Chester J. Pach, Jr. and Elmo Richardson, *The Presidency of Dwight D. Eisenhower* (Lawrence: University Press of Kansas, 1991, 1979), 38; Robert J. Donovan, *Eisenhower: The Inside Story* (New York: Harper and Brothers, 1956), 40, 184; Green, *American Propaganda Abroad*, 29; Jeffreys-Jones, *The CIA and American Democracy*, 86–94; Lawrence C. Soley, *Radio Warfare: OSS and CIA Subversive Propaganda* (New York: Praeger, 1989), 94. For additional information on C. D. Jackson's papers at the Dwight D. Eisenhower Presidential Library, see David Haight, "The Papers of C. D. Jackson: A Glimpse at President Eisenhower's Psychological Warfare Expert," *Manuscript* 28 (1976): 27–37.

8. See Pirsein, *The Voice of America*, 314; Senate Committee on Foreign Relations, *Overseas Information Programs of the United States*, 82d Cong., 2d sess., 1952, 1; and Senate Committee on Foreign Relations, *Overseas Information Programs of the United States*, 83rd Cong., 1st sess., 1953, 229–230.

9. Senate Committee on Foreign Relations, *Overseas Information Programs of the United States*, 83rd Cong., 1st sess., 1953, S. Rept. 406, 8.

10. House Committee on Foreign Affairs, *United States Information and Educational Exchange Act of 1948*, 80th Cong., 2d sess., 1948, H. Rept. 3342, 1014.

11. Senate Committee on Foreign Relations, 1953, S. Rept. 406, 8. See also U.S. Department of State, *Launching the Campaign of Truth, 2nd Phase* (Washington, D.C.: Office of Public Affairs, 1951), 1–50.

12. Senate Committee on Foreign Relations, 1953, 357–358.

13. Staff Memorandum No. 8, April, 1953, "Criticisms and Suggestions on the Overseas Information Program," U.S. President's Committee on International Information Activities (Jackson Committee): Records, 1950–1953, Box 11, DDEPL, 1, 37, 42–43.

14. Senate Committee on Foreign Relations, 1953, 806.

15. Senate Committee on Foreign Relations, 1953, S. Rept. 406, 23–25.

16. "President's Advisory Committee on Government Organization's Report," April, 1953, White House Central Files, 1953–1961, Official File, Box 460, DDEPL, 1–2, 11–13.

17. Walter B. Smith to George A. Morgan, April, 1953, White House Office, NCS Staff: Papers, 1953–1961, PSB Central Files Series, Box 23, DDEPL, 1.

18. Thomas C. Sorensen, *The Word War: The Story of American Propaganda* (New York: Harper & Row, 1968), 42.

19. See Dwight D. Eisenhower to James S. Lay, Jr., January 24, 1953, U.S. President's Committee on International Information Activities (Jackson Committee): Records, 1950–1953, Box 1, DDEPL. See also John Prados, *Presidents' Secret Wars: CIA and Pentagon Covert Operations since World War II* (New York: William Morrow, 1986), 84.

20. The seven other members of the Jackson committee included: C. D. Jackson, Eisenhower's special assistant; Gordon Gray, ex-Army secretary; John C. Hughes, National Committee for a Free Europe; Sigurd Larmon, president of Young and Rubicam; Robert Cutler, special assistant to the president for national security affairs; Berklie McKee Henry, director of corporations and institutions; Roger M. Keyes, undersecretary of defense; and Abbott Washburn, the appointed executive secretary of the Jackson Committee. See Pirsein, *The Voice of America*, 318–319.

21. See James S. Lay, Jr., January 27, 1953, Memorandum for the National Security Council, White House Office, NSC Staff: Papers, 1953–1961, PSB Central Files Series, PSB 334 PCIIA, Box 22, DDEPL, 1; List of Jackson Committee Witnesses, n.d., U.S. President's Committee on International Information Activities (Jackson Committee): Records, 1950–1953, Box 11, DDEPL. See also Tentative List of Witnesses and/or Interviews, n.d., U.S. President's Committee on International Information Activities (Jackson Committee): Records, 1950–1953, Box 11, DDEPL, 1–10; and John W. Henderson, *The United States Information Agency* (New York: Praeger, 1969), 51.

22. "The President's Committee on International Information Activities: Report to the President," June 30, 1953, U.S. President's Committee on International Information Activities (Jackson Committee): Records, 1950–1953, Box 14, DDEPL, 1, 4, 8. (Hereafter cited as the Jackson Committee Report.)

23. Jackson Committee Report, 10, 11, 17.

24. Jackson Committee Report, 17.

25. The Jackson Committee to President Eisenhower, June 30, 1953, The Jackson Committee Report, U.S. President's Committee on International Information Activities (Jackson Committee): Records, 1950–1953, Box 14, DDEPL.

26. Press Release on the Jackson Committee Report, July 8, 1953, C. D. Jackson Papers: 1931–1967, Box 52, DDEPL, 3.

27. Jackson Committee Report, 56–60.

28. "Organizational Changes in the Field of Psychological Strategy under the New Administration," November, 1952, National Security Council Staff: Papers, 1953–1961, PSB Central Files Series, Box 23, DDEPL, 1–2.

29. Walter L. Hixson claimed that "the PSB failed to achieve its 'manifest destiny' of uniting the national security bureaucracy behind a coordinated psychological warfare that would force the retrenchment of Soviet power." See Walter L. Hixson, *Parting the Curtain: Propaganda, Culture, and the Cold War, 1945–1961* (New York: St. Martin's Griffin, 1998), 18–19.

30. Jackson Committee Report, 58, 106.

31. Jackson Committee Report, 99.

32. For more on how the propaganda program furthered Eisenhower's Cold War campaigns, see J. Michael Hogan, "Eisenhower and Open Skies: A Case Study in Psychological Warfare," in *Eisenhower's War of Words: Rhetoric and Leadership*, ed. Martin J. Medhurst (East Lansing: Michigan State University Press, 1994), 137–155.

33. Jackson Committee Report, 75.

34. Speech by C. D. Jackson before the National Security Commission and Committees of the American Legion, August 28, 1953, C. D. Jackson Papers: 1934–1967, Box 82, DDEPL, 7–8 (emphasis in original).

35. "The Study Center for People's Psychology in the Communist Dominated Countries," December, 1952, U.S. President's Committee on International Information Activities (Jackson Committee): Records, 1950–1953, Box 1, DDEPL, 2.

36. "Memorandum on Radio in Psychological Warfare," June 22, 1953, White House Central Files, 1953–1961, Confidential File, Box 61, DDEPL, 8–9.

37. Jackson Committee Report, 68, 73, 71.

38. Jackson Committee Report, 55–56.

39. Jackson Committee Report, 34, 36.

40. Jackson Committee Report, 68.

41. Speech by C. D. Jackson before the National Security Commission and Committees of the American Legion, 3; and Jackson Committee Report, 68.

42. Jackson Committee Report, 76, 35.

43. Jackson Committee Report, 39–40, 41–43.

44. Jackson Committee Report, 11–12, 17.

45. Jackson Committee Report, 11–12, 17.

46. See John W. Henderson, *The United States Information Agency* (New York: Praeger, 1969), 41.

47. Jackson Committee Report, 105, 77, 64, 5.

48. Jackson Committee Report, 104.

49. Cook, *The Declassified Eisenhower*, vi, xxi.

50. James C. Hagerty, June, 1953, Press Release, White House Central Files, 1953–1961, Official File, Box 461, DDEPL, 3.

51. Fred I. Greenstein, *The Hidden-Hand Presidency: Eisenhower as Leader* (New York: Basic Books, 1982), 133.

52. James C. Hagerty, July 8, 1953, Press Release, U.S. President's Committee on International Information Activities (Jackson Committee): Records, 1950–1953, Box 52, DDEPL, 2–3.

53. Bryon K. Enyart to George A. Morgan, July 29, 1953, White House Office, NSC Staff: Papers, 1953–1961, PSB Central Files Series, PSB 040 USIA, Box 10, DDEPL, 1.

54. Hagerty, Press Release, July 8, 1953, 3.

55. Dwight D. Eisenhower to All Executive Departments and the Director for Mutual Security, June, 1953, White House Central Files, 1953–1961, Official File, Box 461, DDEPL, 1.

56. Dwight D. Eisenhower, March, 1953, Draft of Reorganization Plans, White House Central Files, 1953–1961, Official File, Box 460, DDEPL, 1–2. See also National Security Council Meeting, July, 1953, Papers as President of the United States, 1953–1961 (Ann Whitman File), NSC Series, Box 4, DDEPL, 17.

57. See National Security Council Meeting, 17; and Robert Cutler to the Psychological Strategy Board, September 3, 1953, White House Office, NSC Staff:

Papers, 1948–1961, Executive Secretary, Subject Files Series, OCB, Box 14, DDEPL, 1.

58. Stephen F. Knott, *Secret and Sanctioned: Covert Operations and the American Presidency* (New York: Oxford University Press, 1996), 163.

59. National Security Council 5412, March, 1954, National Security Council Directive on Covert Operations, White House Office, Office of Special Assistant for National Security Affairs: Records, 1952–1961, NSC Series, Policy Papers Subseries, Box 10, DDEPL, 1–3. See also National Security Council 5412/1, March, 1955, White House Office of Special Series for National Security Affairs: Presidential Subseries, Box 2, DDEPL, 1–3; and National Security Council 5412/2, December, 1955, White House Office of Special Subseries for National Security Affairs: Presidential Subseries, Box 2, DDEPL, 1–3.

60. Elmer B. Staats, January 3, 1955, Memorandum for the Operations Coordinating Board, White House Office, NSC Staff: Papers, 1948–1961, OCB Central Files Series, OCB 334.OCB, Box 99, DDEPL, 1.

61. See Christopher Andrew, *For the President's Eyes Only: Secret Intelligence and the American Presidency from Washington to Bush* (New York: Harper Collins, 1995), 3–4; and Michael McClintock, *Instruments of Statecraft: U.S. Guerilla Warfare, Counter-Insurgency, and Counter-Terrorism, 1945–1990* (New York: Pantheon, 1992), 137, 161.

62. National Security Council 5412/2, 3.

63. Prados, *Presidents' Secret Wars*, 112.

64. National Security Council 5412/2, 2.

65. See Green, *American Propaganda Abroad*, 30–31; and Pirsein, *The Voice of America*, 328–330.

66. "Progress Report to the National Security Council on Implementation of the Recommendations of the Jackson Committee Report," September 30, 1953, White House Central Files, 1953–1961, Psychological Strategy Board, Box 22, DDEPL, 8.

67. "Progress Report to the National Security Council on Implementation of the Recommendations of the Jackson Committee Report," Annex A, 1.

68. Dwight Eisenhower to William Benton, May, 1953, D. D. E. Diary Series, Box 3, DDEPL, 1–2.

69. Eisenhower to Benton, May, 1953, 1–2.

70. "Progress Report to the National Security Council on Implementation of the Recommendations of the Jackson Committee Report," Annex A, 1, 4.

71. NSC-169, October 27, 1953, Electro-Magnetic Communications, White House Office, Office of the Special Assistant for National Security Affairs: Records, 1952–1961, NSC Series/Policy Papers Subseries, NSC-169, Box 7, DDEPL, 1–15; "Coordination of Broadcasts Directed Towards the USSR and the Satellite Countries," April 21, 1953, White House Office, NSC Staff: Papers, 1948–1961, OCB Central Files Series, 000.77 Radio Broadcasts, Box 3, DDEPL, 1; Elmer B. Staats to Sinclair Weeks, November 10, 1953, White House Office, NSC Staff: Papers, 1948–1961, OCB Central Files Series, 000.77 Radio Broadcasts, Box 3,

DDEPL, 1; Theodore C. Streibert to Elmer B. Staats, December 15, 1953, White House Office, NSC Staff: Papers, 1948–1961, OCB Central Files Series, 000.77 Radio Broadcasts, Box 3, DDEPL, 1.

72. "Proposed Plan for a Psychological Warfare Offensive," n.d, Psychological Strategy Board—White House Office: NSC Staff: Papers, 1948–1961, NSC Series, Box 9, DDEPL, 1–3, 5.

73. Edward P. Lilly, March, 1953, "Report of the Panel to the Director of the PSB," White House Office, NSC Staff: Papers, 1948–1961, OCB Secretariat Series, Doctrinal Warfare (Official), Box 2, DDEPL, 1–2.

74. Jackson Committee Report, 36.

7

The Rhetorical Presidency and the Eisenhower Administration, 1953–1955

Even before Eisenhower moved into the White House, the theme of "peace" represented a central component of his political ideology and served as a primary theme in his 1952 presidential campaign bid. Martin J. Medhurst maintains that Eisenhower's conception of peace emerged from a "direct outcome of strength—military strength, economic strength, and spiritual strength."[1] Robert L. Ivie, though, critiques this so-called peaceful image, arguing that it "severely underestimates [Eisenhower's] . . . impact as an agent of Cold War acculturation."[2]

The synchronization of Eisenhower's rhetorical strategies around a campaign of peace can be seen in the presidential messages delivered during the first years of his presidency—messages that were promulgated by a newly restructured propaganda program. Now in place as the commander-in-chief of a militarized propaganda program, Eisenhower's administration took his campaign theme of peace and transformed it into global propaganda campaigns with both international and domestic implications. The first of these campaigns surrounded the death of Stalin and was publicly referred to as the Chance for Peace campaign. The second was labeled the Atoms for Peace campaign and sought to exacerbate fears over atomic power in the hands of communist leaders, while lessening such apprehensions over U.S. based nuclear activity.[3]

The motives underlying the Chance for Peace and Atoms for Peace campaigns of 1953 reveal the ubiquitous nature and the militarization of the

Eisenhower administration's propaganda campaign of peace. Such plans to exploit Stalin's death began as early as October 1952 and ended with the global efforts surrounding the Atoms for Peace campaign that lasted from 1953 through 1955 and beyond. Within this period, Eisenhower's institutionalization of a militarized structure led to a militarized mindset, resulting in the greater coordination of propaganda strategy, the development of long-range propaganda campaigns more reflective of military philosophy, and most significantly, the articulation of goals that stepped-up rather than reduced the threat of war. The Chance for Peace and the Atoms for Peace campaigns illustrate most clearly the means by which the Eisenhower administration combined bully pulpit activity with covert communication, revealing the changes that Eisenhower brought to the practice of the rhetorical presidency. Eisenhower's propaganda campaigns were complete with defensive (e.g., reactive) and offensive (e.g., proactive) tactics that blended the themes of peace, nuclear disarmament, and scientific superpower status of the United States—themes that held cross-cultural appeal in a world frightened by the threat of nuclear holocaust.[4] Such overt themes, though, masked the complex layering of covert, psychological warfare maneuvers underlying the Eisenhower administration's Cold War motives. As recently declassified materials reveal, the Eisenhower administration initiated plans to transform the Truman administration's communist strategy of containment to one of total extinction that might involve a full-scale war against communism. Such mobilization demanded the production of various propaganda and psychological warfare strategies that would allow the U.S. government to continue nuclear testing and build-up for war, showcasing Eisenhower as a presidential pioneer for the peaceful uses of atomic energy. The psychological strategizing sessions reveal an administration as committed to nuclear proliferation as to negotiating a peaceful solution to the Cold War.

THE CHANCE FOR PEACE CAMPAIGN

Much of the research surrounding Stalin's death centers on Eisenhower's April 16, 1953, Chance for Peace speech. The Eisenhower administration's attempt to gain the propaganda advantage during the Soviet exchange of power, however, extended far beyond the few months surrounding Stalin's death in 1953. Once launched, campaign organizers feared the success of their own propaganda and thus sought to ensure that any peace overture offered by the Soviet Union would be viewed skeptically by the nation's Cold War allies. All of the activities surrounding Eisenhower's Chance for Peace campaign thus provide insight into the psychological strategies of the militarized propaganda program as his presidential message became the center-piece of long-term propaganda campaigns.

Planning for Stalin's Death

Even though Stalin did not die until March 6, 1953, the Psychological Strategy Board (PSB) planners began preparing for his imminent death some five months earlier as part of their doctrinal warfare strategy.[5] In part, the PSB sought to seize "the psychological initiative" with the Soviet leader's death.[6] Additional hidden aims also existed, however, with propagandists wanting to exacerbate the turmoil surrounding a Soviet transfer of power. As PSB staffer William J. Morgan articulated on March 4, 1953, *"Our strategic guiding principle, as well as our secret goal, should be to do everything to encourage and promote chaos within the USSR."*[7] In addition, George A. Morgan, acting director of the PSB, claimed that such a rhetorical exigence offered an opportunity "for world leadership by the President."[8] In order to achieve the psychological advantage, to promote chaos in the Soviet Union and to elevate Eisenhower to a supreme leadership position, the PSB called for "all information media under United States Government control, both overt and covert, [to] . . . be given standing instructions in the event of Stalin's death."[9]

In order to maximize the psychological advantage, the PSB expended considerable energy toward psychologizing and anticipating not only the Kremlin's response to Stalin's death but also the possible reactions of the Soviet public. The PSB presupposed that "like any government the USSR [was] sensitive to any development that Soviet leaders regarded as an actual or potential threat to their power position." Yet in spite of this normal sensitivity, the PSB believed that Soviet leaders represented a psychological anomaly—a "near psychopathic hypersensitivity toward threats" brought about by an "atmosphere of conspiracy," "the tensions of totalitarianism," and "the immutable hostility between Communists and non-Communists." Such views of Soviet vulnerabilities inspired caution among PSB planners. They feared that the Soviet leaders exhibited a "callused insensitivity to the costs of preserving [their] position." Despite such psychological concerns, though, the PSB wanted to adapt U.S. propaganda to the most sensitive communist vulnerabilities that might incite the Soviet people to revolt. PSB planners thus highlighted numerous themes, including the lack of individual freedom, religious oppression, forced labor, desperate living conditions, and alleged Soviet "warmongering"—themes that epitomized PSB's transfer of power campaign.[10]

Members of the PSB also anticipated and prepared for the Soviets' own propaganda moves. Such projections demonstrated the militarized propaganda operations of the U.S. government, complete with defensive and offensive tactics. Edward P. Lilly, a PSB operative, feared, for example, that the "Russian leaders might attribute all the difficulties to Stalin's control and as a propaganda gesture indicate even with specific action that they were willing to terminate the Korean war." In countering such a Soviet action, Lilly recommended that rather than using a high government official to denounce any "peaceful" gesture, that contacts be made with "American columnists and even editorial writers," to warn them of the "dangerous implications . . . of falling into a Soviet trap." These contacts were to be made even before the Soviet Union implemented such a plan so as to thwart its "psychological impact."[11] Toward that end, Lilly viewed any Soviet response as a mere propaganda ploy—even one that brought about the end of the Korean war. This view implied that Lilly privileged the status quo over a peaceful compromise in the Cold War conflict because the former stood to further the propaganda efforts of the United States.

Stalin's eventual death, the PSB members projected, provided a grand opportunity for the Eisenhower administration to gain a psychological advantage in democracy's battle against communism. As Charles R. Norberg, acting deputy assistant director of the PSB, asserted, the Soviet transfer of power and Eisenhower's Chance for Peace address offered "a gold mine of psychological warfare opportunities and obligations."[12] The Chance for Peace address thus marked the first public pronouncement of President Eisenhower in his administration's campaign to "exploit" the changing events in the Soviet Union.

Delivered before the American Society of Newspaper Editors, the Chance for Peace address dichotomized the peaceful intent of the "free world" and the warlike behavior of the Soviet Union in the postwar period. Eisenhower charged that the United States sought "true peace" in the postwar years while the Soviet government exhibited "force: huge armies, subversion, rule of neighbor nations." In looking toward the future in light of the current Cold War tensions, Eisenhower feared either the realization of an "atomic war" or the "perpetual fear" of its probability.[13]

Despite the dim outlook, Eisenhower outlined his vision for achieving a worldwide "peace that [was] neither partial nor punitive." Emphasizing that the United States was "ready to assume its part," and prepared to "dedicate" its "strength to serve the needs, rather than the fears, of the world," the president urged the Soviet Union to take action: to sign the "Austrian treaty"; to offer an "honorable armistice in Korea"; and most importantly, to reduce "the burden of armaments now weighing upon the world." Such measures,

Eisenhower stressed, provided world governments with a "precious chance to turn the black tide of events" and to "conform" to a "firm faith that God created men to enjoy, not destroy, the fruits of the earth and their own toil."[14] Such themes set into motion a multitude of post-address propaganda activities.

Promulgating Eisenhower's Message of "Peace"

Part of the PSB's synchronized plan involved Radio Free Europe (RFE), an organization over which the Eisenhower administration exacted tighter control. John Prados maintains that in 1953, RFE also "introduced a technique of 'saturation broadcasting' to counter Soviet jamming."[15] This saturation can clearly be seen by the manner in which RFE perpetuated the Chance for Peace themes, portraying the United States as the seeker of genuine peace and the Soviet Union as merely providing highly questionable peace overtures. The day of and the day following Eisenhower's speech, governmental radio stations blitzed the airways with his message. In addition to re-airing the speech, RFE constructed U.S. peace as "total," "sincere," "complete," "true," "just," "honest," "lasting," "global," "real," and the peace of the "future," in broadcasts to Poland, Hungary, Albania, and Czechoslovakia.[16] In contrast, RFE, following PSB's prescriptions, questioned the Soviets' peace claims and labeled their peace as "so-called," "false," "maneuvers," "overtures," "ambiguous," and "empty" in broadcasts to Poland, Bulgaria, Hungary and Romania.[17]

As the Eisenhower administration worked to co-opt peace for the United States, RFE helped portray such peace as beneficial to all through a form of defector propaganda. During a broadcast to Albania on April 17, 1953, for example, the anchor who portrayed himself as an Albanian,[18] stressed that Eisenhower "is talking to us. . . . He has laid down . . . the terms of a peace that would . . . benefit all people."[19] In the Czechoslovakian broadcast on the same date, the commentator stressed: "We Czechoslovaks, and the enslaved peoples behind the Iron Curtain can be deeply gratified by Eisenhower's statements. It puts an end to the period of containment."[20] As the PSB directed, the peaceful intentions of the U.S. government were stressed, simultaneously constructing Eisenhower as the newly emerging world leader and the champion of world peace. RFE's broadcasts also met the goals of Jackson committee members who called for the use of more propaganda channels directed by, but not publicly connected to, the U.S. government.

The Chance for Peace campaign not only held international propaganda aims but domestic ones as well. Even though the United States Information Agency (USIA) was supposedly forbidden from propagandizing U.S. citizens, the U.S. Congress allowed the USIA to produce and market one academic journal domestically (and internationally), entitled *Problems of Communism* (POC), which was developed as part of the PSB's Doctrinal Warfare Program to target intellectuals.[21] Attempting to develop an "academic propaganda,"[22] POC's editors maintained that the journal functioned "to make readily available significant background information and documentary material on the theoretical and political aspects of world communism today, with particular emphasis on the policies and aims of the Soviet Union."[23] Originating in 1952 and ending in the aftermath of communism's fall in 1992, the USIA issued this bimonthly publication for forty years to scholars in the United States and abroad.[24] Even though its editors maintained unequivocally that the journal printed only "sober factual accounts," the propagandistic function of the journal becomes most evident by the manner in which Eisenhower's Chance for Peace themes were perpetuated.[25]

For a year following Eisenhower's Chance for Peace address, POC published various stories that promulgated Eisenhower's PSB-generated propaganda aims. In the second issue of 1953, the editor commemorated Stalin's death and rearticulated Eisenhower's dichotomous construction of the future:

The successor regime stands at a crossroads. It can pursue the course set by the Stalin regime since World War II, continuing policies of open aggression and overt hostility toward the non-communist world. Or it can, if it chooses, embark on a new course, repudiating the attitudes and policies linked to Stalin's name and seeking a peaceful *modus vivendi* with the outside world.[26]

The four articles that followed this "editor's note" all related to "A New Chapter in Soviet History," and concerned the Chance for Peace campaign.

The first article of this series centered on "The First Steps of the New Regime" and summarized the events in the Soviet Union during the aftermath of Stalin's death. Just as the PSB proposed and RFE likewise complied, POC writers questioned the sincerity of the Soviet peace activities after Stalin's death, asserting that "a number of contradictory elements should be noted" in the communist's more recent "peace offensive." Along with highlighting and excerpting Eisenhower's April 16th speech, the article also questioned the Soviet Union's most recent peaceful gestures, particularly the new "regime['s] . . . sweeping amnesty affecting millions of prisoners," by placing quotation marks around the word "peace" when referring to the Soviet Union's past conciliatory actions. Following the dictates of Lilly closely, POC writers construed the Soviet's new efforts toward "peace" as "completely erroneous," and they urged their academic readers to "temper hope with utmost caution, keeping in mind the lessons of the past, maintaining a defensive strength, and waiting for concrete demonstration that the communist leadership is ready for a settlement of outstanding issues."[27] Such a move prevented any Soviet action in the wake of Stalin's death from being viewed as a positive step toward détente. The primary goal was to assume the propaganda edge rather than achieve a peaceful resolution to the Cold War.

The RFE and the POC, though, were only two of many media that continued to perpetuate Eisenhower's themes in the months following what the PSB called a "keynote address" that required "re-emphasis . . . every week or ten days." In addition to utilizing "all available media for reaching the people of the Soviet Orbit [in the] exploitation of the President's speech," the PSB also sought to rearticulate subtly the same themes during the president's budget message. In further attempts to "keep . . . the Eisenhower pattern alive and talked about," the PSB planned for key members of Congress to integrate the Chance for Peace ideas in their speeches outside of Congress. As the PSB concluded, the primary task "is to keep the pattern laid out in the [Eisenhower's] speech under active consideration in all parts of the world."[28]

Because U.S. propagandists were so concerned that the world community would embrace the Soviet's conciliatory acts, the PSB revamped the Chance for Peace campaign beginning in May 1953. These new tactics targeted the United Nations and its member countries. The Lodge Project represented the point at which PSB operatives at least became so paranoid of communism's wrath that extinction became an underlying motive of the Eisenhower administration's Cold War plans. The Eisenhower administration's overt strategy of peace thus masked a much more underhanded and aggressive plan to combat communism.

The Lodge Project

In May 1953, the U.S. ambassador to the United Nations, Henry Cabot Lodge, Jr., initiated "a strong anti-Soviet-bloc" psychological warfare campaign. Supported by the PSB, the campaign was designed to use the United Nation's General Assembly (UNGA) for the second stage of the Chance for Peace campaign.[29] Demonstrating the defensive tactics of the propaganda program, the Lodge Project intended to ensure that any peace overture by the USSR would be viewed as yet another propaganda ploy. As defined by Lodge and interpreted by the interdepartmental Working Group of the PSB, the Lodge Project sought to "attack, minimize and ridicule the doctrinal basis of Soviet positions"[30]; to remind "the free world officially of the enduring truth concerning the world communist menace"[31]; "to deflate considerably the Soviet peace offensive; to exert through this project some adverse effects within the enemy camp; and to unify . . . the free world."[32] Attempting to encourage nations to join the United States in its fight against communism beginning in April 1953, the United Nations served as a propaganda venue for this stage of the Eisenhower administration's campaign. As the PSB declared, the United Nations represented the "greatest single sounding board in the world . . . a kind of global amplifier of information."[33]

The Lodge Project clearly became an extension of the Chance for Peace campaign and, once again, targeted Soviet vulnerabilities. It too served to counter the Soviet Union's Hate America campaign and thus represented another dimension of the Eisenhower administration's Doctrinal Warfare Program.[34] Not only did PSB planners call for the perpetuation of Eisenhower's Chance for Peace address, its members asked that "relevant citations" from Eisenhower's address be included in the public presentations and position papers linked to what they called project "Cosmos."[35] As with the initial phases of the Chance for Peace campaign, the PSB wanted to undermine Soviet vincibilities through documents linked to the Lodge Project. In particular, the PSB group working on the project looked to gather information on Soviet weaknesses that would hold "bullet proof authenticity" for audiences so as increase the material's "dramatic attention-getting quality."[36] Specifically, the PSB felt that the Soviet Union and China were particularly assailable on human rights issues linked to religion, the treatment of women and children, and restrictions on thought, speech, and publication.[37] Other Soviet liabilities were associated with alleged "police terror, purges, and political murders"; "slave labor"; and finally, "Soviet aggression" against Poland, Finland, the Baltic States, the European satellites, Korea, Malaya, Laos, and Vietnam. The PSB used refugees and escapees as a major source of information in gathering such information.[38]

In the aftermath of the Chance for Peace address and Stalin's death, the Soviet Union responded with what the PSB considered tokens of peace, which the Eisenhower administration viewed as an extension of the Soviet Union's own propaganda campaign. To the PSB especially, the Cold War context grew more intense and more complicated by the Soviets' words of peace and eagerness to avoid another worldwide conflict. In a "Policy Paper for the Lodge Project," the PSB lamented that "even harsh actions . . . from the communist camp fail[ed] to exert a stiffening effect" among the "free nations" because of confusion, disunification, and economic exigences. The authors of the policy paper believed the free nations sought peace at all costs because the French overlooked Chinese aggression in Vietnam, the British and French reacted passively to the Soviet repression of the June 17 riots in Berlin, and the British (e.g., Churchill) pushed for talks among the

"Big Four" nations. In addition, the PSB worried that the Soviet's development of the H-bomb inspired minimal reaction among allied leaders. The existing Cold War context concerned the PSB to the extent that its members feared that a "project such as that initiated by Ambassador Lodge [could not] be carried out, in the present peace-seeking atmosphere of free world opinion, without doing grave damage to the bonds of unity between the U.S." and its allies. Despite such worries, the PSB concluded that the Eisenhower administration could no longer "tailor [its] expressed views to the actual or supposed sensibilities of [its] allies" for fear of "deepen[ing] the present downward spiral of self-deception in the free world." The PSB thus sought to dramatize "the continuing evils and dangers of Soviet and Chinese Communism," and to "deflate considerably the new Soviet peace offensive" without making the U.S. appear too "trigger-happy."[39]

Toward that end, "Cosmos" was directed toward the elite of neutral nations, who could, in turn, amplify U.S. propaganda themes. C. D. Jackson argued that an "intellectual vacuum" existed in Western Europe apart from the proliferation of Marxism, which required the Eisenhower administration to utilize "intelligence as 'ammunition.'"[40] Journalists once again were selected as the primary agency to transmit Eisenhower's message. As reflected in a working document on the Lodge Project, "neutralist intelligentsia and the unconvinced Satellite leaders" represented the "major target" of this stage of the Doctrinal Warfare Program. Campaign planners thus sought "an intellectual approach [that was] capable of popular exploitation."[41] According to the Lodge Project minutes, Lodge wanted the foreign press to be targeted, which necessitated the gathering of material that emphasized the "journalistic value of the items"[42]—items that could "stand alone as 'hot' journalistic jabs." This latter prescription required the construction of "connected narratives that [could] tell meaningful stories with great cumulative impact."[43] For some members of the PSB, attention-getting sound bites became a way to give "meaning to the [people] in the streets of the world,"[44] a view that Lilly charged was too "sensational" and one that could mean the "death of any doctrinal aspects" of the Lodge Project. As Lilly concluded, the "doctrinal approach" had to be "kept entirely separate" from a journalistic approach.[45]

Lilly's adamant opposition to the journalistic vision grew out of the increased fear that PSB planners began to share—a fear of the Soviets' own propaganda advancements. With Lilly's fear realized via the Korean armistice—a maneuver that the PSB defined as "a Soviet peace offensive deeper than any of its predecessors since World War II"—Lodge and the PSB assumed an even more hardened stance toward their Cold War enemy. The PSB now secretly spoke of communism as a "menace" that could result in "the destruction not only of nations and other free institutions but of the supreme value, the idea of man from which all these institutions derive." Because the PSB now anticipated that the USSR wanted "to impose on all mankind . . . its way of life" so as to create "one nation,"[46] Eisenhower's psychological warfare group revamped its Cold War tactics.

As part of this reconstruction, the PSB critiqued policies based in peace as weak and ineffective and seriously entertained a policy shift from Truman's containment of communism to one centered on its extinction—a goal that could ultimately bring about a global war between democracy and communism. As the PSB articulated in July 1953, "no good policy was ever made with either peace or compromise as its main ingredient."[47] By August of that same year, the PSB was calling for a strengthened foreign policy plan, which could result in the "unequivocal [pronouncement] for the eventual *extinction* of world communism," a mindset undoubtedly inspired by the news of the Soviet's hydrogen bomb capabilities. When referencing this proposed "policy of extinction," the PSB acknowledged that such a policy shift would "increase rather than diminish the likelihood of an early global shooting war." Members of the PSB justified this more strident policy-through-power shift on the grounds that "to balk at action because of an uncertain fear of precipitating war is to increase the risk of defeat in the world struggle." The PSB proposed this policy revision on the grounds that "no amount of persuasion" would reduce the communist threat, which justified a more militaristic response. The PSB warned that if the Eisenhower administration revamped its Cold War mission, it had to be "prepared to use every means, just as our enemy does, limited only by the bounds of moral tolerance in our own way of life," including "force of arms as well as deception."[48] Realizing that such a policy transformation could create an international backlash, the PSB's plans remained hidden from the public for some forty years, with the PSB centering its activities on propaganda and "appropriate non-attributable actions." With the Lodge Project, the PSB sought to "alert the free world [of] the communist peril" in a more vigorous manner,[49] while they planned secretly to expand their military (i.e., nuclear) arsenal.

Although the PSB intended for additional psychological activities at home and abroad to transcend the secretary of state's speech, John Foster Dulles' address before the 8th meeting of the UNGA represented the "keynote" activity of the Lodge Project.[50] In an address entitled, "Easing International Tensions: The Role of the UN,"[51] delivered on September 17, 1953, Dulles constructed the Cold War in a manner that mirrored the prescriptions of the Lodge Project. Reflecting the enhanced threat that emanated from the PSB planners, Dulles discussed the current "disharmony" between the free world and communist world nations as "menacing" and "dangerous." Dulles alluded to the potential for nuclear holocaust, asserting that "physical scientists have now found means which . . . can wipe life off the surface of this planet." Given that potentiality, Dulles urged that the United Nations face the "universal problem of saving the human race from extinction."[52]

In depicting an atmosphere of fear that pitted communism against democracy, Dulles reminded his UN peers that the Soviets could not be trusted. Dulles historicized, for example, that "since 1939 some 600,000,000 people of some 15 nations have been brought into the Soviet camp of dictatorships" involuntarily. Emphasizing the vulnerabilities that the PSB targeted, Dulles spoke in terms of human rights violations in Korea, Indochina, Germany, and Austria in particular, with an emphasis on the lack of freedoms in all communist regions. Just as the PSB charted, Dulles inoculated his audience against Soviet peace claims, arguing that "mere words do not instantly or totally reassure us [because] we have heard them before."[53]

In order to counter this "menacing" communist force, Dulles expanded the peaceful efforts articulated by Eisenhower in the Chance for Peace address to include the entire international community. Speaking in terms of "a community defense system," "international groupings," and a "world community," Dulles attempted to harmonize neutral and satellite countries in the fight against communist imperialism. Portraying U.S. peace efforts as the UN's peace efforts, Dulles returned to Eisenhower's April 16th address, speaking of the necessary "faith" that Eisenhower stressed throughout his address and the need for close surveillance and a reduction in armaments. Finally, Dulles called upon the UN members to "seize [the] moment" and help secure "international agreements limiting armaments."[54]

The Eisenhower administration thus worried that any Soviet actions, which might be viewed as a step toward a peaceful resolution of the Cold War, would thwart U.S. Cold War aims. Such a relaxation of world fears might then allow the Soviet Union to continue its atomic development with lessened resistance. In a defensive maneuver, the PSB countered the Soviets' newest peace ventures in Korea. The intricate and anticipatory strategizing that took place behind closed doors revealed that Eisenhower's message of peace masked the administration's more hardline anticommunist policies. The actual goals of the PSB, while perceived to be more militarily sound, lacked popular appeal, the PSB feared. Much of these policies thus remained hidden from public view. The PSB also directed that someone other than Eisenhower had to deliver the more strident messages in order to preserve the presidential posture of peace. Nevertheless, the Lodge Project was just as coordinated by the Eisenhower administration through the work of the PSB as the Chance for Peace address; RFE, POC, and Lodge thus served as Eisenhower's rhetorical surrogates.

The implementation of this militarized propaganda structure clearly led to more militarized solutions. A propaganda program initially designed to reduce the likelihood of war now became an integral tool that anticipated and assumed an impending global conflict. As Caroline Pruden argues, "the emphasis on psychological warfare therefore may have discouraged more pacific tendencies in the Soviet Union. It [Lodge Project] thus bears at least some responsibility for contributing to the 'lost opportunity' to improve relations between the superpowers."[55] Undoubtedly, this interdepartmental constituency of the PSB/OCB[56] influenced the move toward a stepped-up foreign policy that could have culminated in a third world war. By the summer of 1953, the PSB branch of the Eisenhower administration at least seemed poised to fight this ultimate battle with the intent of "kill[ing] the snake" without "being bitten."[57] Yet, in order for final preparations to occur, the Eisenhower administration had to convince the world community as well as its own public that increased atomic research was a necessary and congruent part of the U.S. campaign of peace.

THE ATOMS FOR PEACE CAMPAIGN

As the PSB planned the Chance for Peace campaign, it was also involved in a domestic propaganda effort that sought to convince the American public of the significant threat that communism posed to the free world. These domestic propaganda strategies targeted the domestic media and were eventually blended into the Eisenhower administration's Atoms for Peace campaign. The Atoms for Peace campaign portrayed the United States as the scientific superpower of peace, which could best supervise all atomic research. Such a propaganda strategy thus was intended to de-legitimize the Soviet's atomic research through a propaganda of fear and to allow the U.S. government to continue its atomic testing and build-up in the event that communism had to be extinguished.

Operation Candor

The next stage of the Eisenhower administration's peace campaign sought to build support for a continued Cold War effort by informing the American people of the potential destructiveness of nuclear weaponry. As conceived, this project contained both apparent and hidden aims. While the campaign intended to celebrate the scientific invention of nuclear power, it also sought to warn "allies" and the country's citizens of the "dark" side of "atomic energy." Such a warning was prompted by the Soviet's stockpiling of weapons, warranting a stepped-up "Civil Defense" program.[58]

As with the Chance for Peace campaign, a speech by President Eisenhower was to serve as the centerpiece of Operation Candor in the summer of 1953. A PSB blueprint for Eisenhower's kick-off address specifically elaborated strategies for this new propaganda offensive against the Soviet Union, one that the United States might pursue "for years if necessary." This offensive was to avoid the appearance of a "propaganda gimmick," yet was to employ the "proven techniques of mass communication to carry" its message "to the farthest corners of the globe." This entire campaign was to emphasize the themes outlined by the PSB in a report known as "The Plan." According to this plan, the campaign sought the shared beliefs between the United States and the rest of "humanity"; the right of "self-determination"; and the need for "disarmament," which would allow for the development of the peaceful uses of atomic energy. The speech and the subsequent campaign were to define what "The Plan" called Eisenhower's message of "the Faith and the Vision,"[59] a popular theme of the Eisenhower administration's peace campaigns.

The fundamental goal of Operation Candor involved mobilizing domestic support for a protracted Cold War battle, which could ultimately expand the national defense system of the United States. C.D. Jackson (Eisenhower's liaison to the PSB/OCB) explained that Operation Candor sought to create a "national will"[60] via what James M. Lambie, Jr., a special White House assistant, referred to as "a job of persuasion or indoctrination or propaganda."[61] Such a propaganda campaign, which was inspired in part by the warnings of the Oppenheimer Panel, was designed to "effect public understanding of the fact that 'we live not in an instant of peril but in an age of peril,'" requiring Americans to "support adequate defense measures" in order to win the "war of endurance" against communism.[62]

The domestic news media became a primary target for Operation Candor. The goal was to convince the U.S. news media that an age of peril existed so that journalists would help "indoctrinate" the American public in much the same way that the Lodge Project used international journalists. The first initiative of this expansive campaign involved the "immediate exploitation [of] U.S. domestic press, radio, television, and newsreels."[63] In order to achieve such exploitation, Abbott Washburn, USIA deputy director, requested that "top opinion molders" be contacted so as to get "the story to their members, readers, listeners."[64] To ensure the requisite coverage, campaign organizers planned a "confidential briefing at [the] White House of top media executives," who, in turn, could help provide a "multiplying effort" for Eisenhower's centerpiece address.[65] But before such media blueprints were operationalized, the plans surrounding Operation Candor were merged with the Atoms for Peace campaign.[66]

Launch of the Atoms for Peace Campaign

The Atoms for Peace campaign, initiated by Eisenhower's UN address of December 8, 1953, eventually targeted not only domestic but international audiences as well, perpetuating the age of peril themes previously outlined. Reflecting the culmination of the Chance for Peace campaign, the Lodge Project, and Operation Candor, the Atoms for Peace campaign sought to fulfill multiple propaganda exigencies while serving to establish new themes for the USIA, the covert propaganda agencies, and the domestic audiences. The Eisenhower administration thus sought an international license to engage in atomic testing—a license that was limited to one scientific superpower—the United States of America.

During the speech, Eisenhower subtly portrayed the United States as the atomic leader who voluntarily chose the path of peace. While ensuring that his audience realized the ability of his country's "defense capabilities" to "inflict terrible losses upon an aggressor," Eisenhower stressed that the United States chose "to be constructive, not destructive." Because the U.S. functioned as the atomic superpower, Eisenhower implied that his nation should logically act as the superpower of "peaceful use[s] of atomic energy," reversing "this greatest of destructive forces . . . for the benefit of all mankind."[67] An Operations Coordinating Board (OCB) document concerning the Atoms for Peace campaign verified that administrative officials wanted the United States to be thought of as the leader of atomic energy development, calling for the country to become the "cream of [the] scientific" community.[68]

In addition to portraying the United States as the atomic superpower, Eisenhower attempted to establish peace as a universal commitment in the Atoms for Peace address. Early in the speech, Eisenhower spoke of a collective and historical commitment to peace: "Occasional pages do record the faces of the 'Great Destroyers' but the whole book of history reveals mankind's never-ending quest for peace." He then juxtaposed the threat of nuclear war with the quest for peace through archetypal (e.g., natural and cross-cultural) metaphors[69]: "So my country's purpose is to move out of the *dark* chamber of horrors into the *light*, to find a way . . . [to] move forward toward peace and happiness."[70]

As with the Lodge Project, the OCB's Working Group for the Exploitation of the President's UN Speech (sanctioned by NSC 5412) wanted the peace overtures of the Soviet Union to be viewed suspiciously by the world community.[71] A January 8, 1954, OCB document on the "exploitation" of the speech indicated that the address sought to associate the "peaceful development of atomic energy" with the United States, thus placing "the USSR in a defensive position."[72] Toward that end, a December 28, 1953, study on "The President's Atomic Proposal Before the UN" stressed: "We must not allow the peaceful image they [Soviets] have attempted to superimpose on ours to become fixed in people's minds."[73] In a letter to the OCB on January 16, 1954, C. D. Jackson called on both covert and overt propaganda channels to help achieve the "psychological" edge.[74] The Eisenhower administration, therefore, assumed that the Soviet Union would *not* meet the stipulations of peace called for in the Atoms for Peace campaign.[75]

As reflected in the internal documents linked to Operation Candor, the Atoms for Peace campaign targeted domestic and international audiences. The administration believed that it needed the support of the American people in order to step up its Cold War efforts and to convince allies to support U.S. foreign policy goals. Regarding the domestic propaganda efforts, C. D. Jackson who chaired the previously mentioned Working Group on the UN Speech, called on the OCB to develop still more "specific programs for follow-up exploitation of the [address] in both the domestic and international public opinion fields."[76] Jackson explained in a January 15, 1954, letter to "Department and Agency Information Centers," that "full understanding of the speech by the American people," would "depend on maximum repetition of the principal points over a period of several months."[77]

According to OCB's minutes of January 19, 1954, part of this domestic campaign included the distribution of some "500,000 illustrated pamphlets" entitled "The Atoms for Peace and Progress," which contained the complete "speech text" and "photographs."[78] In addition, the OCB prepared an *Atomic Power for Peace Action Kit*, containing background information, publicity and speech materials, pictures and pamphlets. Much of this material pointed to the peaceful uses of atomic energy, such as when the "Kit" referred to "radioisotopes" as the "greatest research discovery since the microscope," and emphasized the value of "radioactive iodine in cancer research."[79] According to "The Atoms For Peace and Progress" pamphlet, these materials were to be distributed by "key Federal employers" to "special media," and to "civic, religious, professional, labor, women's, veterans, [and] farmers [groups]."[80] The themes were likewise to be rearticulated in Eisenhower's State of the Union address and the budget message of 1954 in a subtle manner; other cabinet officials spread out across the country voicing Eisenhower's message of peace domestically (e.g., the secretary of state and the chair of the Atomic Energy Commission [AEC]).[81]

The use of the domestic media to promulgate Eisenhower's Atoms for Peace themes appeared successful, based on the *New York Times'* coverage of the campaign. In an editorial the day after Eisenhower's address, the *Times* reiterated the threat that the OCB wanted people in the United States and around the world to grasp, particularly the need to "control this awe-some force that science [had] released."[82] Using language found in the internal working documents previously identified, the editorialists in the *Times* talked of how "the West has now *seized* the initiative," placing the Soviet Union "on the *defensive*, politically and morally." Referring to Eisenhower's proposal as "inspired," the *Times* perpetuated the peaceful dimensions of it by declaring that "an international atomic pool for peaceful purposes [represents] the first step toward breaking the disarmament deadlock and lifting from the world the specter of atomic war."[83] The *Times* also reported on the international reaction to Eisenhower's proposal, stressing that "the President's plan is being hailed with hope and enthusiasm as a practical first step away from the threat of atomic war and toward the promise of atomic peace."[84] The USIA in turn used such positive reviews from American newspapers in their international propaganda, claiming that "newspapers and leaders reflecting the views of both of the major political parties have been unanimous in their praise of the humanitarian purpose expressed in the President's proposals."[85]

In addition to the propaganda distributed domestically, the campaign directed toward international audiences was even more expansive. Even though members of the OCB warned against the "duplication" of U.S. material overseas,[86] the Eisenhower administration went to great lengths to coordinate the domestic and international propaganda strategies.[87] First, the USIA reported to C. D. Jackson on December 10, 1953, that they began translating a version of Eisenhower's speech only twelve minutes after he began speaking.[88] Because the OCB determined that not enough people heard Eisenhower's speech when it was first delivered, the Working Group called for an "aggressive follow-up" campaign that relied on "maximum repetition."[89]

The OCB used all of the USIA's media for the global campaign along with media belonging to the seemingly "private" agencies. According to a document entitled "Summary of Events Planned for Exploitation," scripts and programs were developed for the VOA, the wireless bulletin, motion pictures, information centers, educational exchange services, and covert agencies such as RFE and RL. The VOA carried programs highlighting groups such as the American Federation of Labor, which supposedly hailed the "President's Plan." Movies were also made that depicted the relationship between the "atom" and agriculture, industry, medicine, and physics.[90] On a grander scale, OCB developed exhibits for Brazil, Italy, Belgium, South Asia, and the Middle East, which were operational through 1955.[91]

For the Eisenhower administration, the subject of science served as a major propaganda theme in the Cold War with the Soviet Union; it, too, served the goals of the Doctrinal Warfare Program of targeting intellectuals.[92] In

1957, Arthur Larson, director of the USIA, highlighted the psychological impact of science when he argued that while scientific projects possessed an "inherent scientific value," they simultaneously elevated "our military position and our diplomatic bargaining power."[93] A similar conception of science became evident in the propaganda associated with the Atoms for Peace campaign—a theme that intersected science and peace.

The link between peace, science, and the United States was most noticeable in four "Presidential Statements" that were drafted in July 1953. Even though it is not clear whether or when these drafts were delivered, the National Security Council (NSC) nonetheless sought to equate the United States with a positive use of science and the Soviet Union with the threat of nuclear war. In draft number one, the Soviet Union's science was portrayed through archetypal metaphors, or as "dark clouds over the pathways of scientific advance," which resembled the manner in which Eisenhower depicted the Soviet Union's promises of peace. The use of "dark cloud" imagery in particular, which symbolized nuclear attack, became the vehicle for depicting the Soviet Union. In contrast, the draft outlined the need of Western scientists to "frame a new declaration of scientific independence for all the world to see," establishing "beach-heads of scientific light in the darkness of the Soviet scientific nether world."[94] As the archetypal metaphors suggested, U.S. scientific prowess was connected to light and universal advancements while the Soviet's scientific advancements were engulfed in dark clouds, which threaten all.

The USIA further contextualized the Soviet's scientific advancements in a narrative of fear through articles published in *Problems of Communism*. Featuring excerpts from a book entitled *Soviet Science*, published by the American Association for the Advancement of Science, POC accented the governmental control over science in the Soviet Union, a practice that reportedly thwarted academic freedom. In discrediting Soviet science, Lazar Volin, the book's author, charged that scientists in the Soviet Union were "forced to pay the Kremlin the heavy price of general subservience to the state," a common practice of the early 1930s, with the "systematic tightening of government and party control over science." While the majority of the article critiqued Soviet scientific techniques, Volin ended the piece by cautioning readers that all must still fear the Soviet's science because of its state sponsorship. As Volin maintained, "The deterioration of science in the U.S.S.R. has not had apparent adverse effects on the Soviet military potential."[95] Ignoring the U.S. government's own influence over scientific advancements, particularly atomic research, the POC editors clearly sought to expose what they saw as a flaw within Soviet research, targeting the all-important academic value of scholarly freedom.

In contrast to the construction of Soviet science, U.S. scientific advancements were naturalized in the government's propaganda.[96] In a U.S. pamphlet entitled *Atomic Power for Peace*, America's scientific virility was emphasized, with "power" assuming a primary focus over the secondary emphasis of "peace." The word "POWER" appeared on the opening page of this USIA pamphlet. "Power" symbolized the atom; it was called "the greatest [power] ever known on earth." Questioning whether or not "man will use [this power] for good or evil," the USIA emphasized U.S. advancements in such vital fields as medicine, agriculture, industry, and energy production. The USIA thus subtly answered the question by placing this unleashed form of power into the peaceful hands of the United States, a country dedicated to "progress, instead of destruction; peace, instead of war." The naturalization of this energy form is furthered by a scene that appeared in the end of the pamphlet, where two men, one dressed in a military uniform and shaped not unlike that of General Dwight Eisenhower, are shown walking into the visualized sunset.[97] Such an image emphasized the serenity of nature and the comforting vision of a lasting peace.

The naturalization of atomic power was perpetuated in another propaganda text created for the Atoms for Peace campaign. In a thirty-minute video entitled *Blessing of Atomic Energy*, the United States once again emerged as the "natural" leader over this powerful, and potentially dangerous, scientific advancement. While attempting to connect science and peace with the United States, campaign officials went to great lengths to adjust the propaganda to the individual needs of audiences. Japan, of course, represented one of those countries that posed unique propaganda problems because of the U.S. nuclear attack in 1945.[98] In response to this exigence, the USIA attempted to lessen Japanese fears of atomic energy while emphasizing its significant benefits in the *Blessing of Atomic Energy* video. The use of an archetypal metaphor simultaneously reinforced the need for U.S. supervision over future scientific advancements. The narrator of the USIA film asserted: "Just as when primitive man first discovered fire and gradually learned to make it serve his needs, so men of today are learning how the tremendous power of the atom—the second fire—can be used by mankind now and for all generations to come." The comparisons of atomic energy to "fire" heightened the atom's archetypal utility while also lessening apprehensions about its use because fire represented a universal and natural phenomenon. Because of the destructive power of fire, however, the metaphor was imbued with an element of fear. Such fear was transferred to atomic energy, which necessitated the need for a scientific superpower to "control" its potentially destructive forces, even for peaceful purposes. The United States, not surprisingly, represented that superpower, with its atomic advancements in the fields of medicine, agriculture, and industry accented in the beginning of the film.[99]

The Eisenhower administration thus equated peace and science with the United States while casting Soviet peace and science in a context of fear and suspicion. Many scholars have addressed the possible impact of such rhetorical strategies.[100] Blanche Wiesen Cook calls Eisenhower's Chance for Peace speech "stunning"; Fred I. Greenstein proclaims that the Atoms for Peace address was "one of the rhetorical landmarks of Eisenhower's eight years in office."[101] In addressing the impact of the peace themes on international and domestic publics, Medhurst argues "that Eisenhower's speech raised the hope of turning weapons into plowshares can hardly be denied."[102] While the Eisenhower administration's propaganda and psychological warfare messages did not incite liberation in the target countries as planned, Walter L. Hixson maintains that messages emanating from the United States "unnerved the Kremlin, and often achieved the desired effect of spurring unrest behind the Iron Curtain."[103] The Eisenhower administration's own evaluation team, the Sprague committee, maintained that the "Atoms for Peace" campaign in particular, "contributed greatly to the positive image of the United States as a peace-keeping nation."[104]

Despite the Eisenhower administration's perceived success in promulgating a rhetoric of peace,[105] it faced obstacles in its bid to become the scientific superpower. To begin with, the Soviet Union responded to the Atoms for Peace speech by calling for a "general and complete abolition of all major weapons." The OCB anticipated this response because of their own intelligence on the issue and because such a reply paralleled previous Soviet calls for a reduction in conventional arms in the post-World War I era. Simultaneously, the Soviet Union claimed that Eisenhower's proposal would "lead to the production of more and more destructive atomic weapons and to the sanctioning of such production."[106] This latter claim was perhaps most troublesome because the Eisenhower administration did seek to continue nuclear testing and build-up in the face of strong international and domestic opposition. Such testing was integral to the Eisenhower administration's preparation for what the PSB/OCB felt, at least, could be the eventual world war designed to extinguish communism. Such a changing political climate thus required new propaganda strategies that addressed a formidable Soviet counterattack.

Atomic Testing and the Atoms for Peace Campaign

An acknowledged contradiction existed between the Eisenhower administration's campaign of peace and its plan for nuclear testing—a central feature of the Soviet's response to the Atoms for Peace campaign. To address the nuclear testing exigence, the OCB established another Working Group, empowered by NSC-5412, to manage the backlash against such testing and to plan propaganda activities associated with such testing. In relation to the latter, the group sought to further the propaganda aims of Eisenhower's Atoms for Peace speech as it planned new psychological initiatives. Of central concern was Operation CASTLE, which represented the code name for the May 13, 1954, nuclear tests in the Pacific. With Operation CASTLE, the Working Group sought "to debunk the widespread fantasies about effects of radiation on sea life, ocean currents, etc." while "re-emphasizing the deterrent effects on agression [sic] of the U. S. position in weapons development."[107]

Most disconcerting for the administration were the ongoing questions linked to the negative environmental and human side effects of nuclear testing. An NSC document revealed, for example, that people in the United States and other countries alleged that weather abnormalities such as increased tornadoes and nuclear fallout dust accompanied the nuclear tests.[108] Certain people that lived near the test sites in places such as the Marshall Islands also experienced medical abnormalities.[109] As the OCB stipulated, its task became to "minimize such [a] climate of opinion [concerning] the adverse effects of such testing,"[110] so as to continue nuclear experimentation by the U.S. government.

In addressing the newly emerging propaganda exigence, the OCB charted several responses. First, the OCB strong-armed a reluctant National Weather Bureau into issuing a report which denied "that nuclear tests [had] observable effects on the weather." A President's Advisory Committee on Weather Controls also emitted an announcement, which cited an Atomic Energy Commission (AEC) report that "no health hazard exist[ed]" from the tests; the committee also reiterated that the U.S. Weather Bureau found "no evidence to link these weather abnormalities with atomic explosions."[111] In addition, the U.S. government also sent a medical team to the Marshall Islands for follow-up care in the aftermath of the testing. Beyond that, a series of motion pictures identifying the peaceful uses of nuclear testing were also distributed in the islands for some six months.[112] Finally, the OCB sought to involve allied countries in the nuclear testing process, while seeking to maintain the "technical leadership [of the United States] over the USSR."[113]

The OCB Working Group also developed new propaganda strategies that would feature President Eisenhower's justification of U.S. atomic energy. In the summer of 1954, members of the Working Group drafted a speech for Eisenhower entitled "The United States in the Nuclear Age." Their intent was to "remind the nation of the substance of the December 8 [1953] speech" and to move ahead without the Soviet Union on the need for an international conference to develop "peaceful applications of nuclear energy." In the end, the OCB, in consultation with Eisenhower, decided the speech would be delivered at the dedication of the first nuclear power reactor site (Shippingport, Pennsylvania) on Labor Day, September 6, 1954. Even though the speech was scaled down from earlier drafts, Eisenhower still called for the establishment of an international atomic energy agency and rearticulated a familiar theme: "I am confident that the atom will not be devoted *exclusively* to the destruction of man, but will be his mighty servant and tireless benefactor."[114] Eisenhower's insertion of the word "exclusively" implies that the atom could still be used for the "destruction of man," which points to the deterrent aspects of atomic weapons and puts the Soviets on notice of their potential use. These same themes were likewise promulgated by Lodge during the 1954 United Nations General Assembly as well as by other U.S. delegates to the United Nations. Films were also produced to support the most recent development of the Atoms for Peace speech. Regarding this latter issue, Eisenhower personally halted the public release of one film ("A New Look at the H-Bomb"), demonstrating his close involvement and supervision over such propaganda activities.[115]

In the final analysis, the OCB's Working Group created a propaganda of deflection as it sought to lessen concerns over U.S. nuclear testing. The OCB wanted to delay "public announcements on nuclear weapons effects" as long as possible in order to promulgate Eisenhower's Atoms for Peace themes further. Toward that end, the OCB recommended that the U.S. practice of "establishing the conditions of an enduring peace" be emphasized, along with the theme that the "nuclear weapons" of the United States, "together with those of our Allies, have rightly been called the defense shield of the free world."[116] A propaganda of deflection and a "peace through strength" policy ultimately helped the Eisenhower administration continue testing in the Pacific Ocean and Nevada, with minimal opposition in 1954 and 1955.[117] Propaganda posturing thus kept the Eisenhower administration on track in its preparation for a potential war with the Soviet Union—a goal that seemingly placed U.S. Cold War motives above all other ethical issues. Though the Eisenhower administration did not follow through on its policy of extinction, such a hardline stance undoubtedly prevented the administration from seeking peaceful resolutions to the Cold War conflict.

Overall, Eisenhower's newly centralized propaganda program increased the importance of propaganda and psychological warfare for his administration's foreign policy operations. Such a militarized structure also showed signs of organizational success. Wilson P. Dizard maintains that for the "first time the overseas information program was to participate officially in both the formulation and the development of foreign policies";[118] Medhurst concurs, arguing that both the NSC and the OCB "became powerful voices in the articulation of policy" for the Eisenhower administration.[119] Members of Eisenhower's staff concurred. C. D. Jackson told Eisenhower that the OCB's "relationship with the National Security Council is good, [with] the flow from NSC Planning Board, to NSC, to you for decision, and then back to OCB for allocation of responsibility, coordination of action plans, and follow-through on action, is working well."[120] According to a progress report on the implementation of the Jackson committee report, the VOA allegedly broadcast more "factual news," with less material attributed to the U.S. government. Finally, the American public figured more heavily in the propaganda program's goals as the Jackson committee wished, with additional material released in order to elevate the success of the presidential propaganda campaigns.[121] In fact, once C. D. Jackson returned to *Time* magazine in 1954, he continued promulgating the Atoms for Peace themes for Eisenhower in his magazine, evidencing the means of production involved between the private press and the Eisenhower administration.[122] Medhurst locates Eisenhower's rhetorical effectiveness in his clear understanding of the "power of language," where he "considered rhetoric to be a weapon in the arsenal of democracy."[123]

In the end, the Eisenhower administration's militarized propaganda structure brought about shifts in the role of propaganda in U.S. foreign policy. Designed initially as a program to promote peace, propaganda eventually became a key agent in planning for the possible extinction of communism through a war of global and devastating proportions. As institutionalized, the propaganda program helped mask the Eisenhower administration's covert activities that remained hidden from public view for thirty to forty years and beyond. Just as the Jackson committee stipulated, the USIA became a mouth-piece for presidential initiatives, extending the rhetorical powers of the president. This chapter reveals most explicitly the means by which Cold War propaganda and the rhetorical presidency were practiced by the Eisenhower administration. Through the militarized structure initiated by the Truman administration and institutionalized by the Eisenhower administration, the rhetorical presidency extended beyond the bully pulpit to include covert means of communication. The conclusion examines the propaganda legacies of the Truman and Eisenhower administrations by reviewing successor presidents' actions in relation to propaganda and Cold War policy.

NOTES

1. Martin J. Medhurst, *Dwight D. Eisenhower: Strategic Communicator* (Westport, CT: Greenwood Press, 1993), 30, 86.

2. Robert L. Ivie, "Eisenhower as Cold Warrior," in *Eisenhower's War of Words: Rhetoric and Leadership*, ed. Martin J. Medhurst (East Lansing: Michigan State University Press, 1994), 7.

3. See Ivie, "Eisenhower as Cold Warrior," 19; and Hans N. Tuch, *Communicating with the World: U.S. Public Diplomacy Overseas* (New York: St. Martin's Press, 1990), 62. Other scholars who address the Chance for Peace and the Atoms for Peace campaigns include Martin J. Medhurst, "Eisenhower's 'Atoms for Peace' Speech: A Case Study in the Strategic Use of Language" *in Cold War Rhetoric: Strategy, Metaphor, and Ideology*, eds. Martin J. Medhurst, Robert L. Ivie, Philip Wander, and Robert L. Scott (East Lansing: Michigan State University Press, 1997), 29–50; Martin J. Medhurst, "Eisenhower's Rhetorical Leadership: An Interpretation," in *Eisenhower's War of Words: Rhetoric and Leadership*, ed. Martin J. Medhurst (East Lansing: Michigan State University Press, 1994), 287–297; and Martin J. Medhurst, "Atoms for Peace and Nuclear Hegemony: The Rhetorical Structure of a Cold War Campaign," *Armed Forces & Society* 23 (1997): 571–593.

4. Shawn J. Parry-Giles, "Rhetorical Experimentation and the Cold War, 1947–1953: The Development of an International Approach to Propaganda," *Quarterly Journal of Speech* 80 (1994): 463.

5. Truman established the Psychological Strategy Board (PSB) in the spring of 1951. Eisenhower abolished the PSB in September 1953 and replaced it with the Operations Coordinating Board (OCB). For the first few months of the Eisenhower presidency, the PSB remained in place. The United States Information Agency (USIA) was created by the Eisenhower administration on August 1, 1953. See James C. Hagerty, June, 1953, Press Release, White House Central Files, 1953–1961, Official File, Box 461, Dwight D. Eisenhower Presidential Library (hereafter cited as DDEPL); Edward Lilly, December, 1951, "PSB: A Short History," White House Office, National Security Council Staff Papers, 1953–1961, PSB Central Files Series, Box 6, DDEPL; and "The President's Committee on International Activities: Report to the President," June 30, 1953, U.S. President's Committee on International Information Activities (Jackson Committee): Records, 1950–1953, Box 14, DDEPL. Eisenhower's newly titled agencies (e.g., OCB and the USIA) extended the activities that were initiated by the Truman administration's PSB and his overt propaganda channels.

6. See Psychological Strategy Board Minutes, October, 1952, White House Office, NSC Staff: Papers, 1948–1961, NSC Registry Series, 1947–1962, Box 17, DDEPL, 2; Summary Statement, April 14, 1953, White House Office, NSC Staff: Papers, 1948–1961, OCB Secretariat Series, Doctrinal Warfare (Official), Box 2, DDEPL, 2; and Working Draft, January, 1953, White House Office, NSC Staff: Papers, 1953–1961, PSB Central Files Series, Box 8, DDEPL, 1–2.

7. William J. Morgan to Dr. H. S. Craig, March, 1953, White House Office, NSC Staff: Papers, 1953–1961, PSB Central Files Series, Box 8, DDEPL, 1 (emphasis in original).

8. George A. Morgan to the Psychological Strategy Board, March, 1953, White House Office, NSC Staff: Papers, 1953–1961, PSB Central Files Series, Box 8, DDEPL, 1.

9. Working Draft, 1.

10. "Soviet Sensitivities," January, 1953, White House Office, NSC Staff: Papers, 1953–1961, PSB Central Files Series, Box 8, DDEPL, 1–15.

11. Edward P. Lilly to George A. Morgan, March, 1953, White House Office, NSC Staff: Papers, 1953–1961, PSB Central Files Series, Box 8, DDEPL, 1–2.

12. See Charles R. Norberg to Paul B. Comstock, April, 1953, White House Office, NSC Staff: Papers, 1953–1961, PSB Central Files Series, Box 8, DDEPL, 1. According to Medhurst, the announcement of Joseph Stalin's death on March 6, 1953, represented the "opening shot in the psychological warfare [activities] advocated by [C. D.] Jackson" as a means to halt potential Soviet peace offensives. See Medhurst, "Eisenhower's 'Atoms for Peace' Speech," 30–31. See also Robert L. Ivie, "Dwight D. Eisenhower's 'Chance for Peace': Quest or Crusade?" *Rhetoric & Public Affairs* 1 (1998): 227–243.

13. Dwight D. Eisenhower, "Address 'The Chance for Peace' Delivered Before the American Society of Newspaper Editors," *Public Papers of the Presidents of the United States: Dwight D. Eisenhower, 1953* (Washington, D.C.: Government Printing Office, 1960), 179–182.

14. Eisenhower, "Chance for Peace," 183–188.

15. John Prados, *Presidents' Secret Wars: CIA and Pentagon Covert Operations since World War II* (New York: William Morrow, 1986), 123, 126.

16. See "Sunday Talk," No. 51, April, 1953, Radio Free Europe—Poland, White House Office, NSC Staff: Papers, 1953–1961, PSB Central Files Series, Box 8, DDEPL; Radio Free Hungary, n.d., White House Office, NSC Staff: Papers, 1953–1961, PSB Central Files Series, Box 8, DDEPL; Eisenhower's Speech, April, 1953, Radio Free Europe—Albania Desk, White House Office, NSC Staff: Papers, 1953–1961, PSB Central Files Series, Box 8, DDEPL; "Our New York Correspondent Reports," April, 1953, Radio Free Europe—Czechoslovak Desk, White House Office, NSC Staff: Papers, 1953–1961, PSB Central Files Series, Box 8, DDEPL, 1–4; and "International Commentary," April, 1953, Radio Free Europe—Poland, White House Office, NSC Staff: Papers, 1953–1961, PSB Central Files Series, Box 8, DDEPL, 1–8.

17. See "International Commentary," April, 1953, Radio Free Europe—Poland; "Special Commentary on the Occasion of President Eisenhower's Speech," Radio Free Europe—Bulgaria, April, 1953, White House Office, NSC Staff: Papers, 1953–1961, PSB Central Files Series, Box 8, DDEPL; "Daily Commentary," Radio Free Europe—Hungary; and Radio Free Europe—Romania, April, 1953,

White House Office, NSC Staff: Papers, 1953–1961, PSB Central Files Series, Box 8, DDEPL.

18. See Cord Meyer, *Facing Reality: From World Federalism to the CIA* (New York: Harper & Row, 1980), 120; and Paul A. Smith, Jr., *On Political War* (Washington, D.C.: National Defense University Press, 1989), 199. Meyer and Smith discuss RFE's practice of recruiting exiled indigenous news personnel.

19. Eisenhower's Speech, Radio Free Europe—Albania, 6–8.

20. "International Commentary"—Radio Free Europe—Czechoslovakia, 4.

21. Psychological Strategy Board, "U.S. Doctrinal Program," June 29, 1953, White House Office, NSC Staff: Papers, 1948–1961, OCB Secretariat Series, Doctrinal Periodicals–Dr. Lilly, Box 1, DDEPL, Annex C, 9.

22. Tuch, *Communicating with the World*, 24, 61. Tuch also explains that the U.S. Congress allowed one other periodical to be published by the USIA and marketed in the United States. This second periodical is entitled *English Teaching Forum* and is targeted to English teachers.

23. Editorial Statement, *Problems of Communism* 3 (1954): i.

24. Wayne Hall et al., "Toward a Postcommunist World," *Problems of Communism* 41 (1992): 1–3.

25. W. Phillips Davison, *International Political Communication* (New York: Praeger, 1965), 258–259.

26. "A New Chapter in Soviet History," *Problems of Communism* 2 (1953): 1.

27. "The First Steps of the New Regime," *Problems of Communism* 2 (1953): 1–5.

28. Edward M. O'Connor to George Morgan, April 21, 1953, White House Office, NSC Staff: Papers, 1953–1961, PSB Central Files Series, Box 031, Box 10, DDEPL, 3–6.

29. Wallace Irwin, Jr., to George A. Morgan, May, 1953, PSB, Office of Evaluation and Review, White House Office, NSC Staff: Papers, 1953–1961, PSB Central Files Series, Box 23, DDEPL, 1–2.

30. "Lodge Project within the United Nations," n.d., White House Office, NSC Staff: Papers, 1953–1961, PSB Central Files Series, Box 23, DDEPL, 1. The PSB working group for the Lodge Project consisted of members from the PSB (Wallace Irwin, Jr., Chair), the CIA, and the Departments of State (Richard L. Sneider) and Defense (Major James J. Kelleher, Jr.) with a special intelligence advisor (Louis T. Olom). See PSB, June 30, 1953, Committee on the 8th General Assembly, White House Office, NSC Staff: Papers, 1953–1961, PSB Central Files Series, PSB 334 UN, Box 23, DDEPL, 1.

31. "The Lodge Project and the World Conflict: Notes for a General Policy Approach," August, 1953, White House Office, NSC Staff: Papers, 1953–1961, PSB Central Files Series, Box 24, DDEPL, 1.

32. "Notes for a General Policy Approach to the Lodge Project," July, 1953, White House Office, NSC Staff: Papers, 1953–1961, PSB Central Files Series, Box 23, DDEPL, 2–3.

33. Notes on Ambassador Lodge's Meeting with Contributors to GA Project, August, 1953, White House Office, NSC Staff: Papers, 1953–1961, PSB Central Files Series, Box 23, DDEPL, 2–3.

34. See Wallace Irwin, Jr., to Dr. Edward P. Lilly, May 29, 1953, White House Office, NSC Staff: Papers, 1948–1961, OCB Secretariat Series, Lodge's Human Rights Project, Box 4, DDEPL, 1–2; and "Subjects for Possible UN Exploitation," April 28, 1953, White House Office, NSC Staff: Papers, 1948–1961, OCB Secretariat Series, Lodge's Human Rights Project, Box 4, DDEPL, 2–3.

35. "Cosmos," July, 1953, White House Office, NSC Staff: Papers, 1953–1961, PSB Central Files Series, Box 24, DDEPL, Annex A, 1.

36. Wallace Irwin, Jr., to George A. Morgan, September 1, 1953, White House Office, NSC Staff: Papers, 1953–1961, PSB Central Files Series, Box 24, DDEPL, 5.

37. "Suggested Topics for Intelligence Development on Communist China Vulnerabilities in Support of Ambassador Lodge's 'Human Rights' Project," June, 1953, White House Office, NSC Staff: Papers, 1953–1961, PSB Central Files Series, Box 23, DDEPL, 1–4; "Preliminary Statement of Suggested Vulnerability Topics on Communist China," June, 1953, White House Office, NSC Staff: Papers, 1953–1961, PSB Central Files Series, Box 23, DDEPL, 1–2.

38. See "List of Soviet Vulnerabilities for Possible Exploitation at the UN," n.d., White House Office, NSC Staff: Papers, 1953–1961, PSB Central Files Series, Box 23, DDEPL, 1–2; PSB, August 28, 1953, Committee on the 8th General Assembly, White House Office, NSC Staff: Papers, 1953–1961, PSB Central Files Series, PSB 334 UN, Box 24, DDEPL, 6.

39. PSB, August 26, 1953, Policy Paper for the Lodge Project, White House Office, NSC Staff: Papers, 1948–1961, OCB Secretariat Series, Lodge's Human Rights Project, Box 4, DDEPL, 1–25.

40. See C. D. Jackson to David McCord Wright, March 31, 1953, White House Office, NSC Staff: Papers, 1948–1961, OCB Secretariat Series, Lodge's Human Rights Project, Box 4, DDEPL, 1; and George A. Morgan to Frank G. Wisner, June 3, 1953, White House Office, NSC Staff: Papers, 1953–1961, PSB Central Files Series, PSB 334 UN, Box 23, DDEPL, 2.

41. "Lodge Project within the United Nations," 2–3.

42. Notes on Ambassador Lodge's Meeting with Contributors to GA Project, 1.

43. Wallace Irwin, Jr., to George A. Morgan, July, 1953, White House Office, NSC Staff: Papers, 1953–1961, PSB Central Files Series, Box 23, DDEPL, 1–2.

44. Notes on Ambassador Lodge's Meeting with Contributors to GA Project, 1.

45. See Edward P. Lilly to George A. Morgan, July 31, 1953, White House Office, NSC Staff: Papers, 1953–1961, PSB Central Files Series, Box 23, DDEPL, 1.

46. Notes for a General Policy Approach to the Lodge Project, 1–6.

47. Notes for a General Policy Approach to the Lodge Project, 14–15.

48. Policy Paper for the Lodge Project, 17–20.

49. The Lodge Project and the World Conflict: Notes for a General Policy Approach, 1, 23, Annex A (emphasis in original).

50. George A. Morgan to Frank G. Wisner, June 3, 1953, 3.

51. The same speech was titled "Harmonizing the Actions of Nations: Major Causes of Present Tension," in *Vital Speeches of the Day*. This version of the speech also contains content variations from the one included in the *Department of State Bulletin*. See John Foster Dulles, "Harmonizing the Actions of Nations: Major Causes of Present Tension," *Vital Speeches of the Day* 19 (October 1953): 748–751. I examine and cite the speech in the *Department of State Bulletin* because it is considered the official version of the speech from the Department of State.

52. John Foster Dulles, "Easing International Tensions: The Role of the U.N.," *Department of State Bulletin* 29 (September 1953): 403–404.

53. Dulles, "Easing International Tensions," 403–406.

54. Dulles, "Easing International Tensions," 403, 407, 408.

55. Caroline Pruden, *Conditional Partners: Eisenhower, the United Nations, and the Search for a Permanent Peace* (Baton Rouge: Louisiana State University Press, 1998), 85.

56. "Operations Coordinating Board Established by the President," *Department of State Bulletin* 29 (September 1953): 420–421. The PSB became the OCB in September 1953.

57. "Policy Paper for the Lodge Project," 20.

58. See "Ad Hoc Committee on Armaments and American Policy," July 14, 1953, White House Office, NSC Staff: Papers, 1953–1961, PSB Central Files Series, Box 17, DDEPL; and "Draft Presidential Speech on Atomic Energy," July 10, 1953, White House Office, NSC Staff: Papers, 1953–1961, PSB Central Files Series, Box 17, DDEPL.

59. See "Proposed Plan for a Psychological Warfare Offensive," n.d., White House Office, NSC Staff: Papers, 1953–1961, PSB Central Files Series, Box 9, DDEPL, 2, 5–6; and "The USIA Program for 1953," July 15, 1953, White House Central Files, 1953–1961, Confidential File, Institute for International-American Affairs, Box 909, DDEPL, 2–5.

60. C. D. Jackson to Ted S. Repplier, June, 1953, White House Central Files, 1953–1961, Confidential File, Box 12, DDEPL, 1.

61. James M. Lambie, Jr., to C. D. Jackson, July, 1953, White House Central Files, 1953–1961, Confidential File, Box 12, DDEPL, 1.

62. Memorandum on a Public Information Program, July, 1953, White House Central Files, 1953–1961, Confidential File, Box 12, DDEPL, 2. The Oppenheimer Panel, which was led by Los Alamos director, J. Robert Oppenheimer, issued a report to Secretary of State Dean Acheson that was also widely studied by the Eisenhower administration. Even though the administration and the PSB/OCB ignored much of the warnings of a nuclear build-up emanating from the panel's report, the administration nevertheless took heed the panel's call for an approach of "candor" with the American people related to civil defense matters

and nuclear arms proliferation. For more details on the Oppenheimer Report, see: J. Michael Hogan, "The Science of Cold War Strategy: Propaganda and Public Opinion in the Eisenhower Administration's 'War of Words,'" in *Critical Reflections on the Cold War: Linking Rhetoric and History*, eds. Martin J. Medhurst and H. W. Brands (College Station: Texas A&M University, 2000),154–160.

63. Suggested Check List for Presidential Speech Implementation, November, 1953, Jackson, C. D.: Papers, 1931–1967, Box 30, DDEPL, 1.

64. Abbott Washburn to C. D. Jackson, June, 1953, White House Central Files, 1953–1961, Official File, Box 524, DDEPL, 1.

65. "The Safety of the Republic Series: A Suggested Public Education Support Program," n.d., White House Central Files, 1953–1961, Confidential File, Box 12, DDEPL, 3–4.

66. See "Project 'Candor,'" July 22, 1953, White House Office, NSC Staff: Papers, 1953–1961, PSB Central Files Series, Box 17, DDEPL; and Horace S. Craig to Roy Snapp, August 26, 1953, White House Office, NSC Staff: Papers, 1953–1961, PSB Central Files Series, Box 17, DDEPL. According to Craig, a "draft of the President's Speech on Candor dated August 13, 1953" was "destroyed as classified waste" on August 18, 1953. See also Medhurst, "Eisenhower's 'Atoms for Peace' Speech," 32.

67. Dwight D. Eisenhower, "Address before the General Assembly of the United Nations on Peaceful Uses of Atomic Energy," *Public Papers of the Presidents of the United States, Dwight D. Eisenhower, 1953* (Washington, D.C.: Government Printing Office, 1960), 817–821.

68. "Check List for Possible Exploitation of President's Atomic Energy Speech," December, 1953, White House Central Files, 1953–1961, Confidential File, Box 13, DDEPL, 1.

69. See Michael Osborn, "Archetypal Metaphor in Rhetoric: The Light-Dark Family," *Quarterly Journal of Speech* 53 (1967): 116. Osborn maintains that "archetypal metaphors" are "grounded in prominent features of experience, in objects, action, or conditions which are inescapably salient in human consciousness."

70. Dark/light images serve as archetypal metaphors that portray U.S. peace in a positive light and emphasize the troubling darkness of a Soviet peace. Dwight D. Eisenhower, "Address before the General Assembly of the United Nations on Peaceful Uses of Atomic Energy," *Public Papers of the Presidents of the United States, Dwight D. Eisenhower, 1953* (Washington, D.C.: Government Printing Office, 1960), 817 (emphasis added).

71. OCB, December, 18, 1953, Minutes of the Working Group for the Exploitation of the President's UN Speech, White House Office, NSC Staff: Papers, 1948–1961, OCB Central Files Series, OCB 383.3, Box 121, DDEPL, 1. The OCB Working Group included representatives from the Departments of State (Joseph Phillips) and Defense (William H. Godel), the CIA (Tracy Barnes), the USIA (Andrew Berding), the AEC (Morse Salisbury), the FDCA (John DeChant), the OCB (Richard Hirsch), and C. D. Jackson as chairperson.

72. "A Program to Exploit the President's UN Speech of December 8, 1953, in Domestic and International Public Opinion Fields," January 8, 1954, White House Central Files, 1953–1961, Confidential File, Box 13, DDEPL.

73. "The President's Atomic Proposal before the UN," December 28, 1953, White House Central Files, 1953–1961, Confidential File, Box 13, DDEPL, 1.

74. C. D. Jackson to members of the Operations Coordinating Board, January, 16, 1954, White House Central Files, 1953–1961, Confidential File, Box 13, DDEPL.

75. National Security Council 5431/1, August, 1954, "Cooperation with Other Nations in the Peaceful Uses of Atomic Energy," White House Office: Office of Special Assistant for National Security Affairs: Records, 1952–1961, NSC Series, Policy Papers Subseries, Box 12, DDEPL, 5.

76. Memorandum for the Operations Coordinating Board, December 9, 1953, White House Office, NSC Staff: Papers, 1953–1961, PSB Central Files Series, Box 28, DDEPL.

77. C. D. Jackson to Department and Agency Information Centers, January 19, 1954, White House Central Files, 1953–1961, Confidential File, Box 13, DDEPL, 1.

78. Operations Coordinating Board Minutes, January 19, 1954, White House Central Files, 1953–1961, Confidential File, Box 13, DDEPL, 1–2.

79. *Atomic Power for Peace*, Background and Action Kit No. 24, n.d., White House Central Files, 1953–1961, Confidential File, Box 13, DDEPL.

80. "The Atom for Peace and Progress: Suggested Domestic Implementation Actions," n.d., White House Central Files, 1953–1961, Confidential File, Box 13, DDEPL.

81. See OCB, January 6, 1954, Minutes of the Working Group for the Exploitation of the President's UN Speech, White House Office, NSC Staff: Papers, 1948–1961, OCB Central Files Series, OCB 388.3, Box 121, DDEPL, 2; OCB, January 6, 1954, Extracts from Mr. C. D. Jackson's Report on Follow-up Action to the President's Speech, White House Office, NSC Staff: Papers, 1948–1961, OCB 388.3, Box 121, DDEPL, 3; and OCB, January 19, 1954, Minutes of the Working Group for the Exploitation of the President's UN Speech, White House Office, NSC Staff: Papers, 1948–1961, OCB Central Files Series, OCB 388.3, Box 121, DDEPL, 3.

82. "A Pool of Atomic Power," *New York Times*, December 9, 1953, 10.

83. "The Western Initiative," *New York Times*, December 10, 1953, 46 (emphases added).

84. "Only the Soviets Say 'No,'" *New York Times*, December 11, 1953, 30.

85. "Americans Eager to Share Peaceful Uses of Atomic Energy," n.d., White House Central Files, 1953–1961, Confidential File, Box 13, DDEPL, 2.

86. Operations Coordinating Board Minutes, January 19, 1954, 1.

87. Lewis Strauss to Dwight D. Eisenhower, February, 1957, White House Central Files, 1953–1961, Confidential File, Box 531, DDEPL, 1–5.

88. USIA to C. D. Jackson, December 10, 1953, White House Central Files, 1953–1961, Confidential File, Box 13, DDEPL.

89. OCB, January 6, 1954, Extracts from Mr. C. D. Jackson's Report, 3; and C. D. Jackson to Department and Agency Information Offices, January 19, 1954, White House Office, NSC Staff: Papers, 1948–1961, OCB Central Files Series, OCB 388.3, Box 121, DDEPL, 1.

90. "Summary of Events Planned for Exploitation: President Eisenhower's Speech before the UN, December 8, 1953," February 17, 1954, White House Central Files, 1953–1961, Confidential File, Box 13, DDEPL, 1–5.

91. See OCB, October 25, 1954, "Progress Report of the OCB on Nuclear Energy Projects and Related Information Programs," White House Office, NSC Staff: Papers, 1948–1961, OCB Central Files Series, 000.9 Atomic Energy, Box 8, DDEPL, 4–5; and "Preliminary Outline for USIA: Exhibit at Sao Paulo Quadricentennial Exposition," n.d, White House Central Files, 1953–1961, Confidential File, Box 13, DDEPL, 1.

92. See USIA, January 15, 1954, "United States Doctrinal Program," White House Office, NSC Staff: Papers, 1948–1961, OCB Central Files Series, OCB 091.4 Ideological Programs, Box 70, DDEPL, 19. For additional readings on the relationship between science and the Cold War, see Stuart W. Leslie, *The Cold War and American Science* (New York: Columbia University Press, 1994); and Jessica Wang, *American Science in an Age of Anxiety: Scientists, Anticommunism, and the Cold War* (Chapel Hill: University of North Carolina Press, 1999).

93. Arthur Larson to Dwight D. Eisenhower, October, 1957, Eisenhower, Dwight D.: Papers as President of the United States, 1953–1961 (Ann Whitman File), Administrative Series, Box 37, DDEPL, 1.

94. "Presidential Statement," July, 1953, White House Office, NSC Staff: Papers, 1953–1961, PSB Central Files Series, Box 10, DDEPL, 1–4.

95. Lazar Volin, "Science and Intellectual Freedom in Russia," *Problems of Communism* 3 (1954): 35–37.

96. By naturalization I mean that the human qualities are "removed" and the entity seemingly embodies characteristics found only in nature. The politicization of the entity is masked by its construction in more natural terms. See Roland Barthes, *Mythologies* (New York: Hill and Wang, 1972), 142–143.

97. *Atomic Power for Peace*, n.d., White House Central Files (Official File), 1953–1961, Box 524, DDEPL, 1–21.

98. OCB, "Overseas Reaction to the AEC Report on the Effects of High-Yield Nuclear Explosions," March, 1955, White House Office, NSC Staff: Papers, 1948–1961, OCB Central Files Series, Box 9, DDEPL, 1.

99. The United States Information Agency, *Blessing of Atomic Energy*, 1956, Record Group 306, The National Archives Motion Picture Collection.

100. See Ivie, "Eisenhower as Cold Warrior," 16.

101. Blanche Wiesen Cook, *The Declassified Eisenhower: A Divided Legacy* (Garden City, NY: Doubleday, 1981), 180–181; and Fred I. Greenstein, *The Hid-*

den-Hand Presidency: Eisenhower as Leader (New York: Basic Books, 1982), 181.

102. Medhurst, "Eisenhower's 'Atoms for Peace' Speech," 47.

103. Walter L. Hixson, *Parting the Curtain: Propaganda, Culture, and the Cold War, 1945–1961* (New York: St. Martin's Griffin, 1998), 223.

104. "President's Committee on Information Activities Abroad Conclusions and Recommendations," December, 1960, Eisenhower, Dwight D.: Papers as President of the United States, 1953–1961 (Ann Whitman File), Administrative Series, Box 33, DDEPL, 21–22. Eisenhower formed this committee, popularly known at the Sprague committee, to evaluate the USIA and other areas of psychological warfare at the end of his presidency. The Sprague committee thus served as the bookend to the Jackson committee. While the objectivity of committee members may be called into question because Eisenhower appointed them, the credibility of their assessment is heightened by their critical assessment of the USIA in other areas. In addition, this report remained classified for almost forty years, indicating its results were less likely to be used for public relations purposes.

105. For other interpretations of the effectiveness of Eisenhower's peace campaigns, see Wilson P. Dizard, *The Strategy of Truth: The Story of the U.S. Information Service* (Washington, D.C.: Public Affairs Press, 1961), 44; and Leo Bogart, *Cool Words, Cold War: A New Look at USIA's Premises for Propaganda* (Washington, D.C.: American University Press, 1995), 212–225.

106. See OCB, December 18, 1953, Minutes of the Working Group, 3; and Stefan T. Possony, December 12, 1953, Notes on Soviet Statement Concerning President Eisenhower's Proposal for an Atomic Energy Pool, White House Office, NSC Staff: Papers, 1948–1961, OCB Central Files Series, OCB 388.3, Box 121, DDEPL, 1–2.

107. Richard Hirsch, "Status of OCB Guidance on Operation CASTLE Public Reporting Problems," May 18, 1954, White House Office, NSC Staff: Papers, 1948–1961, OCB Central Files Series, 000.9 Atomic Energy, Box 8, DDEPL, 1–2. See also OCB, "Progress Report of the OCB," October 24, 1954, 1; Elmer B. Staats, April 26, 1954, Letter to Lewis L. Strauss, White House Office, NSC Staff: Papers, 1948–1961, OCB Central Files Series, 000.9 Atomic Energy, Box 8, DDEPL, 1. Members of the OCB Working Group on the Coordination of Nuclear Energy Projects and Related Information Programs included Gerard Smith, chairperson; Walter Radius and George Spiegel (Department of State); Gen. Herbert B. Loper (Department of Defense); Robert E. Matteson (FOA); And.ew Berding and Allen Haden (USIA); Gen. Willard S. Paul (ODM); Morse Sali .bury (AEC); John DeChant (FCDA); and Horace S. Craig and Richard Hirsch (OCB). See OCB, June, 1, 1954, Minutes of the OCB Working Group on Coordination of Nuclear Energy Projects and Related Information Programs, White House Office, NSC Staff: Papers, 1948–1961, OCB Central Files Series, 000.9 Atomic Energy, Box 8, DDEPL, 1.

108. Operations Coordinating Board Minutes, August, 1954, White House Office, NSC Staff: Papers, 1948–1961, OCB Central Files Series, Box 8, DDEPL,

1–2; and James J. Kelleher, Jr., to Mr. Button, August, 1954, White House Office, NSC Staff: Papers, 1948–1961, OCB Central Files Series, Box 8, DDEPL, 2.

109. Operations Coordinating Board Minutes, August, 1954, 1–2.

110. Operations Coordinating Board, "Progress Report to the OCB on Nuclear Energy Projects and Related Information Programs," December, 1954, White House Office, NSC Staff: Papers 1948–1961, OCB Central Files Series, OCB 000.9 Atomic Energy, Box 8, DDEPL, 4.

111. Gerard C. Smith to Richard B. Hirsch (including a Draft of the Proposed Press Release), October 12, 1954, White House Office, NSC Staff: NSC Papers, 1948–1961, OCB Central Files Series, 000.9 Atomic Energy, Box 8, DDEPL, 1–5.

112. OCB Minutes, August, 1954, 1–2. See also Kelleher to Mr. Button, August, 1954, 1.

113. OCB, "Progress Report," December, 1954, 5.

114. See OCB, June 30, 1954, Minutes of the OCB Working Group on Coordination of Nuclear Energy Projects and Related Information Programs (including a Check List of Suggested Themes), White House Office, NSC Staff: Papers, 1948–1961, OCB Central Files Series, 000.9 Atomic Energy, Box 8, DDEPL, 1–2; OCB, August 18, 1954, "Nuclear Energy Projects and Related Information," White House Office, NSC Staff: Papers, OCB Central Files Series, 000.9 Atomic Energy, Box 8, DDEPL, 1; OCB, October 14, 1954, Draft State Department Contribution for Progress Report to OCB, White House Office, NSC Staff: Papers, 1948–1961, OCB Central Files Series, 000.9 Atomic Energy, Box 8, DDEPL, 1–2; and Dwight D. Eisenhower, "Radio and Television Remarks on the Occasion of the Ground-Breaking Ceremony for the Shippingport Atomic Power Plant," *Public Papers of the Presidents: Dwight D. Eisenhower, 1954* (Washington, D.C.: U.S. Government Printing Office, 1960), 840–841 (emphasis added).

115. See OCB, August 18, 1954, "Nuclear Power Projects," 1; OCB, "Progress Report, December 1954, 1; Gerard C. Smith to Elmer B. Staats, December 21, 1954, White House Office, NSC Staff: Papers, 1948–1961, OCB 000.9 Atomic Energy, Box 8, DDEPL, 1.

116. OCB, "Overseas Reaction," 2–3.

117. OCB, "Progress Report, December, 1954," 1–2.

118. Dizard, *The Strategy of Truth*, 44.

119. Medhurst, *Dwight D. Eisenhower: Strategic Communicator*, 74.

120. C. D. Jackson to Dwight D. Eisenhower, March, 1954, Eisenhower, Dwight D.: Papers as President of the United States, 1953–1961 (Ann Whitman File), Administration Series, Box 22, DDEPL, 1.

121. OCB, "Progress Report to the National Security Council on Implementation of the Recommendations of the Jackson Committee Report," September, 1953, PSB Central Files Series, Box 22, DDEPL, Annex B, 1, 4.

122. Shawn J. Parry-Giles, "'Camouflaged' Propaganda: The Truman and Eisenhower Administrations' Covert Manipulation of the News," *Western Journal of Communication* 60 (1996): 158–159.

123. Medhurst, "Eisenhower's Rhetorical Leadership," 289, 296.

Conclusion: Expanding the Rhetorical Presidency

According to Louis J. Halle, "most persons regard the Cold War as essentially an ideological war"[1]—a "war of words," where propaganda replaced bombs and tanks. In the early post-World War II years, though, propaganda was an ill-understood practice, or at least one known only in terms of the negative connotations attached to its uses in World War I and II. As the United States progressed from two world wars into a cold war, Washington insiders became more interested in the strategic potential of propaganda. Over time, its practitioners replaced a language of peace and news with a language of war and weaponry in deliberations over propaganda's utility. By 1952, the presidential election brought not only a military general to the White House, but a general who had also experienced *and* championed the practice of propaganda during wartime.[2] Only months before his death, Dwight D. Eisenhower still referred to the directorship of the United States Information Agency (USIA) as "one of the most important jobs in the entire United States Government."[3] Not unexpectedly, then, this general-turned-president completed what Truman started. He institutionalized a militarized vision of the propaganda program with the president acting as its commander-in-chief, expanding the rhetorical powers of the presidency in the process.

It is not surprising that the enhanced use of propaganda by the U.S. government mirrors the development of the rhetorical presidency: both require an appreciation for the power of persuasion; both serve to bolster the power of the presidency; and both target larger publics, lessening congressional involvement in foreign policy matters especially. Jeffrey K. Tulis maintains that twentieth century presidents "speak to 'the people' more" than their "nineteenth-century predecessors," as they "defend themselves publicly . . . promote policy initiatives nationwide, and . . . inspirit the population."[4] The Truman and Eisenhower administrations' move, though, to more secret operations provided presidential administrations a much more *covert* means of rhetorical influence. Technological sophistication and classified executive orders increased the available modes of communication capable of servicing the president,[5] expanding the parameters of the rhetorical presidency to include more "hidden hand" communication tactics.[6] The public proliferation of presidential policies so vital to the rhetorical effectiveness of a presidential administration,[7] could now be conducted by various institutions and individuals, whose articulation of the same themes could perpetuate an illusion of widespread consensus. Certainly, Eisenhower's Chance for Peace and Atoms for Peace campaigns demonstrate just how coordinated, centralized, and covert such presidentially inspired messages could actually become.

Even though scholars have increased attention devoted to the expansion of rhetorical leadership by twentieth-century presidents,[8] many overlook the changes that the presidential administrations of Harry S. Truman and Dwight D. Eisenhower brought to the rhetorical presidency. When introducing the concept of the rhetorical presidency in 1981, James W. Ceaser et al. address the rhetorical influences of such presidents as Theodore Roosevelt, Woodrow Wilson, Franklin D. Roosevelt, John F. Kennedy, Richard Nixon, and Jimmy Carter.[9] Jeffrey K. Tulis offers a similar focus yet acknowledges the work of Lyndon Johnson;[10] others also point to Ronald Reagan's persuasive prowess,[11] as well Bill Clinton's rhetorical acumen.[12] In very recent scholarship on the subject, Truman and Eisenhower were virtually ignored by Richard J. Ellis and his colleagues in their historical review of the rhetorical presidency.[13] Philip Abbott barely mentions the country's first two Cold War presidents in his work about presidential leadership. Even though Abbott notes Truman's alleged "spiritedness," neither Truman nor Eisenhower were identified as one of the author's "eleven poet-presidents."[14] Fred I. Greenstein's hidden-hand thesis did not even inspire political scientists to reassess their attention to Eisenhower's rhetorical actions.[15]

What both Truman and Eisenhower bring to an understanding of the rhetorical presidency is the way in which covert actions expand, supplement, and supplant the bully pulpit, transforming and enhancing the presidential-rhetorical paradigm. Bruce E. Gronbeck argues that "the age of secondary orality" involving radio, television, and film refashioned presidential rhetoric.[16] As a result, radio stations such as the VOA, RFE, and RL could promulgate Truman's and Eisenhower's messages either overtly or covertly even though the latter two stations were not even associated with the U.S. government. Surrogates working on behalf of the executive branch could present speeches that were strategized by the presidential administration; books that reflected presidential themes could be disseminated in such a way that masked the U.S. government's involvement. These messages, though, reinforced the bully pulpit themes that both Truman and Eisenhower promulgated and furthered the means by which to by-pass congressional influence. The repetitive and covert nature of these themes also expanded the power of the bully pulpit because of the impression of narrative substantiation. In other instances, the covert messages replaced presidential statements yet still reinforced discursive goals of the executive branch. To divorce such covert messages from the rhetorical presidency is naïve and misreads the practice of presidential communication in this "age of secondary orality." In the early Cold War period in particular, covert means of discourse represented a standard mode of rhetorical influence for the presidential administrations as they relied on, among others, a camouflaged and defector propaganda as part of their militarized structure.

The depths of the covert operations and the institutionalization of a militarized structure had clear and concerning consequences. To begin with, it must be understood that the communists were principal agents in the intensification of the Cold War. Thus, the Truman and Eisenhower operatives should not shoulder the brunt of the critique; from the presidents' vantage point, the Cold War necessitated such a clandestine structure. Yet, such a militarized mindset helped promote private plans for the extinction of communism as the Eisenhower administration, in fact, lessened its commitment to peace; privately, operatives planned for a war of wars that could extinguish the enemy as it publicly promoted a rhetoric of peace. Peace in the Psychological Strategy Board (PSB) framework connoted weakness while war and weaponry equaled a show of strength. The administration recognized that such controversial policies had to remain secret, which is why we are only now just beginning to discover the magnitude of such covert actions.

Covert activities thus further eroded the checks and balances of congressional review and public scrutiny and aided in the production of more ethically questionable solutions as the presidential administrations operated, at least partially, in a covert vacuum. In the process, the American media acted, willingly and unwittingly, as the domestic arm of the presidential propaganda program, and Congress, willingly and unwittingly, was excluded from many of the covert planning sessions. The power of the presidency and, in particular, presidential-rhetorical power, though, continued to grow, and the administration was also able to promulgate a more monolithic Cold War ideology with limited opposition. While public knowledge of such plans may not have changed the course of the Cold War, the secretization of such planning ensured that the United States remained steadfast in its determination to contain and potentially extinguish communism internationally, prolonging a deadly and costly war.

Because of the actions of Truman and Eisenhower, the narrative repetition of the Cold War message from 1945 to 1960 helped normalize the Cold War ideology that resonates in the U.S. collective memory of that battle. The creation and the perpetuation of such a Cold War narrative represent yet another contribution of the Truman and Eisenhower administrations to the rhetorical presidency. They established an apparatus that allowed for the dissemination of a more ideologically consonant message that became naturalized by the time that the Kennedy administration came to Washington. Obviously, there were other political operatives and institutions (e.g., the media, McCarthy) that helped create such a message; the Truman and Eisenhower administrations, nevertheless, both fashioned the machination, the political ideology, and the political strategies that outlived the Cold War—influencing American media coverage in the process. In order to understand how ideology is presidentially constructed and promulgated, we must move beyond the confines of the bully pulpit to the secret strategies and the multifarious messages involved in the performance of the rhetorical presidency. To fully appreciate the legacies of the Truman and Eisenhower administration's rhetorical presidencies is to understand the way in which future administrations molded the USIA into their own presidential "voice."

THE LEGACY OF A MILITARIZED PROPAGANDA PROGRAM

In reorganizing the U.S. propaganda program, the Eisenhower administration freed propaganda from the political whims of Congress. Yet such a structure did not entirely insulate the agency from continued disagreements over the meaning or purposes of propaganda. Eisenhower's reorganization shifted the focus of debate over U.S. propaganda from Congress to the White House, revealing, in part, Truman's and Eisenhower's propaganda legacy. In reviewing presidential propaganda prerogatives over the past forty years, the actions of these two presidential administrations are still evident in the structural, strategic, and symbolic actions made by more contemporary presidential administrations. As presidents sought to mold the propaganda program to fit within their individualized foreign policy aims, many also mirrored the propaganda philosophies of the two presidents who most influenced its practice.

Thirteen months before he left office, Eisenhower appointed yet another committee to assess the effectiveness of the USIA—the Committee on Information Activities Abroad (Sprague committee)—the bookend to the Jackson committee. While the Sprague committee urged that foreign opinion needed even further consideration in policy formation and execution, its members also applauded the work by the Operations Coordinating Board (OCB) and recommended its continuation.[17] When John F. Kennedy assumed office, however, he abolished the OCB, bringing to an end the first and last official peacetime psychological warfare agency—a move that astounded USIA officials, given the PSB/OCB presidential utility.[18]

Kennedy's actions, though, brought other important changes to the USIA. Most significantly, Kennedy appointed famed radio personality Edward R. Murrow as USIA's new director. Such a move enhanced the credibility of the USIA, while also perpetuating the journalistic paradigm used by the Truman administration during the Smith-Mundt hearings.[19] Even though some scholars contend that Murrow was excluded from Kennedy's "inner circle," others argue that the administration accepted the USIA "as a genuine arm of American diplomacy."[20] The status of the USIA, at least, was most noticeably seen in the prominent role it played in such operations as the Bay of Pigs, the Cuban Missile Crisis, and the country's space mission.[21] USIA's activities were also expanded in developing regions such as Africa, another domestic propaganda venture began during Kennedy's term, with the inauguration of the *English Teaching Forum*. This journal targeted English teachers in the United States and abroad and accompanied the *Problems of Communism* (POC) as the only other *official* domestic publication authorized by the USIA.[22]

Like Eisenhower, Kennedy relied on the USIA to help the United States obtain its foreign policy objectives. But unlike Eisenhower, the tone of the agency grew more hardline under Kennedy's administration. Murrow openly called himself a propagandist, and he refuted the dictum that the USIA should emit primarily straight news. As a result, the USIA sponsored, for example, more strident propaganda films that were shown to international and domestic audiences.[23] Such an aggressive approach with the USIA resembled the strategies amassed by the Truman administration during the Campaign of Truth and countered Eisenhower's attempt to remake the USIA into a seemingly more "objective" news source.

The next two presidential administrations continued to rely on the USIA to broadcast their foreign policy goals, particularly in relation to the country's newest Cold War exigency. During Vietnam, the USIA flourished as it sought to win approval of U.S. military goals. Noted journalist John Chancellor headed the Voice of America for part of the Lyndon Johnson administration,[24] reflecting once again the journalistic paradigm of USIA's overt stations. Johnson also appointed Carl T. Rowan, another renowned journalist and the first African American, as director of the USIA. Even though Johnson was initially skeptical of the USIA's utility, he eventually grew to appreciate its ability to spotlight his activities. Thus, Johnson expanded the use of still photography for domestic and international public relations efforts to document presidential activity.[25] Toward that end, Johnson fashioned the rhetorical presidency to include visual as well as verbal discourse for propaganda purposes.

President Richard M. Nixon's primary propaganda concern was that his foreign policy aims be "sold" abroad. Nixon was most interested in the propaganda program's covert capabilities, which were initiated by the Truman administration in the late 1940s and early 1950s.[26] According to Cold War information specialist Hans N. Tuch, the USIA's primary mission under Nixon "was to conduct a vigorous, aggressive anti-communist campaign to 'defeat' Soviet imperialism"—a strategy that stood in direct contrast to Nixon's public policy of détente.[27] Such a policy, which used covert propaganda tactics that contradicted the overt strategies, mirrored the propaganda philosophies of both the Truman and Eisenhower administrations. As the Vietnam conflict came to an end, though, agency officials grew concerned that support for the propaganda program would wane during peacetime.[28]

When President Jimmy Carter entered office, he lessened tensions over the program's future. He also brought the greatest changes to the USIA's structure since its creation. Carter renamed the program the United States International Communication Agency (USICA), and vowed to make the agency a two-way communication medium. While USICA told the nation's story to the international public, it was also designed to educate U.S. citizens about international nations.[29] As Carter expressed, "It is in our interest—and in the interest of other nations—that Americans have the opportunity to understand the histories, cultures and problems of others, so that we can come to understand their hopes, perceptions and aspirations."[30] The agency thus functioned to help the United States "win understanding and acceptance" of foreign policy aims abroad,[31] while teaching the American public about the cultures of the world. Such a move clearly evidences how presidential philosophy molds propaganda into a presidential tool.

Unlike his predecessor, President Ronald Reagan reinvigorated the aggressive Cold War posture of the USIA reminiscent of the Truman administration, simultaneously expanding its budget.[32] To begin with, Reagan restored the original name of the USIA when he entered office. He also reinstituted a program of "hard-hitting" propaganda against communism—a program resembling Truman's even in name: "Project Truth."[33] According to Tuch, the Campaign of Truth-like program was devised to combat Soviet "disinformation," by "exposing the source of the lies, documenting their falseness, and condemning the Soviets' venality in spreading them."[34] Such an approach reflected Truman's response to the Hate America campaign in particular.

Reagan's propaganda philosophy also revealed a style similar to that of Eisenhower. Reagan's Project Truth, for example, stressed the "common moral, spiritual, and cultural values" of the United States and its allies,[35] themes perpetuated in both the Chance for Peace and the Atoms for Peace campaigns. Also like Eisenhower, Reagan awarded propaganda strategy a more prominent place in his administration, giving the USIA director, Charles Z. Wick, a prominent position in national security policy making.[36] Part of Wick's attractiveness centered on his outspoken anticommunist views and his close friendship with Reagan—a relationship similar to the one between Truman and Gordan Gray and Eisenhower and C. D. Jackson. Also like the USIA of the Eisenhower years, the propaganda program under Reagan was awarded an advisory role to the National Security Council (NSC), with the same authority as the Central Intelligence Agency (CIA) and the Joint Chiefs of Staff. Most significantly, Reagan formed a Special Planning Group on Public Diplomacy, similar to the secret "5412 group" that Eisenhower assembled, both of which were managed by the White House.[37] Finally, the Reagan administration also developed a holistic and domestic propaganda campaign to influence the debate surrounding the funding of the Nicaraguan contras—a domestic propaganda effort not unlike that of Eisenhower's and Truman's because of the focus on influencing the U.S. private press corps.[38]

Reminiscent of the McCarthy-like tactics of the 1950s, Reagan also reportedly "black list[ed]" a group of "potential USIA speakers declared by [the USIA] . . . to be 'unsuitable' for participation" in the government's propaganda programs. These individuals included scholars and educators. Such an act created a considerable partisan outcry, since most of the speakers were members of the Democratic Party.[39] This dispute served to accentuate the partisan-nature of the propaganda program. With propaganda institutionalized as an executive tool by the Eisenhower administration, the agency cannot only meet foreign policy aims but presidential partisan goals as well.

By exhibiting a heightened interest in propaganda strategy, the Reagan administration also expanded the propaganda program. Early in Reagan's first term, the USIA introduced Radio Marti, beamed by the VOA to Cuba, and designed to promote the cause of freedom there. Almost simultaneously, the Reagan administration enhanced the USIA's Television and Film Service Activities in 1983 via Worldnet, a closed-circuit satellite television system that transmitted twenty-four hours a day in English, French, Spanish, and Arabic. This represented the USIA's venture into what Richard C. Levy calls "video diplomacy."[40] Worldnet provides foreign journalists who gather at U.S. embassies the opportunity to interview U.S. political officials, including cabinet members, congressional leaders, and other distinguished citizens.[41] While airing original programming, Worldnet also features such domestic programs as the *MacNeil/Lehrer News Hour*,[42] which blurs the international and domestic propaganda practices so common in the Truman and Eisenhower eras.

Also reflective of the two earliest Cold War administrations is the language that Reagan administration officials employed to characterize their newest propaganda medium. In a speech entitled "Global Interdependence and the *War* of Ideas," Wick asserted that the "USIA entered the age of 'satellite television diplomacy,'" with the addition of Worldnet, "by launching a new and potent *weapon*."[43] Like the presidential administrations that legalized and institutionalized a militarized propaganda program, the Reagan administration also used the militarized language associated with this governmental agency. As Laurien Alexandre notes, Reagan's version of the USIA exemplifies "the ideological campaign being waged by the executive branch."[44]

Formalizing the propaganda program in his own image, President George Bush perpetuated the propaganda strategies instituted by his former boss. Bush continued targeting Cuba by adding TV Marti to the USIA in 1990 at a cost of $65 million. The Bush administration also called for the establishment of Radio Free Asia (RFA); its structure was to reflect that of Radio Free Europe (RFE) and Radio Liberty (RL). Like RFE and RL under the Truman administration, radio broadcasts were intended to target particular regions, including China, North Korea, Vietnam, Laos, Cambodia, and Burma through an alleged "nonprofit" agency, brought about, in part, by opposition to government sponsorship. Such a structure, of course, sounds all too familiar. While the official sponsorship of such Asian broadcasts is not fully known, the USIA did eventually open in-country propaganda services in Laos and Cambodia in 1992.[45] This proposed expansion of Asian broadcasts through public, and presumably private channels, represents a familiar propaganda practice that can be traced to the Truman and Eisenhower presidencies.

As intended in 1948 with the Smith-Mundt Act, the U.S. propaganda program also figured quite heavily in the eventual cessation of the Cold War. In 1991, Radio Liberty served as a major source of information and support for those who resisted the military coup in Moscow. With an office in Moscow, RL championed Mikhail Gorbachev's glasnost policy, which aided the fall of Soviet communism.[46] But because of the historical connections between the Cold War and the propaganda program, propagandists feared that the end of the Cold War would simultaneously mark the demise of the USIA.

Although the Clinton administration brought changes to the organizational structure of the USIA, it still reflected the organizing principles of the earliest Cold War presidents. In commemorating the country's Cold War propaganda efforts, President Bill Clinton claimed, "Our victory in the cold war was due not only to the strength of our forces but also to the power of our ideas." Calling propaganda one of "the most effective foreign policy tools we have," Clinton sought to sculpt propaganda into the image of his personal presidential philosophy in the post-Cold War period:

I have said that my foreign policy is premised on promoting democracy, improving our security, and revitalizing our economy. The [propaganda] plan we are announcing today assists us in doing all three [by] . . . telling America's story to the rest of the world, reporting objective international news, providing accurate in-country news where a free press is not yet developed, and . . . helping to transmit our Government's official views abroad.[47]

In 1994, Clinton signed into law the United States International Broadcasting Act (P.L. 103–236), establishing the International Broadcasting Bureau (IBB) that existed under USIA control. The IBB supervises all nonmilitary governmental broadcast services: RFE, RL, VOA, Worldnet, Radio and TV Marti, and the newly established Radio Free Asia (1994). All of these stations operate under the oversight of the Broadcasting Board of Governors (BBG), which exists to "promote the open communication of information and ideas, in support of democracy, and the freedom to seek, receive, and impart information, worldwide." On October 1, 1999, the BBG became an "independent, autonomous entity responsible for all U.S. government and government sponsored, nonmilitary, international broadcasting." The USIA was folded back into the Department of State and became known as the International Information Programs. In essence, the autonomy offered the BBG stations reflects the same structure of Eisenhower's USIA, awarding the presidential administration greater control over the broadcast mediums that were situated in the Department of State.[48]

Such a tribute to the U.S. propaganda program in the aftermath of the Cold War demonstrates the impact of the Truman and Eisenhower administrations' propaganda legacies. By equating propaganda with military, economic, and diplomatic activities in U.S. foreign policy, Truman and Eisenhower ensured its longevity. By making the USIA and its covert counterparts a mouthpiece for the president, Truman and Eisenhower cemented its executive status, which ensured the expansion of the rhetorical presidency to include their successors.

An examination of presidential propaganda strategies thus acts as a representation of a president's communication and governmental philosophies. Both Truman and Eisenhower demonstrated a predisposition toward synchronizing not only overt and covert propaganda strategy, but also overt and covert military action. Based on the revisionist histories of Eisenhower, his public persona countered his private one.[49] Viewed by many during his presidency as an inactive and grandfatherly figure, Eisenhower secretly embarked on a fierce battle against communism through what many believe were unethical, if not unconstitutional, means.[50] This strategy also characterized his overall foreign policy activities, the covert depths of which we are just beginning to discover. To that end, the configuration of the U.S. propaganda program becomes a representation of each president's personal/political philosophy. Interestingly, though, the propaganda program also serves as a key instrument in the *construction* of each president's public image as well as the public understanding of the U.S. presidency in general, making it an agency worthy of further scholarly examination.[51]

While Truman was forced to reconcile propaganda with democratic principles before legalizing a peacetime propaganda program, propaganda today exists as a less controversial and more naturalized part of the government's foreign policy apparatus. The eventual militarization of the U.S. propaganda program through a language of war and a militarized structure, helped secure this naturalization. The military arguably acts as one of the least controversial arms of government in the sense that it operates with limited civilian and public influence. The military also serves as that arm of the government in which the president assumes the most significant and often the least questioned authority. By militarizing propaganda, both the Truman and Eisenhower administrations, whether intentionally or not, managed to expand the rhetorical powers of the presidency, while simultaneously legitimizing what many scholars, journalists, and political officials previously labeled as an "undemocratic" activity.

NOTES

1. Louis J. Halle, *The Cold War as History* (New York: Harper Torchbooks, 1967), 3.

2. See Fitzhugh Green, *American Propaganda Abroad: From Benjamin Franklin to Ronald Reagan* (New York: Hippocrene Books, 1988), 28; and Rhodri

Jeffreys-Jones, *The CIA and American Democracy* (New Haven, CT: Yale University Press, 1989), 85.

3. Frank Shakespeare, "Comment," in *Ike and USIA: A Commemorative Symposium*, eds. Hans N. Tuch and G. Lewis Schmidt (Washington, D.C.: The U.S. Information Agency Alumni Association, The Public Diplomacy Foundation, 1991), 56.

4. Jeffrey K. Tulis, *The Rhetorical Presidency* (Princeton, NJ: Princeton University Press, 1987), 6.

5. See James W. Ceaser, Glen E. Thurow, Jeffrey Tulis, and Joseph M. Bessette, "The Rise of the Rhetorical Presidency," *Presidential Studies Quarterly* 11 (1981): 164; Roderick P. Hart, *The Sound of Leadership: Presidential Communication in the Modern Age* (Chicago: University of Chicago Press, 1987), 209; Kathleen Hall Jamieson and David S. Birdsell, *Presidential Debates: The Challenge of Creating an Informed Electorate* (New York: Oxford University Press, 1988), 180; James Oliver Robertson, *American Myth, American Reality* (New York: Hill & Wang, 1980), 312; and David Zarefsky, *President Johnson's War on Poverty: Rhetoric and History* (University: University of Alabama Press, 1986), 8.

6. Fred I. Greenstein discusses the "hidden-hands" of the Eisenhower presidency. See Fred I. Greenstein, *The Hidden-Hand Presidency: Eisenhower as Leader* (New York: Basic Books, 1982).

7. Zarefsky, *President Johnson's War on Poverty*, 14.

8. See Leroy G. Dorsey, "The Frontier Myth in Presidential Rhetoric: Theodore Roosevelt's Campaign for Conservation," *Western Journal of Communication* 59 (1995): 1–19; Gerald Gamm and Reneé M. Smith, "Presidents, Parties, and the Public: Evolving Patterns of Interaction, 1877–1929, in *Speaking to the People: The Rhetorical Presidency in Historical Perspective*, ed. Richard J. Ellis (Amherst: University of Massachusetts Press, 1998), 87–110; Sidney M. Milkis, "Franklin D. Roosevelt, Progressivism, and the Limits of Popular Leadership," in *Speaking to the People: The Rhetorical Presidency in Historical Perspective*, ed. Richard J. Ellis (Amherst: University of Massachusetts Press, 1998), 182–210; Halford Ross Ryan, *Franklin D. Roosevelt's Rhetorical Presidency* (Westport, CT: Greenwood, 1998); and Jeffrey K. Tulis, "Reflections on the Rhetorical Presidency in American Political Development," in *Speaking to the People: The Rhetorical Presidency in Historical Perspective*, ed. Richard J. Ellis (Amherst: University of Massachusetts Press, 1998), 211–222.

9. Ceaser et al., "The Rise of the Rhetorical Presidency," 158–171.

10. Tulis, *The Rhetorical Presidency*, 1987; and Jeffrey K. Tulis, "Revising the Rhetorical Presidency," in *Beyond the Rhetorical Presidency*, ed. Martin J. Medhurst (College Station: Texas A&M University Press, 1996), 3–14.

11. William Ker Muir, Jr., *The Bully Pulpit: The Presidential Leadership of Ronald Reagan* (San Francisco: Institute for Contemporary Studies, 1992), 2.

12. See Tulis, "Revising the Rhetorical Presidency," 3–14.

13. See Richard J. Ellis, ed., *Speaking to the People: The Rhetorical Presidency in Historical Perspective* (Amherst: University of Massachusetts Press, 1998).

14. Philip Abbott, *Strong Presidents: A Theory of Leadership* (Knoxville: University of Tennessee Press, 1996), 228, 14.

15. Greenstein, *The Hidden-Hand Presidency*.

16. Bruce E. Gronbeck, "The Presidency in the Age of Second Orality," in *Beyond the Rhetorical Presidency*, ed. Martin J. Medhurst (College Station: Texas A&M University Press, 1996), 49.

17. "Conclusions and Recommendations of the President's Committee on Information Activities Abroad," December, 1960, Papers as President of the United States, 1953–1961 (Ann Whitman File), Administration Series, Box 33, Dwight D. Eisenhower Presidential Library, 4, 60.

18. See Green, *American Propaganda Abroad*, 35–37; and Thomas C. Sorensen, *The Word War: The Story of American Propaganda* (New York: Harper & Row, 1968), 118–119.

19. For more background material on how Edward R. Murrow became a noted journalist, see Thomas Rosteck, "Irony, Argument, and Reportage in Television Documentary: *See It Now* Versus Senator McCarthy," *Quarterly Journal of Speech* 75 (1989): 277–298. See also Hans N. Tuch, *Communicating with the World: U.S. Public Diplomacy Overseas* (New York: St. Martin's Press, 1990), 25. Tuch discusses credibility issues regarding the USIA.

20. See Green, *American Propaganda Abroad*, 37; and Julian Hale, *Radio Power: Propaganda and International Broadcasting* (Philadelphia, PA: Temple University Press, 1975), 35.

21. Green, *American Propaganda Abroad*, 36–37.

22. Hans N. Tuch, ed., *USIA: Communicating with the World in the 1990s* (Washington, D.C.: The U.S. Information Agency Alumni Association, The Public Diplomacy Foundation, 1994), 37.

23. Green, *American Propaganda Abroad*, 35–37.

24. Tuch, *USIA*, 2–3.

25. Green, *American Propaganda Abroad*, 38.

26. Leo Bogart, *Cool Words, Cold War: A New Look at USIA's Premises for Propaganda* (Washington, D.C.: American University Press, 1995), xxii.

27. Tuch, *USIA*, 40.

28. Green, *American Propaganda Abroad*, 38–39.

29. Green, *American Propaganda Abroad*, 42–43.

30. Tuch, *USIA*, n.p.

31. Green, *American Propaganda Abroad*, 42–43.

32. Robin Andersen, "USIA: Propaganda as Public Diplomacy," *Covert Action Information Bulletin* 39 (1991–1992): 40–41.

33. Green, *American Propaganda Abroad*, 192.

34. Tuch, *Communicating with the World*, 115.

35. Green, *American Propaganda Abroad*, 189–193.

36. David D. Newsom, *Diplomacy and the American Democracy* (Bloomington: Indiana University Press, 1988), 183.

37. Laurien Alexandre, "In the Service of the State: Public Diplomacy, Government Media and Ronald Reagan," *Media, Culture and Society* 9 (1987): 31–32. Alexandre does not discuss the similarities between the Reagan and the Eisenhower administrations' structure of the USIA.

38. Robin Andersen, "Propaganda and the Media: Reagan's 'Public Diplomacy,'" *CovertAction Information Bulletin* 31 (1989): 20–24. Andersen does not discuss the Truman or Eisenhower administrations.

39. See Andersen, "USIA," 41; and Tuch, *USIA*, 42.

40. Richard C. Levy, "Discussion," in *Public Diplomacy: USA versus USSR*, ed. Richard F. Starr (Stanford, CA: Hoover Institution Press, 1986), 195. See also Paul P. Blackburn, "The Post-Cold War Public Diplomacy of the United States," *The Washington Quarterly* 15 (1992): 78; and Bogart, *Cool Words, Cold War*, xliv–xxxviii.

41. Alexandre, "In the Service of the State," 30.

42. Bogart, *Cool Words, Cold War*, xxxviii.

43. Charles Z. Wick, "Global Interdependence and the War of Ideas: The Free Flow of Ideas," *Vital Speeches of the Day* 54 (March 15, 1988): 330 (emphasis added).

44. Alexandre, "In the Service of the State," 31.

45. See Bogart, *Cool Words, Cold War*, xliv–xlv; and Tuch, *USIA*, 43.

46. Bogart, *Cool Words, Cold War*, xlii.

47. William J. Clinton, "Statement on International Broadcasting Programs," *Weekly Compilation of Presidential Documents* 29 (June 21, 1993): 1088–1089.

48. See International Broadcasting Bureau, International Broadcasting Bureau Homepage, www.ibb.gov/ibbfact.html; U.S. International Broadcasting Chronology, International Broadcasting Bureau Homepage, www.ibb.gov/bbg/chron.html; An Organization of U.S. International Broadcasters, BBG Organization, www.ibb.gov/bbg/bbgorg.htlm; Our Mission–Message from the BBG Chairman, BBG Mission, www.ibb.gov/bbg/mission.html.

49. See Blanche Wiesen Cook, *The Declassified Eisenhower: A Divided Legacy* (Garden City, NY: Doubleday, 1981), xv–xix; and Greenstein, *The Hidden-Hand Presidency*, 4–5.

50. Greenstein, *The Hidden-Hand Presidency*, 5–9.

51. For more information on constructions of the presidency, see Thomas W. Benson, "'To Lend a Hand': Gerald R. Ford, Watergate, and the White House Speechwriters," *Rhetoric & Public Affairs* 1 (1998): 201–225.

Bibliography

ARCHIVES AND MANUSCRIPT COLLECTIONS

American Society of Newspaper Editors' Archives, Reston, Virginia.

William Benton Oral History Interview, Columbia University Oral History Collection, 1968, New York, New York.

The William Benton Papers, Department of Special Collections, The University of Chicago Library, Chicago, Illinois.

Dwight D. Eisenhower Presidential Library, Abilene, Kansas:

Dwight D. Eisenhower: Papers as President of the United States, 1953–1961 (Ann Whitman File)
    Administrative Series
    DDE Diary Series
    Name Series
    NSC Series

Dwight D. Eisenhower: Records as President, White House Central Files, 1953–1961
    Confidential File
    Official File
    Psychological Strategy Board File

U.S. President's Committee on Information Activities Abroad (Sprague Committee): Records, 1960–1961

U.S. President's Committee on International Information Activities (Jackson Committee): Records, 1950–1953

White House Office: National Security Council Staff: Papers, 1948–1961

Executive Secretary Subject Files Series
NSC Registry Series, 1947–1962
OCB Central Files Series
OCB Secretariat Series
PSB Central Files Series
White House Office, Office of the Special Assistant for National Security Affairs:
Records, 1952–1961
NSC Series/Policy Papers Subseries
White House Office of Special Series for National Security Affairs
Presidential Subseries
Personal Papers
Gordon Gray
C. D. Jackson
James M. Lambie, Jr.
The National Archives Motion Picture Collection, Washington, D.C.
The United States Information Agency
Record Group 306
Harry S. Truman Presidential Library, Independence, Missouri:
Papers of Harry S. Truman
Official File
Records of Organizations in the Executive Office of the President
Record Group 429
State Department File
Psychological Strategy Board
Personal Papers
Paul G. Hoffman
Charles Hulten
Howland H. Sargeant
Charles Thayer

BOOKS

Abbott, Philip. *Strong Presidents: A Theory of Leadership*. Knoxville: University of Tennessee Press, 1996.

Abshire, David. M. *International Broadcasting: A New Dimension of Western Diplomacy*. Beverly Hills, CA: Sage Publications, 1976.

Acheson, Dean. *Present at the Creation: My Years in the State Department*. New York: W. W. Norton, 1969.

Alexandre, Laurien. *The Voice of America: From Detente to the Reagan Doctrine*. Norwood, NJ: Ablex, 1988.

Allen, Craig. *Eisenhower and the Mass Media: Peace, Prosperity, & Prime-Time TV*. Chapel Hill: University of North Carolina Press, 1993.

Ambrose, Stephen E. *Eisenhower: The President*. vol. 2. New York: Simon and Schuster, 1984.

————. *Ike's Spies: Eisenhower and the Espionage Establishment*. Garden City, NY: Doubleday & Company, Inc., 1981.

Andrew, Christopher. *For the President's Eyes Only: Secret Intelligence and the American Presidency from Washington to Bush*. New York: HarperCollins, 1995.

Aronson, James. *The Press and the Cold War*. New York: Monthly Review Press, 1990.

Barclay, C. N. *The New Warfare*. New York: Philosophical Library, 1954.

Barmine, Alexander. *One Who Survived: The Life Story of a Russian under the Soviets*. New York: G. P. Putnam's Sons, 1945.

Barrett, Edward W. *Truth Is Our Weapon*. New York: Funk and Wagnalls, 1953.

Barthes, Roland. *Mythologies*. New York: Hill and Wang, 1972.

Bartlett, F. C. "The Aims of Political Propaganda." In *Public Opinion and Propaganda*, edited by Daniel Katz et al. New York: Dryden Press, 1954.

Bayley, Edwin R. *Joe McCarthy and the Press*. New York: Pantheon Books, 1981.

Beer, Francis A., and Robert Hariman, "Realism and Rhetoric in International Relations." In *Post-Realism: The Rhetorical Turn in International Relations*, edited by Francis A. Beer and Robert Hariman. East Lansing: Michigan State University Press, 1996.

Bell, Daniel. "Status Politics and New Anxieties." In *The Meaning of McCarthyism*, edited by Earl Latham. Lexington, MA: D. C. Heath, 1973.

Bennett, W. Lance. *Public Opinion in American Politics*. New York: Harcourt Brace Jovanovich, 1980.

Benton, William. "My Overview of the Nineteen Forties." *The Times in Review: 1940–1949*. New York: Arno Press, 1973.

————. *The Voice of Latin America*. New York: Harper & Brothers, 1961.

Bernhard, Nancy E. *U.S. Television News and Cold War Propaganda, 1947–1960*. New York: Cambridge University Press, 1999.

Bimes, Terri, and Stephen Skowronek. "Woodrow Wilson's Critique of Popular Leadership: Reassessing the Modern-Traditional Divide in Presidential History." In *Speaking to the People: The Rhetorical Presidency in Historical Perspective*, edited by Richard J. Ellis. Amherst: University of Massachusetts Press, 1998.

Bogart, Leo. *Cool Words, Cold War: A New Look at USIA's Premises for Propaganda*. Washington, D.C.: American University Press, 1995.

————. *Premises for Propaganda: The United States Information Agency's Operating Assumptions in the Cold War*. New York: Free Press, 1976.

Boorstin, Daniel J. *The Image: A Guide to Pseudo-Events in America*. New York: Harper Colophon Books, 1964.

Bowie, Robert R., and Richard H. Immerman. *Waging Peace: How Eisenhower Shaped an Enduring Cold War Strategy*. New York: Oxford University Press, 1998.

Brendon, Piers. *Ike: His Life and Times*. New York: Harper & Row, 1986.

Broadwater, Jeff. *Eisenhower and the Anti-Communist Crusade.* Chapel Hill: University of North Carolina Press, 1992.

Brockriede, Wayne, and Robert L. Scott. *Moments in the Rhetoric of the Cold War.* New York: Random House, 1970.

Buckley, William F., Jr., and L. Brent Bozell. *McCarthy and His Enemies: The Record and Its Meaning.* Chicago: Henry Regnery, 1954.

Burk, Robert F. *Dwight D. Eisenhower: Hero and Politician.* Boston: Twayne Publishers, 1986.

Campbell, James. *Exiled in Paris: Richard Wright, James Baldwin, Samuel Beckett, and Others on the Left Bank.* New York: Scribner, 1995.

Cater, Douglass. *The Fourth Branch of Government.* New York: Vintage Books, 1965.

Catlin, George E. Gordon. "Propaganda as a Function of Democratic Government." In *Propaganda and Dictatorship*, edited by Harwood Lawrence Childs. Princeton, NJ: Princeton University Press, 1936.

Chilton, Paul A. "The Meaning of Security." In *Post-Realism: The Rhetorical Turn in International Relations*, edited by Francis A. Beer and Robert Hariman. East Lansing: Michigan State University Press, 1996.

Clark, Peter B. "The Opinion Machine: Intellectuals, the Mass Media, and American Government." In *The Mass Media and Modern Democracy*, edited by Harry M. Clor. Chicago: Rand McNally, 1974.

Cohen, Bernard C. *The Press and Foreign Policy.* Princeton, NJ: Princeton University Press, 1963.

————. *The Public's Impact on Foreign Policy.* Boston: Little, Brown, 1973.

Cook, Blanche Wiesen. *The Declassified Eisenhower: A Divided Legacy.* Garden City, NY: Doubleday, 1981.

Corry, John. *TV News and the Dominant Culture.* Washington, D.C.: The Media Institute, 1986.

Creel, George. *How We Advertised America.* 1920. Reprint. New York: Arno Press, 1972.

Critchlow, James. *Radio Hole-in-the-Head: Radio Liberty: An Insider's Story of Cold War Broadcasting.* Washington, D.C.: American University Press, 1995.

Crossman, Richar, ed. *The God That Failed.* New York: Harper & Brothers, 1949.

Curtin, Michael. *Redeeming the Wasteland: Television Documentary and Cold War Politics.* New Brunswick, NJ: Rutgers University Press, 1995.

Cuthbertson, Ken. *Inside: The Biography of John Gunther.* Chicago: Bonus Books, 1992.

Dalyell, Tam. *Dick Crossman: A Portrait.* London: Weidenfeld and Nicolson, 1989.

Daugherty, William E. "Post-World War II Developments." In *A Psychological Warfare Casebook*, edited by William E. Daugherty and Morris Janowitz. Baltimore, MD: Johns Hopkins University Press, 1958.

———. "Richard H. S. Crossman." In *A Psychological Warfare Casebook*, edited by William E. Daugherty and Morris Janowitz. Baltimore, MD: Johns Hopkins University Press, 1958.

David, Hugh. *Stephen Spender: A Portrait with Background*. London: Heinemann, 1992.

Davis, David Brion. *The Slave Power Conspiracy and the Paranoid Style*. Baton Rouge: Louisiana State University Press, 1969.

Davis, Richard. *The Press and American Politics: The New Mediator*. New York: Longman, 1992.

Davison, W. Phillips. *International Political Communication*. New York: Praeger, 1965.

Denton, Robert E., Jr., and Dan F. Hahn. *Presidential Communication: Description and Analysis*. New York: Praeger, 1986.

Dizard, Wilson P. *The Strategy of Truth: The Story of the U.S. Information Service*. Washington, D.C.: Public Affairs Press, 1961.

Donovan, Robert J. *Conflict and Crisis: The Presidency of Harry S. Truman, 1945–1948*. New York: W. W. Norton, 1977.

———. *Eisenhower: The Inside Story*. New York: Harper & Brothers, 1956.

Doob, Leonard W. *Public Opinion and Propaganda*. 1948. Reprint. Hamden, CT: Archon Books, 1966.

Eisenhower, Dwight D. *Mandate for Change, 1953–1956*. Garden City, NY: Doubleday, 1963.

Elder, Robert E. *The Information Machine: The United States Information Agency and American Foreign Policy*. Syracuse, NY: Syracuse University Press, 1968.

Ellis, Richard J., ed. *Speaking to the People: The Rhetorical Presidency in Historical Perspective*. Amherst: University of Massachusetts Press, 1998.

———. "Introduction." In *Speaking to the People: The Rhetorical Presidency in Historical Perspective*, edited by Richard J. Ellis. Amherst: University of Massachusetts Press, 1998.

Ellul, Jacques. *Propaganda: The Formation of Men's Attitudes*. New York: Vintage Books, 1965.

Emery, Edwin. *The Press and America: An Interpretive History of the Mass Media*, 3d ed. Englewood Cliffs, NJ: Prentice-Hall, 1972.

Entman, Robert M. *Democracy without Citizens: Media and the Decay of American Politics*. New York: Oxford University Press, 1989.

Epstein, Edward Jay. "The Selection of Reality." In *What's News: The Media in American Society*, edited by Elie Abel. San Francisco: Institute for Contemporary Studies, 1981.

Ewald, William Bragg, Jr. *Eisenhower the President: Crucial Days, 1951–1960*. Englewood Cliffs, NJ: Prentice-Hall, 1981.

Fabre, Michel. *The Unfinished Quest of Richard Wright*. Urbana: University of Illinois Press, 1993.

Fiedler, Leslie. "McCarthy as Populist." In *The Meaning of McCarthyism*, edited by Earl Latham. Lexington, MA: D. C. Heath, 1973.

Florig, Dennis. *The Power of Presidential Ideologies*. Westport, CT: Praeger, 1992.

Frazier, Robert. *Anglo-American Relations with Greece: The Coming of the Cold War, 1942–1947*. New York: St. Martin's Press, 1991.

Fried, Richard M. *Men Against McCarthy*. New York: Columbia University Press, 1976.

Friedman, Norman. *The Fifty-Year War: Conflict and Strategy in the Cold War*. Annapolis, MD: Naval Institute Press, 2000.

Gaddis, John Lewis. *Strategies of Containment: A Critical Appraisal of Postwar American National Security Policy*. Oxford: Oxford University Press, 1982.

————. *The United States and the Origins of the Cold War, 1941–1947*. New York: Columbia University Press, 1972.

Gamm, Gerald, and Reneé M. Smith. "Presidents, Parties, and the Public: Evolving Patterns of Interaction, 1877–1929." In *Speaking to the People: The Rhetorical Presidency in Historical Perspective*, edited by Richard J. Ellis. Amherst: University of Massachusetts Press, 1998.

Gans, Herbert J. *Deciding What's News*. New York: Vintage Books, 1979.

Goldsmith, John, ed. *Stephen Spender: Journals 1939–1983*. London: Faber and Faber, 1985.

Goldston, Robert. *The American Nightmare: Senator Joseph R. McCarthy and the Politics of Hate*. Indianapolis, IN: Bobbs-Merrill, 1973.

Graber, Doris A. *Mass Media and American Politics*, 4th ed. Washington, D.C.: Congressional Quarterly Press, 1993.

Green, Fitzhugh. *American Propaganda Abroad*. New York: Hippocrene Books, 1988.

Greenstein, Fred I. *The Hidden-Hand Presidency: Eisenhower as Leader*. New York: Basic Books, 1982.

————. *The Presidential Difference: Leadership Style from FDR to Clinton*. New York: Martin Kessler Books, 2000.

Griffith, Robert. *The Politics of Fear: Joseph R. McCarthy and the Senate*. Amherst: University of Massachusetts Press, 1987.

Gronbeck, Bruce E. "The Presidency in the Age of Second Orality." In *Beyond the Rhetorical Presidency*, edited by Martin J. Medhurst. College Station: Texas A&M University Press, 1996.

Gunther, John. "Foreword." In *This Is the Challenge: The Benton Reports of 1956–1958 on the Nature of the Soviet Threat*, edited by Edward W. Barrett. New York: Associated College Presses, 1958.

————. *Inside U.S.A.* New York: Harper and Brothers, 1947.

Hale, Julian. *Radio Power: Propaganda and International Broadcasting*. Philadelphia, PA: Temple University Press, 1975.

Halle, Louis J. *The Cold War as History*. New York: Harper Torchbooks, 1967.

Hamilton, Iain. *Koestler: A Biography*. New York: Macmillan, 1982.

Hart, Roderick P. *The Sound of Leadership: Presidential Communication in the Modern Age*. Chicago: University of Chicago Press, 1987.

Hartley, John. *Understanding News*. London: Methuen, 1982.

Henderson, John W. *The United States Information Agency*. New York: Praeger, 1969.

Henry, William A., III. "News as Entertainment: The Search for Dramatic Unity." In *What's News: The Media in American Society*, edited by Elie Abel. San Francisco: Institute for Contemporary Studies, 1981.

Herzstein, Robert Edwin. *The War that Hitler Won: The Most Infamous Propaganda Campaign in History*. New York: G. P. Putnam's Sons, 1978.

Hinckley, Barbara. *The Symbolic Presidency: How Presidents Portray Themselves*. New York: Routledge, 1990.

Hinds, Lynn Boyd, and Theodore Otto Windt, Jr. *The Cold War as Rhetoric: The Beginnings, 1945–1950*. New York: Praeger, 1991.

Hixson, Walter L. *Parting the Curtain: Propaganda, Culture, and the Cold War, 1945–1961*. New York: St. Martin's Griffin, 1998.

Hofstadter, Richard. "The Paranoid Style in American Politics." In *The Paranoid Style in American Politics and Other Essays*, edited by Richard Hofstadter. New York: Knopf, 1966.

Hogan, J. Michael. "Eisenhower and Open Skies: A Case Study in Psychological Warfare." In *Eisenhower's War of Words: Rhetoric and Leadership*, edited by Martin J. Medhurst. East Lansing: Michigan State University Press, 1994.

———. "The Science of Cold War Strategy: Propaganda and Public Opinion in the Eisenhower Administration's 'War of Words.' " In *Critical Reflections on the Cold War: Linking Rhetoric and History*, edited by Martin J. Medhurst and H. W. Brands. College Station: Texas A&M University, 2000.

Hogan, Michael J. *The Marshall Plan: America, Britain, and the Reconstruction of Western Europe, 1947–1952*. Cambridge: Cambridge University Press, 1987.

Howard, Anthony. *Crossman: The Pursuit of Power*. London: Jonathon Cape, 1990.

Hyman, Sidney. *The Lives of William Benton*. Chicago: University of Chicago Press, 1969.

Ivie, Robert L. "Cold War Motives and the Rhetorical Metaphor: A Framework of Criticism." In *Cold War Rhetoric: Strategy, Metaphor, and Ideology*, edited by Martin J. Medhurst, Robert L. Ivie, Philip Wander, and Robert L. Scott; East Lansing: Michigan State University Press, 1997.

———. "Metaphors and the Rhetorical Invention of Cold War 'Idealists.'" In *Cold War Rhetoric: Strategy, Metaphor, and Ideology*, edited by Martin J. Medhurst, Robert L. Ivie, Philip Wander, and Robert L. Scott. East Lansing: Michigan State University Press, 1997.

———. "Declaring a National Emergency: Truman's Rhetorical Crisis and the Great Debate of 1951." In *The Modern Presidency and Crisis Rhetoric*, edited by Amos Kiewe. Westport, CT: Praeger, 1994.

———. "Eisenhower as Cold Warrior." In *Eisenhower's War of Words: Rhetoric and Leadership*, edited by Martin J. Medhurst. East Lansing: Michigan State University Press, 1994.

Jamieson, Kathleen Hall, and David S. Birdsell. *Presidential Debates: The Challenge of Creating an Informed Electorate*. New York: Oxford University Press, 1988.

Jeffreys-Jones, Rhodri. *The CIA and American Democracy*. New Haven, CT: Yale University Press, 1989.

Jowett, Garth S., and Victoria O'Donnell. *Propaganda and Persuasion*, 2d ed. Newbury Park, CA: Sage Publications, 1992.

Karabell, Zachary. *Architects of Intervention: The United States, the Third World, and the Cold War, 1946–1962*. Baton Rouge: Louisiana State University Press, 1999.

Kimble, James Jerry. "Mobilizing the Home Front: War Bonds, Morale, and the U.S. Treasury's Domestic Propaganda Campaign, 1942–1945." Ph.D. diss., University of Maryland, 2001.

Knott, Stephen F. *Secret and Sanctioned: Covert Operations and the American Presidency*. New York: Oxford University Press, 1996.

Kravchenko, Victor. *I Chose Freedom: The Personal and Political Life of a Soviet Official*. New York: Scribner's Sons, 1946.

Krippendorff, Klaus. "On the Ethics of Constructing Communication." In *Rethinking Communication: Paradigm Issues*, edited by Brenda Dervin, Lawrence Grossberg, Barabara J. O'Keefe, and Ellen Wartella. Newbury Park, CA: Sage, 1989.

Krugler, David F. *The Voice of America and the Domestic Propaganda Battles, 1945–1953*. Columbia: University of Missouri Press, 2000.

Lakoff, George. *Women, Fire, and Dangerous Things: What Categories Reveal about the Mind*. Chicago: University of Chicago Press, 1987.

Lakoff, George, and Mark Johnson. *Metaphors We Live By*. Chicago: University of Chicago Press, 1980.

Laracey, Mel. "The Presidential Newspaper: The Forgotten Way of Going Public." In *Speaking to the People: The Rhetorical Presidency in Historical Perspective*, edited by Richard J. Ellis. Amherst: University of Massachusetts Press, 1998.

Lasswell, Harold D. *Propaganda Technique in World War*. New York: Peter Smith, 1938.

———. "The Scope of Research on Propaganda and Dictatorship." In *Propaganda and Dictatorship*, edited by Harwood Lawrence Childs. Princeton, NJ: Princeton University Press, 1936.

Latham, Earl. *The Meaning of McCarthyism*. Lexington, MA: D. C. Heath, 1973.

Lerner, Daniel, ed. *Propaganda in War and Crisis*. New York: George W. Stewart, 1951.

Leslie, Stuart W. *The Cold War and American Science*. New York: Columbia University Press, 1994.

Levy, Richard C. "Discussion." In *Public Diplomacy: USA versus USSR*, edited by Richard F. Starr. Stanford, CA: Hoover Institution Press, 1986.

Lipper, Elinor. *Eleven Years in Soviet Prison Camps*. Chicago: Henry Regnery, 1951.

Lippmann, Walter. *Public Opinion*. New York: Harcourt, Brace, 1922.

Lumley, Frederick. *The Propaganda Menace*. New York: The Century Co., 1933.

MacDonald, J. Fred. *Don't Touch that Dial! Radio Programming in American Life, 1920–1960*. Chicago: Nelson-Hall, 1979.

———. *Television and the Red Menace: The Video Road to Vietnam*. New York: Praeger, 1985.

Markel, Lester. *Public Opinion and Foreign Policy*. New York: Harper & Brothers, 1949.

Matusow, Allen J. *Joseph R. McCarthy*. Englewood Cliffs, NJ: Prentice-Hall, 1970.

Matusow, Harvey. *False Witness*. New York: Cameron & Kahn, 1955.

Mayo, H. B. *Democracy and Communism*. New York: Oxford University Press, 1955.

McClintock, Michael. *Instruments of Statecraft: U.S. Guerrilla Warfare, Counter-Insurgency, and Counter-Terrorism, 1945–1990*. New York: Pantheon, 1992.

McEnaney, Laura. *Civil Defense Begins at Home: Militarization Meets Everyday Life in the Fifties*. Princeton, NJ: Princeton University Press, 2000.

Medhurst, Martin J. "Eisenhower's 'Atoms for Peace' Speech: A Case Study in the Strategic Use of Language." In *Cold War Rhetoric: Strategy, Metaphor, and Ideology*, edited by Martin J. Medhurst, Robert L. Ivie, Philip Wander, and Robert L. Scott. East Lansing: Michigan State University Press, 1997.

———. "Rhetoric and Cold War: A Strategic Approach." In *Cold War Rhetoric: Strategy, Metaphor, and Ideology*, edited by Martin J. Medhurst, Robert L. Ivie, Philip Wander, and Robert L. Scott. East Lansing: Michigan State University Press, 1997.

———. "A Tale of Two Constructs: The Rhetorical Presidency Versus Presidential Rhetoric." In *Beyond the Rhetorical Presidency*, edited by Martin J. Medhurst. College Station: Texas A&M University Press, 1996.

———. *Beyond the Rhetorical Presidency*. College Station: Texas A&M University Press, 1996.

———. "Eisenhower, Little Rock, and the Rhetoric of Crisis." In *Modern Presidency and Crisis Rhetoric*, edited by Amos Kiewe. Westport, CT: Praeger, 1994.

————. "Eisenhower's Rhetorical Leadership: An Interpretation." In *Eisenhower's War of Words: Rhetoric and Leadership*, edited by Martin J. Medhurst. East Lansing: Michigan State University Press, 1994.

————. *Dwight D. Eisenhower: Strategic Communicator*. Westport, CT: Greenwood Press, 1993.

Merson, Martin. *The Private Diary of a Public Servant*. New York: Macmillan, 1955.

Meyer, Cord. *Facing Reality: From World Federalism to the CIA*. New York: Harper & Row, 1980.

Meyerhoff, Arthur E. *The Strategy of Persuasion: The Use of Advertising Skills in Fighting the Cold War*. New York: Coward-McCann, 1965.

Mickelson, Sig. *America's Other Voice: The Story of Radio Free Europe and Radio Liberty*. New York: Praeger, 1983.

Milkis, Sidney M. "Franklin D. Roosevelt, Progressivism, and the Limits of Popular Leadership." In *Speaking to the People: The Rhetorical Presidency in Historical Perspective*, edited by Richard J. Ellis. Amherst: University of Massachusetts Press, 1998.

Muir, William Ker, Jr. *The Bully Pulpit: The Presidential Leadership of Ronald Reagan*. San Francisco: Institute for Contemporary Studies, 1992.

Nelson, Michael. *War of the Black Heavens: The Battles of Western Broadcasting in the Cold War*. Syracuse, NY: Syracuse University Press, 1997.

Neustadt, Richard E. *Presidential Power: The Politics of Leadership*. New York: John Wiley & Sons, 1960.

Newsom, David D. *Diplomacy and the American Democracy*. Bloomington: Indiana University Press, 1988.

O'Donnell, Victoria, and Garth S. Jowett. "Propaganda as a Form of Communication." In *Propaganda: A Pluralist Perspective*, edited by Ted J. Smith, III. New York: Praeger, 1989.

Oshinsky, David M. *A Conspiracy So Immense: The World of Joe McCarthy*. New York: Free Press, 1983.

Pach, Chester J., Jr., and Elmo Richardson. *The Presidency of Dwight D. Eisenhower*. 1979. Reprint. Lawrence: University Press of Kansas, 1991.

Packer, Herbert L. *Ex-Communist Witnesses: Four Studies in Fact Finding*. Stanford, CA: Stanford University Press, 1962.

Parenti, Michael. *Inventing the Politics of News Media Reality*, 2d ed. New York: St. Martin's Press, 1993.

Parry-Giles, Shawn J. "Militarizing America's Propaganda Program, 1945–1955." In *Critical Reflections on the Cold War: Linking Rhetoric and History*," edited by Martin J. Medhurst and H. W. Brands. College Station: Texas A&M Press, 2000, 95–133.

Pease, Stephen E. *Psywar: Psychological Warfare in Korea, 1950–1953*. Harrisburg, PA: Stackpole Books, 1992.

Pirsein, Robert William. *The Voice of America: An History of the International Broadcasting Activities of the United States Government, 1940–1962*. New York: Arno Press, 1979.

Prados, John. *Presidents' Secret Wars: CIA and Pentagon Covert Operations since World War II*. New York: William Morrow, 1986.

Pratte, Paul Alfred. *Gods Within the Machine: A History of the American Society of Newspaper Editors, 1923–1993*. Westport, CT: Praeger, 1995.

Price, Harry Bayard. *The Marshall Plan and Its Meaning*. New York: Cornell University Press, 1955.

Pridmore, Jay. *John Gunther: Inside Journalism*. Chicago: University of Chicago Press, 1990.

Pruden, Caroline. *Conditional Partners: Eisenhower, the United Nations, and the Search for a Permanent Peace*. Baton Rouge: Louisiana State University Press, 1998.

Puddington, Arch. *Broadcasting Freedom: The Cold War Triumph of Radio Free Europe and Radio Liberty*. Lexington: University of Kentucky Press, 2000.

Qualter, Terence H. *Opinion Control in the Democracies*. New York: St. Martin's Press, 1985.

———. *Propaganda and Psychological Warfare*. New York: Random House, 1962.

Rawnsley, Gary D. *Cold-War Propaganda in the 1950s*. New York: St. Martin's Press, 1999.

———. *Radio Diplomacy and Propaganda: The BBC and VOA in International Politics, 1956–1964*. New York: St. Martin's Press, 1996.

Reeves, Thomas C. *The Life and Times of Joe McCarthy: A Biography*. New York: Stein and Day, 1982.

Robertson, James Oliver. *American Myth, American Reality*. New York: Hill & Wang, 1980.

Roshco, Bernard. *Newsmaking*. Chicago: University of Chicago Press, 1975.

Rossiter, Clinton. *The American Presidency*. New York: Harcourt, Brace & World, 1960, 1956.

Rosteck, Thomas. "The Case of Eisenhower Versus McCarthyism." In *Eisenhower's War of Words: Rhetoric and Leadership*, edited by Martin J. Medhurst. East Lansing: Michigan State University, 1994.

———. *"See It Now" Confronts McCarthyism: Television and Representation*. Tuscaloosa: The University of Alabama Press, 1994.

Rovere, Richard H. *Senator Joe McCarthy*. New York: Harper Torchbooks, 1959.

Rubin, Ronald I. *The Objectives of the U.S. Information Agency: Controversies and Analysis*. New York: Frederick A. Praeger, 1966.

Ryan, Halford Ross. *Franklin D. Roosevelt's Rhetorical Presidency*. Westport, CT: Greenwood Press, 1998.

Saunders, Frances Stonor. *The Cultural Cold War: The CIA and the World of Arts and Letters*. New York: New Press, 2000.

Shakespeare, Frank. "Comment." In *Ike and USIA: A Commemorative Symposium*, edited by Hans N. Tuch and G. Lewis Schmidt. Washington, D.C.:

The U.S. Information Agency Alumni Association, The Public Diplomacy Foundation, 1991.

Sheehan, Marion Turner, ed. *The World at Home: Selections from the Writings of Anne O'Hare McCormick*. New York: Alfred A. Knopf, 1956.

Shulman, Holly Cowan. *The Voice of America: Propaganda and Democracy, 1941–1945*. Madison: University of Wisconsin Press, 1990.

Simpson, Christopher. *Science of Coercion: Communication Research and Psychological Warfare, 1945–1960*. New York: Oxford University Press, 1994.

Smith, Paul A., Jr. *On Political War*. Washington, D.C.: National Defense University Press, 1989.

Smith, Ted. J., III. "Propaganda and the Techniques of Deception." In *Propaganda: A Pluralist Perspective*, edited by Ted J. Smith, III. New York: Praeger, 1989.

Snyder, Alvin A. *Warriors of Disinformation: American Propaganda, Soviet Lies, and the Winning of the Cold War: An Insider's Account*. New York: Arcade Publishing, 1997.

Soley, Lawrence C. *Radio Warfare: OSS and CIA Subversive Propaganda*. New York: Praeger, 1989.

Sorensen, Thomas C. *The Word War: The Story of American Propaganda*. New York: Harper & Row, 1968.

Sproule, J. Michael. *Propaganda and Democracy: The American Experience of Media and Mass Persuasion*. New York: Cambridge University Press, 1997.

———. "Propaganda: The Ideological Rhetoric." In *Rhetoric and Ideology: Compositions and Criticisms of Power*, edited by Charles W. Kneupper. Arlington, TX: Rhetoric Society of America, 1989.

———. "Social Responses to Twentieth-Century Propaganda." In *Propaganda: A Pluralistic Perspective*, edited by Ted J. Smith, III. New York: Praeger, 1989.

Stephens, Oren. *Facts to a Candid World: America's Overseas Information Program*. Stanford, CA: Stanford University Press, 1955.

Stern, Frederick Martin. *Capitalism in America: A Classless Society*. New York: Rinehart, 1950.

Stevens, Edmund. *This Is Russia, Uncensored*. New York: Didier, 1950.

Stid, Daniel. "Rhetorical Leadership and 'Common Counsel' in the Presidency of Woodrow Wilson." In *Speaking to the People: The Rhetorical Presidency in Historical Perspective*, edited by Richard J. Ellis. Amherst: University of Massachusetts Press, 1998.

Straight, Michael. *Trial by Television and Other Encounters*. New York: Devon Press, 1979.

Summers, Robert E. *America's Weapons of Psychological Warfare*. New York: H. W. Wilson, 1951.

Theoharis, Athan. *Seeds of Repression: Harry S. Truman and the Origins of McCarthyism*. Chicago: Quadrangle Books, 1971.

Thomson, Charles A., and Walter H. C. Laves. *Cultural Relations and U.S. Foreign Policy*. Bloomington: Indiana University Press, 1963.

Thomson, Charles A. H. *Overseas Information Service of the United States Government*. Washington, D.C.: The Brookings Institution, 1948.

Thurow, Glen E. "Dimensions of Presidential Character." In *Beyond the Rhetorical Presidency*, edited by Martin J. Medhurst. College Station: Texas A&M University Press, 1996.

Truman, Harry S. *Years of Trial and Hope: Memoirs by Harry S. Truman*. Vol. 2. New York: New American Library, 1956.

Tuch, Hans N. *Communicating with the World: U.S. Public Diplomacy Overseas*. New York: St. Martin's Press, 1990.

————, ed. *USIA: Communicating with the World in the 1990s*. Washington, D.C.: The U.S. Information Agency Alumni Association, The Public Diplomacy Foundation, 1994.

Tulis, Jeffrey K. "Reflections on the Rhetorical Presidency in American Political Development." In *Speaking to the People: The Rhetorical Presidency in Historical Perspective*, edited by Richard J. Ellis. Amherst: University of Massachusetts Press, 1998.

————. "Revising the Rhetorical Presidency." In *Beyond the Rhetorical Presidency*, edited by Martin J. Medhurst. College Station: Texas A&M University Press, 1996.

————. *The Rhetorical Presidency*. Princeton, NJ: Princeton University Press, 1987.

Urban, George R. *Radio Free Europe and the Pursuit of Democracy: My War within the Cold War*. New Haven, CT: Yale University Press, 1997.

Vaughn, Stephen. *Holding Fast the Inner Lines: Democracy, Nationalism, and the Committee on Public Information*. Chapel Hill: University of North Carolina Press, 1980.

Wang, Jessica. *American Science in the Age of Anxiety: Scientists, Anticommunism, and the Cold War*. Chapel Hill: University of North Carolina Press, 1999.

Wasburn, Philo C. *Broadcasting Propaganda: International Radio Broadcasting and the Construction of Political Reality*. Westport, CT: Praeger, 1992.

Watkins, Arthur V. *Enough Rope: The Inside Story of the Censure of Senator Joe McCarthy by His Colleagues—The Controversial Hearings that Signaled the End of a Turbulent Career and a Fearsome Era in American Public Life*. Englewood Cliffs, NJ: Prentice-Hall, 1969.

Wechsler, James A. *The Age of Suspicion*. New York: Random House, 1953.

Whelan, Joseph G. *Radio Liberty: A Study of Its Origins, Structure, Policy, Programming, and Effectiveness*. Washington, D.C.: Congressional Research Service, 1972.

Whitfield, Stephen J. *The Culture of the Cold War*. Baltimore, MD: Johns Hopkins University Press, 1996.

Whitton, John B., and Arthur Larson. *Propaganda: Towards Disarmament in the War of Words*. Dobbs Ferry, NY: Oceana Publications, 1964.

Whitton, John Boardman. *Propaganda and the Cold War*. Westport, CT: Greenwood Press, 1984.

Winkler, Allan M. *The Politics of Propaganda: The Office of War Information, 1942–1945*. New Haven, CT: Yale University Press, 1978.

Zarefsky, David. *President Johnson's War on Poverty: Rhetoric and History*. University: University of Alabama Press, 1986.

ARTICLES

Abbott, Philip. "Do Presidents Talk Too Much? The Rhetorical Presidency and Its Alternative." *Presidential Studies Quarterly* 18 (1988): 347–362.

Alexandre, Laurien. "In the Service of the State: Public Diplomacy, Government Media and Ronald Reagan." *Media, Culture and Society* 9 (1987): 29–46.

Andersen, Robin. "Propaganda and the Media: Reagan's 'Public Diplomacy.'" *CovertAction Information Bulletin* 31 (1989): 20–24.

———. "USIA: Propaganda as Public Diplomacy." *Covert Action Information Bulletin* 39 (1991–1992): 40–44.

Benson, Thomas W. "Rhetoric and Autobiography: The Case of Malcolm X." *Quarterly Journal of Speech* 60 (1974): 1–13.

———. " 'To Lend a Hand': Gerald R. Ford, Watergate, and the White House Speechwriters." *Rhetoric & Public Affairs* 1 (1998): 201– 225.

Benton, William. "Europe and Senator McCarthy." *The Fortnightly Review* (April 1954): 3–14 (reprint).

Blackburn, Paul P. "The Post-Cold War Public Diplomacy of the United States." *The Washington Quarterly* 15 (1992): 75–86.

Block, Ralph. "Propaganda and the Free Society." *Public Opinion Quarterly* 12 (1948–1949): 677–686.

Ceaser, James W., Glen E. Thurow, Jeffrey Tulis, and Joseph M. Bessette. "The Rise of the Rhetorical Presidency." *Presidential Studies Quarterly* 11 (1981): 158–171.

Cochran, Thomas C. "Media as Business: A Brief History." *Journal of Communication* 25 (1975): 155–165.

Cranberg, Gil. "Propaganda and the United States." *Etc.* 41 (1984): 184–186.

Cunningham, Stanley B. "Sorting Out the Ethics of Propaganda." *Communication Studies* 43 (1992): 233–245.

Davis, Elmer. "The Government's News Service: Shall It Be Continued?" *Journalism Quarterly* 23 (1946): 146–154.

Dewey, Donald O. "America and Russia, 1939–1941: The Views of the *New York Times*." *Journalism Quarterly* 44 (1967): 62–70.

Dorsey, Leroy G. "The Frontier Myth in Presidential Rhetoric: Theodore Roosevelt's Campaign for Conservation." *Western Journal of Communication* 59 (1995): 1–19.

Emery, Walter B. "Verbal Warfare." *Quarterly Journal of Speech* 30 (1944): 154–157.

Evensen, Bruce J. "The Limits of Presidential Leadership: Truman at War with Zionists, the Press, Public Opinion and His Own State Department over Palestine." *Presidential Studies Quarterly* 23 (1993): 269–287.

Feinstein, Donald. "Free Voices in the Battle for Men's Minds." *Journalism Quarterly* 31 (1954): 193–200.

Grey, Robin. "Inside the Voice of America." *Columbia Journalism Review* 21 (1982): 23–30.

Hackett, Robert A. "Decline of a Paradigm? Bias and Objectivity in News Media Studies." *Critical Studies in Mass Communication* 1 (1984): 229–259.

Haight, David. "The Papers of C. D. Jackson: A Glimpse at President Eisenhower's Psychological Warfare Expert." *Manuscripts* 28 (1976): 27–37.

Hardt, Hanno. "Newsworkers, Technology, and Journalism History." *Critical Studies in Mass Communication* 7 (1990): 346–365.

Hollihan, Thomas A. "Propagandizing the Interest of War: A Rhetorical Study of the Committee on Public Information." *Southern Speech Communication Journal* 49 (1984): 241–257.

Hoxie, R. Gordon. "Dwight David Eisenhower: Bicentennial Considerations." *Presidential Studies Quarterly* 20 (1990): 253–264.

Ivie, Robert L. "Dwight D. Eisenhower's 'Chance for Peace': Quest or Crusade?" *Rhetoric & Public Affairs* 1 (1998): 227–243.

———. "Images of Savagery in American Justifications for War." *Communication Monographs* 47 (1980): 279–294.

———. "Literalizing the Metaphor of Soviet Savagery: President Truman's Plain Style." *Southern Speech Communication Journal* 51 (1986): 91–105.

———. "Presidential Motives for War." *Quarterly Journal of Speech* 60 (1974): 337–345.

King, Erika G. "Exposing the 'Age of Lies': The Propaganda Menace as Portrayed in American Magazines in the Aftermath of World War I." *Journal of American Culture* 12 (1989): 35–40.

Knoll, Steve. "The Voice of America: Banned in the Land of the Free." *Washington Journalism Review* 10 (1988): 43–46.

Kohler, Foy D. "The Voice of America: Spokesman of the Free World." *Proceedings of the Academy of Political Science* 24 (1951): 92–100.

Larson, Cedric. "Religious Freedom as a Theme of the Voice of America." *Journalism Quarterly* 29 (1952): 187–193.

McGee, Michael Calvin. "The 'Ideograph': A Link Between Rhetoric and Ideology." *Quarterly Journal of Speech* 66 (1980): 1–16.

Medhurst, Martin J. "Atoms for Peace and Nuclear Hegemony: The Rhetorical
    Structure of a Cold War Campaign." *Armed Forces & Society* 23 (1997):
    571–593.
———. "Eisenhower and the Crusade for Freedom: The Rhetorical Origins of the
    Cold War Campaign." *Presidential Studies Quarterly* 27 (1997): 646–
    661.
———. "Truman's Rhetorical Reticence, 1945–1947: An Interpretive Essay."
    Quarterly Journal of Speech 74 (1988): 52–70.
"Non-Military Weapons in Cold War Offensive." *Editorial Research Reports* 1
    (1951): 259–276.
Osborn, Michael. "Archetypal Metaphor in Rhetoric: The Light-Dark Family."
    Quarterly Journal of Speech 53 (1967): 115–126.
Padover, Saul K. "Psychological Warfare and Foreign Policy." *American Scholar*
    20 (1951): 151–161.
Parry-Giles, Shawn J. " 'Camouflaged' Propaganda: The Truman and Eisenhower
    Administrations' Covert Manipulation of News." *Western Journal of Com-
    munication* 60 (1996): 146–167.
———. "The Eisenhower Administration's Conceptualization of the USIA: The
    Development of Overt and Covert Propaganda Strategies." *Presidential
    Studies Quarterly* 24 (1994): 263–276.
———. "Propaganda, Effect, and the Cold War: Gauging the Status of America's
    'War of Words.'" *Political Communication* 11 (1994): 203–213.
———. "Rhetorical Experimentation and the Cold War, 1947–1953: The Devel-
    opment of an Internationalist Approach to Propaganda." *Quarterly Jour-
    nal of Speech* 80 (1994): 448–467.
Parry-Giles, Trevor. "Character, the Constitution, and the Ideological Embodi-
    ment of 'Civil Rights' in the 1967 Nomination of Thurgood Marshall to
    the Supreme Court." *Quarterly Journal of Speech* 82 (1996): 364–382.
Pollard, James E. "President Truman and the Press." *Journalism Quarterly* 28
    (1951): 457–468.
———. "Truman and the Press: Final Phase, 1951–1953." *Journalism Quarterly*
    39 (1953): 273–286.
Raucher, Alan. "Beyond the God That Failed: Louis Fischer, Liberal Internation-
    alist." *The Historian* 44 (1982): 174–189.
Reese, Stephen D. "The News Paradigm and the Ideology of Objectivity: A So-
    cialist at the *Wall Street Journal*." *Critical Studies in Mass Communica-
    tion* 7 (1990): 390–409.
Rosteck, Thomas. "Irony, Argument, and Reportage in Television Documentary:
    See It Now Versus Senator McCarthy." *Quarterly Journal of Speech* 75
    (1989): 277–298.
Rubin, Amy Magaro. "Clinton Agrees to Fold USIA and Its Exchange Program
    into the State Department." *The Chronicle of Higher Education*, May 2,
    1997: A50.

Scanlan, Ross. "Two Views of Propaganda." *Communication Quarterly* 1 (1953): 13–14.

Schiller, Dan. "An Historical Approach to Objectivity and Professionalism in American News Reporting." *Journal of Communication* 29 (1979): 46–57.

Sloan, John W. "The Management and Decision-Making Style of President Eisenhower." *Presidential Studies Quarterly* 20 (1990): 295–313.

Sproule, J. Michael. "Progressive Propaganda Critics and the Magic Bullet Myth." *Critical Studies in Mass Communication* 6 (1989): 225–246.

———. "Propaganda Studies in American Social Science: The Rise and Fall of the Critical Paradigm." *Quarterly Journal of Speech* 73 (1987): 60–78.

Stuckey, Mary E., and Frederick J. Antczak. "The Rhetorical Presidency: Deepening Vision, Widening Change." *Communication Yearbook* 21 (1998): 405–441.

Tuchman, Gaye. "Objectivity as Strategic Ritual: An Examination of Newsmen's Notions of Objectivity." *American Journal of Sociology* 77 (1972): 660–679.

Whittington, Keith E. "The Rhetorical Presidency, Presidential Authority, and President Clinton." *Perspectives on Political Science* 26 (1997): 199–207.

PUBLIC DOCUMENTS

The following sources are organized alphabetically; the material, however, within each heading is organized chronologically.

Barnard, Thurman L. "Truth Propaganda and the U.S. Information Program." *Department of State Bulletin* 25 (November 26, 1951): 851–853.

Barrett, Edward W. "U.S. Informational Aims in the Cold War." *Department of State Bulletin* 22 (June 19, 1950): 992–995.

———. "USIE Capitalizes on Soviet Propaganda Blunders." *Department of State Bulletin* 23 (September 11, 1950): 414–416.

———. "Mobilization of American Strength for World Security." *Department of State Bulletin* 23 (November 6, 1950): 735–737.

———. "Expanding Techniques for a Truth Strategy." *Department of State Bulletin* 23 (December 11, 1950): 945–948.

———. "The Turn of the Tide." *Department of State Bulletin* 24 (February 26, 1951): 352–354.

Begg, John M. "The American Idea: Package It for Export." *Department of State Bulletin* 24 (March 21, 1951): 409–412.

Benton, William. "Position of Department of State on AP Action." *Department of State Bulletin* 14 (January 27, 1946): 92–93.

———. "Freedom of the Press—World-Wide." *Department of State Bulletin* 14 (February 3, 1946): 156–162.

———. "Protest by the Department of State on AP and UP Action." *Department of State Bulletin* 14 (February 10, 1946): 217–218.

———. "The American Press Associations: An Opportunity and Responsibility." *Department of State Bulletin* 14 (April 7, 1946): 574–578.

Clinton, William J. "Statement on International Broadcasting Programs," *Weekly Compilation of Presidential Documents* 29 (June 21, 1993): 1088–1089.

Compton, Wilson. "An Organization for International Information." *Department of State Bulletin* 26 (March 26, 1952): 443–447.

———. "Mutual Security Requires Mutual Understanding." *Department of State Bulletin* 26 (April 28, 1952): 668–672.

———. "The Voice of America at the Water's Edge." *Department of State Bulletin* 26 (June 2, 1952): 864–867.

———. "Crusade of Ideas." *Department of State Bulletin* 27 (September 8, 1952): 343–348.

———. "Paving a Road to Peace." *Department of State Bulletin* 27 (October 20, 1952): 604–608.

Congressional Record. Washington, D.C., 1947–1953.

Cowan, Geoffrey. "The Voice of America: Our Mission Is More Important than Ever." *Vital Speeches of the Day* 60 (1994): 649–652.

"Draft of a Treaty on Freedom of Information." *Department of State Bulletin* 17 (September 14, 1947): 529.

Dulles, John Foster. "Easing International Tensions: The Role of the U.N." *Department of State Bulletin* 29 (September 1953): 403–408.

———. "Harmonizing the Actions of Nations: Major Causes of Present Tension." *Vital Speeches of the Day* 19 (October 1953): 748–751.

Eisenhower, Dwight D. "The State of the Union, 1953." *Department of State Bulletin* 28 (1953): 207–211.

———. "Address 'The Chance for Peace' Delivered before the American Society of Newspaper Editors." *Public Papers of the Presidents of the United States: Dwight D. Eisenhower, 1953*. Washington, D.C.: Government Printing Office, 1960.

———. "Address before the General Assembly of the United Nations on Peaceful Uses of Atomic Energy." *Public Papers of the Presidents of the United States: Dwight D. Eisenhower, 1953*. Washington, D.C.: Government Printing Office, 1960.

———. "Radio and Television Remarks on the Occasion of the Ground-Breaking Ceremony for the Shippingport Atomic Power Plant," *Public Papers of the Presidents of the United States: Dwight D. Eisenhower, 1954* (Washington, D.C.: U.S. Government Printing Office, 1960), 840–841.

"Government Calls Conference with Radio Industries to Discuss International Broadcasting." *Department of State Bulletin* 26 (May 11, 1947): 951–952.

"Operations Coordinating Board Established by the President." *Department of State Bulletin* 29 (September 1953): 420–422.

"Plan for Agreement on International Freedom of Information." *Department of State Bulletin* 17 (September 14, 1947): 527.

"Radio Advisory Committee Urges Strengthening of Voice of America." *Department of State Bulletin* 16 (May 25, 1947): 1038.

The Refugee Act of 1953. 80th Cong., 1st sess., 1953, P. L. 203.

"Report of Radio Advisory Committee to the Assistant Secretary of State for Public Affairs." *Department of State Bulletin* 16 (May 25, 1947): 1041.

"Status of American International Broadcasting." *Department of State Bulletin* 15 (May 26, 1946): 900–904.

Truman, Harry S. "Going Forward with a Campaign of Truth." *Department of State Bulletin* 22 (May 1, 1950): 669–672.

———. Letter from the President to Senator Flanders. *Department of State Bulletin* 23 (1950): 424–425.

———. "The Objective Is Our Efforts in Peace, Not Conflict," *Department of State Bulletin* 22 (July 19, 1950): 996–998.

———. "Expanded Information Program Vital to National Security," *Department of State Bulletin* 23 (July 31, 1950): 194.

———. "The Defense of Freedom," *Department of State Bulletin* 25 (July 16, 1951): 83–86.

———. "President Urges USSR to Inform People of U.S. Friendship," *Department of State Bulletin* 25 (July 16, 1951): 87.

———. "Continued Efforts Urged Against Soviet Propaganda," *Department of State Bulletin* 25 (September 3, 1951): 381.

U.S. Department of State. *The World Audience for America's Story*. Washington, D.C.: Office of Public Affairs, 1949.

———. *Launching the Campaign of Truth, 1st Phase*. Washington, D.C.: Office of Public Affairs, 1950.

———. *Launching the Campaign of Truth, 2nd Phase*. Washington, D.C.: Office of Public Affairs, 1951.

———. *Waging the Truth Campaign*. Washington, D.C.: Office of Public Affairs, 1951.

———. *The International Information Administration*. July–December 1952. Washington, D.C.: Office of Public Affairs, Division of Publications, 1953.

U.S. House Committee on Appropriations. *Department of State Appropriation Bill for 1948*. 80th Cong., 1st sess., 1947.

———. *Supplemental Appropriations Bill for 1951*. 81st Cong., 2d sess., 1950.

———. *Department of State Appropriations for 1952*. 82d Cong., 1st sess., 1951.

———. *Departments of State, Justice, Commerce and the Judiciary Appropriations for 1953*. 82d Cong., 2d sess., 1952.

U.S. House Committee on Expenditures in the Executive Departments. *Investigation of the State Department Voice of America Broadcasts*. 80th Cong., 2d sess., 1948.

————. Fourteenth Intermediate Report. *Investigation of the State Department Voice of America Broadcasts*. 80th Cong., 2d sess., 1948, H.R. 2350.

U.S. House Committee on Foreign Affairs. *United States Information and Educational Exchange Program of 1947*. 80th Cong., 1st sess., 1947, H.R. 416.

————. *United States Information and Educational Exchange Act of 1947*. 80th Cong., 1st sess., 1947.

————. *United States Information and Educational Exchange Act of 1948*. 80th Cong., 2d sess., 1948, H.R. 3342.

U.S. House Committee on Foreign Affairs and Senate Committee on Foreign Relations. *The Voice of America*. 82d Cong., 1st sess, 1951.

U.S. House Committee on Un-American Activities. 80th Cong., 1st sess., 1947.

U.S. House Committee on Un-American Activities, 81st Cong., 1st sess., 1949.

U.S. Senate Committee on Appropriations. *Departments of State, Justice, Commerce, and the Judiciary Appropriation Bill for 1948*. 80th Cong., 1st sess., 1947.

————. *Departments of State, Justice, Commerce, and the Judiciary Appropriation Bill for 1950*. 81st Cong., 1st sess., 1949.

———— *Departments of State, Justice, Commerce and the Judiciary Appropriations for 1951*. 81st Cong., 2d sess., 1950.

————. *Supplemental Appropriations for 1951*. 81st Cong., 2d sess., 1950.

————. *Departments of State, Justice, Commerce, and the Judiciary Appropriations for 1952*. 82nd Cong., 1st sess., 1951.

————. *Departments of State, Justice, Commerce and the Judiciary Appropriations for 1953*. 82d Cong., 2d sess., 1952.

U.S. Senate Committee on Foreign Relations. *Enabling the Government of the United States More Effectively to Carry On Its Foreign Relations by Means of Promotion of the Interchange of Persons, Knowledge, and Skills between the People of the United States and Other Countries, and by Means of Public Dissemination Abroad of Information about the United States, Its People, and Its Policies*. 80th Cong., 1st sess., 1947 S. Rept. 573.

————. *United States Information and Educational Exchange Act of 1947*. 80th Cong., 1st sess., 1947.

————. *United States Information and Educational Exchange Act of 1948*. 80th Cong., 2d sess., 1948.

————. *Investigation of "Voice of America" and "Know North America" Series of Broadcasts*. 80th Cong., 2d sess., 1948.

————. *Promoting the Better Understanding of the United States among the People of the World and to Strengthen Cooperative International Relations*. 80th Cong., 2d sess., 1948, S. Rept. 811.

————. *The United States Information Service in Europe*. 80th Cong., 2d sess., 1948, S. Rept. 855.

————. *Expanded International Information and Education Program*. 81st Cong., 2d sess., 1950, S. Rept. 243.

————. *Reaffirming the Friendship of the American People for All Peoples of the World, Including the Soviet Union.* 82d Cong., 1st sess., 1951, S. Rept. 298.

————. *Overseas Information Programs of the United States.* 82d Cong., 2d sess., 1952.

————. *Overseas Information Programs of the United States.* 83rd Cong., 1st sess., 1953.

————. Overseas Information Programs of the United States. 83rd Cong., 1st sess., 1953, S. Rept. 406.

U.S. Senate Committee on Government Operations. *State Department Information Program—Information Centers.* 83rd Cong., 1st sess., 1953.

————. *State Department Information Program—Voice of America.* 83rd Cong., 1st sess., 1953.

————. *State Department Information Program—Information Centers.* 83rd Cong., 2d sess., 1954, S. Rept. 879.

————. *Waste and Management in Voice of America Engineering Projects.* 83rd Cong., 2d sess., 1954, S. Res. 40, 10.

U.S. Public Law 402. *United States Information and Educational Exchange Act of 1948.* 80th Cong., 2d sess., January 27, 1948.

Wick, Charles Z. "Global Interdependence and the War of Ideas: The Free Flow of Ideas." *Vital Speeches of the Day* 54 (March 15, 1988): 327–330.

Index

About the Author

SHAWN J. PARRY-GILES is Assistant Professor of Communication, Affiliate Assistant Professor of Women's Studies, and the Director of the Center for Political Communication Civic Leadership in the Department of Communication, University of Maryland. Parry-Giles has published in numerous communication journals.